Pope.L Campaign

Edited by Dieter Roelstraete
Mousse Publishing

Under Our Breath
Dieter Roelstraete

This book is a three-part report on the long-term collaboration between artist Pope.L and curator Dieter Roelstraete, which began in the spring of 2016 with an invitation, extended to the artist by Roelstraete and his colleagues Monika Szewczyk and Adam Szymczyk, to participate in the fourteenth edition of documenta, the internationally renowned quinquennial exhibition of contemporary art, which took place in Athens, Greece, and its traditional home of Kassel, Germany, in the spring and summer of 2017. Pope.L's contribution to this sprawling, multicity mega-event took on the fitting guise of an immersive, seemingly omnipresent sound installation titled *Whispering Campaign*, consisting of thousands of hours of whispered content broadcast throughout the two cities using both speakers and live "whisperers"—or, as an enthusiastic *New York Times* put it on March 2, 2018, "a bravura undertaking in which live performers wandered the cities broadcasting prerecorded monologues in English, German and Greek about nationhood and borders, with hidden speakers in public locations across both cities transmitting still more, the words seeming to haunt the exhibition itself." It is this *Whispering Campaign* that gives this book its title and that forms the subject of its opening chapter, consisting of contributions by Monika Szewczyk, Klea Charitou, and Leon Hösl, the curatorial assistants based in Athens and Kassel, respectively, who were tasked with the work's realization on the ground, providing the testimonial perspective from which they here recount their experiences as whisper masters extraordinaire.

A mere month after the closing of documenta 14 in Kassel, a second chapter of our titular campaign was inaugurated at the University of Chicago's Logan Center for the Arts, revolving centrally around the exhibition and art intervention project *Brown People Are the Wrens in the Parking Lot*, curated by Yesomi Umolu. In these pages, Zachary Cahill looks back upon this complex, multifaceted enterprise that involved a more or less conventional art exhibit, a DIY media campaign, a thematic library, video interviews, and a series of events ranging from impromptu performances and DJ sets to an expansive program of talks, presentations, and debates. Likewise reflecting on pressing issues of connectedness, home, and migration, this campaign-cum-exhibition, so acutely anchored in the precarious fabric of Chicago's South Side, took place at a significant moment in US history dominated by debates over immigration, race, and the plight of the ninety-nine percent—dominated, in a sense, by constant *campaigning*.

The third and final chapter of the artist's campaign, and the closing chapter of this book, unfolded as a course co-taught at the University of Chicago by Pope.L and Roelstraete titled "Art and Knowledge," which, in part at least, sought to address one of *Whispering Campaign*'s catchiest and most puzzling slogans—namely, "ignorance is a virtue." The students who constituted this query's primary audience were invited to contribute their observations and intuitions concerning art's at times proudly tenuous relationship to knowledge, prompting all of us wonder whether "art *and* knowledge" should really be read as "art *or* knowledge."

With these wise words of consternation, we hit the trail.

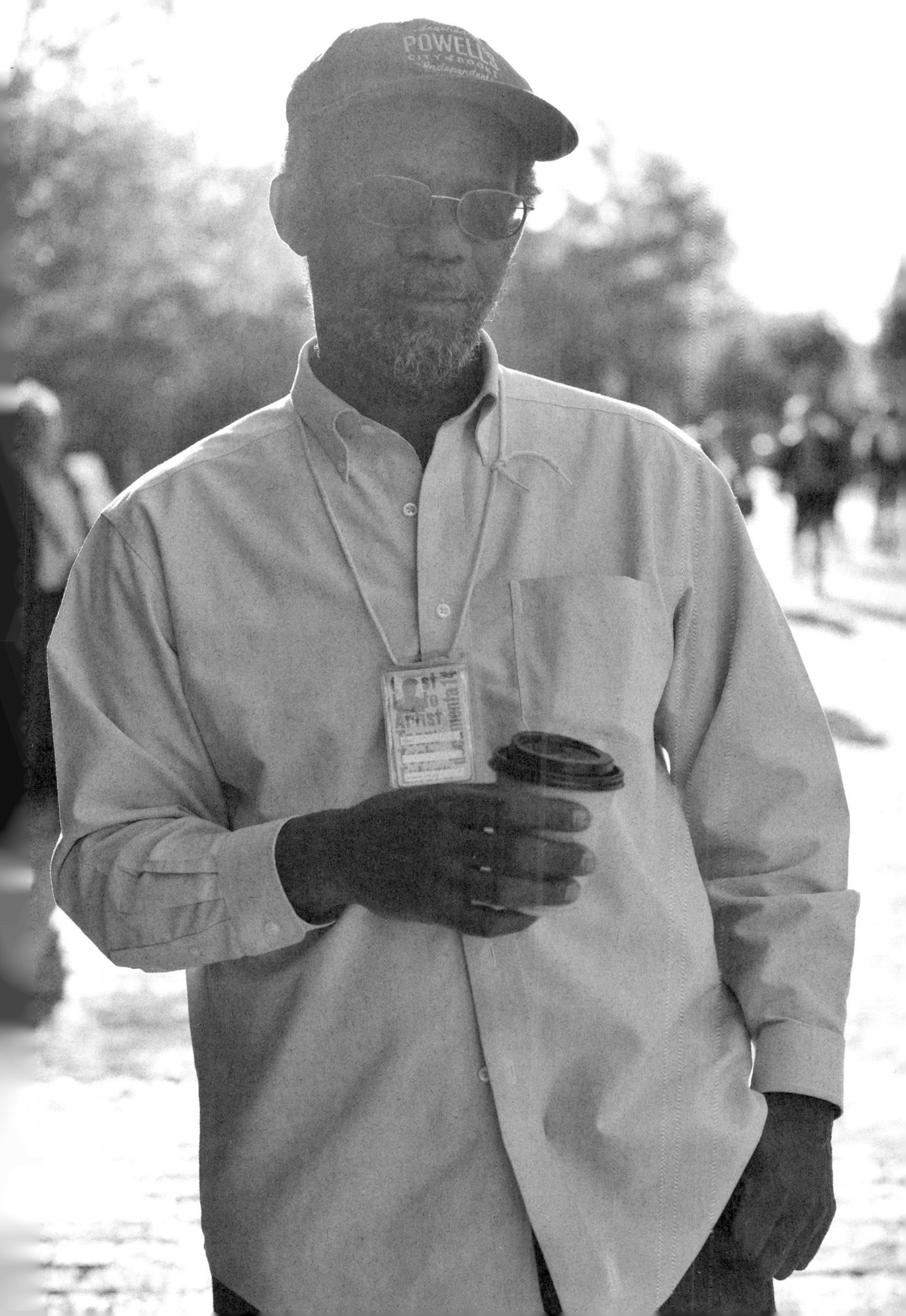
POWEL

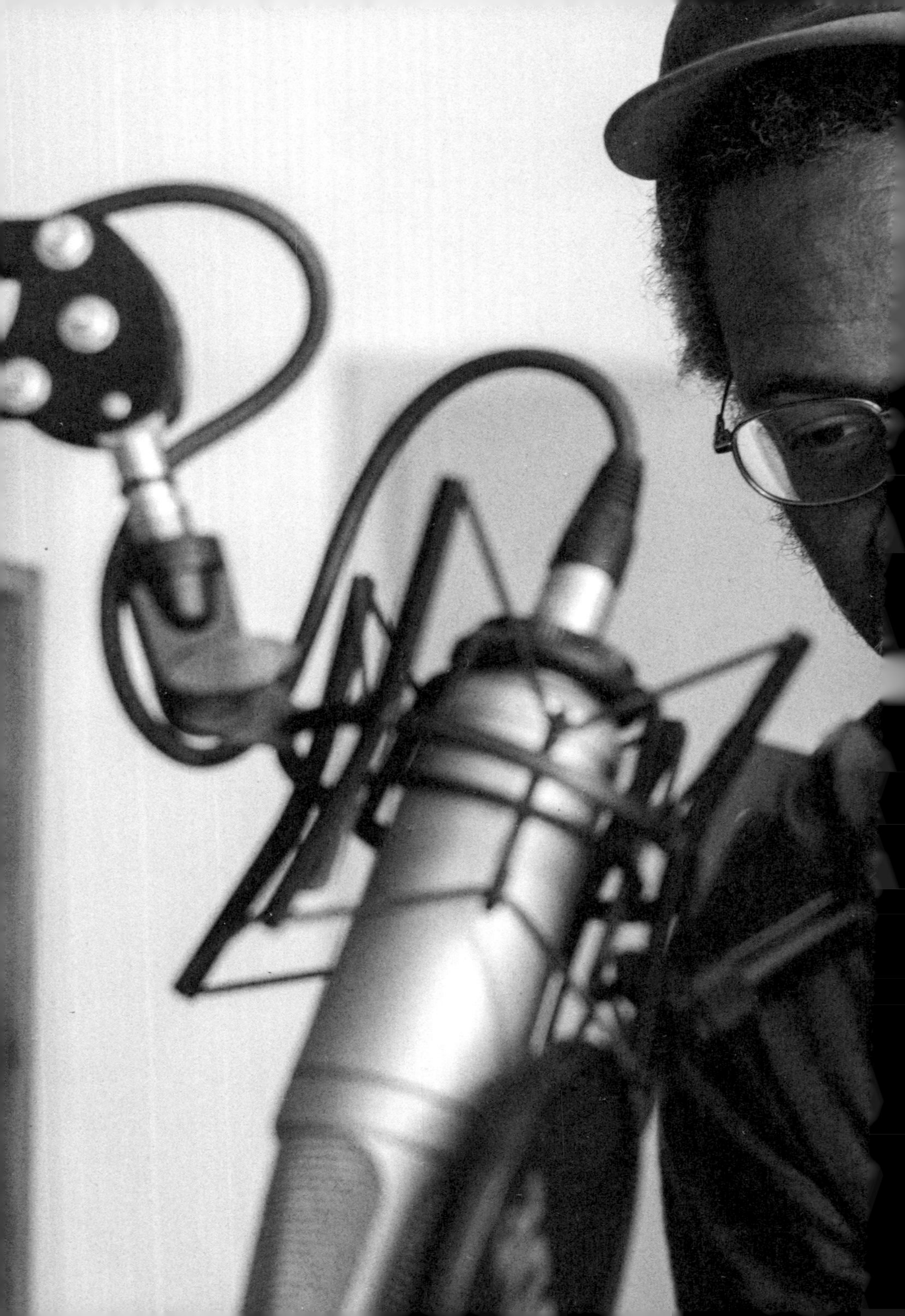

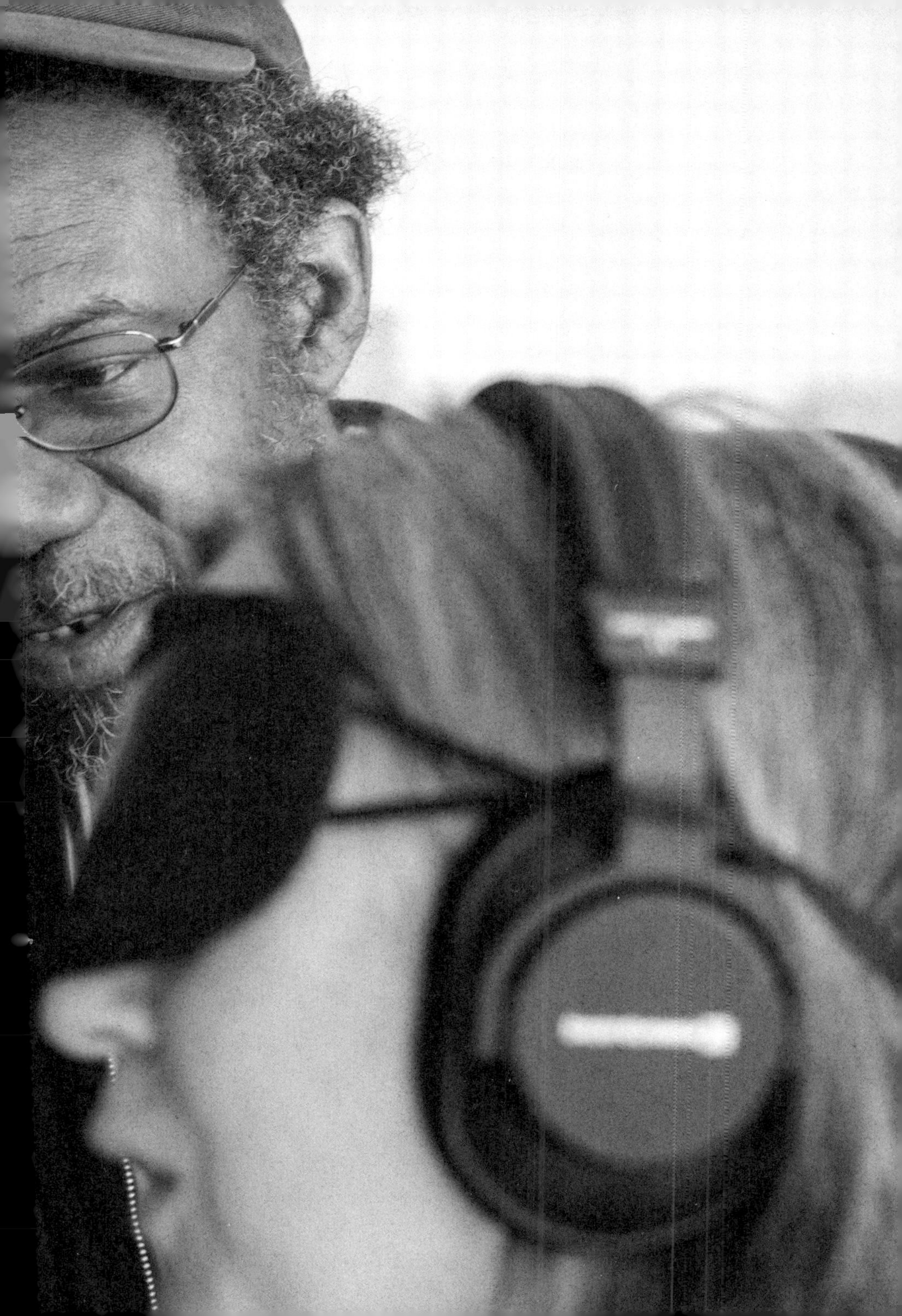

The Virtues of Ignorance Zachary Cahill in Conversation with Pope.L and Dieter Roelstraete

Whispering Campaign was the title of a sound installation created by Pope.L for documenta 14, the quinquennial exhibition of contemporary art that took place in Athens (Greece) and Kassel (Germany), in the spring and summer of 2017. The work was installed using sound sources scattered throughout both cities, in places one might expect to find art, such as the museum, as well as unexpected locations like a restaurant bathroom or a parked or passing car. *Whispering Campaign* was at once subtle and unsettling, addressing—among other things—the paranoia that immigrants and refugees are often faced with, as well as the various ways innuendo is mobilized to cast suspicion in the public sphere. In the fall of 2017, I invited the artist to join a conversation with documenta 14 curator Dieter Roelstraete about their collaborative work on that project as it extended to Chicago in the shape of an exhibition at the Logan Center Gallery at the University of Chicago titled *Brown People Are the Wrens in the Parking Lot* (November 2017–January 2018), as well as a course taught at the university by the artist and the curator titled "Art and Knowledge" (January–March 2018). The resulting interview covers topics as wide-ranging as immigration, art, knowledge, and ignorance.
—Zachary Cahill

ZACHARY CAHILL: Let's start with a question for you, Dieter. How does someone actually *curate* a whispering campaign? Can a whispering campaign ever be intentional? Can it even be "inaugurated"? Or does it always have a life of its own? Can artists or cultural producers ever really manipulate public opinion, or do they just create space to simply have one of their own?

DIETER ROELSTRAETE: Here's one thing I learned from working on the *Whispering Campaign*, in my capacity as a curator for documenta 14 involved in the realization of this project in particular:

the sheer *power* of this invisible, sprawling, ubiquitous "thing" that is, was, just impossible to grasp.... I remember initially having some qualms about the viability of this project, fearing that a *sound* piece scattered all around Athens and Kassel, with no real emphatic physical point of anchorage or spatial compression, would quite simply get drowned out, lost, dilute, and dissolve. In many ways, the opposite appears to have been true: this most immaterial and fleeting of works is precisely what appears to have caught people's attention in a way that I certainly did not expect, producing not just a standout work of art, but among documenta 14's most talismanic. It was somewhat amusing, even, to see the *Whispering Campaign* mentioned in publications like the *New York Times* without there ever being an image to go along with it. Anyway, I think that the enthusiastic public reception, more so even than the critical success, is quite telling—a sign of the times, to be sure. I mean, this is a work of which many will remember the one endlessly repeated mantra more than anything else: "ignorance is a virtue"—not an innocent slogan to go around by any means, in 2017.... In any case, I do not want to deduct too much from this or otherwise get lost in idle speculation, but I do look back upon it as a reminder of the fact that we can never really *know* an artwork: there is no way of knowing what it will do, and in this sense there's also no *owning* it—it does have a life of its own in the most literal sense imaginable. This, to me, is one of the great lessons of any curatorial work: it consists of *listening* to the work of art, obeying it, and following its lead. It's works of art that make exhibitions—not artists, and certainly not curators. So if you're asking me whether a "whispering campaign" can ever be intentional—yes, the artwork has its own intent. For sure. The work of art is the origin of everything that constitutes art.

ZC: Pope.L, could you talk a little bit about this phrase, "ignorance is a virtue"? Why was this an important phrase to disseminate throughout the exhibition? Where does it come from, and what does it mean to you? And what kind of questions were you hoping it would catalyze for documenta's audience?

POPE.L: The phrase "ignorance is a virtue" came out of failure, my inability to arrive at an anchor or pivot from which to make many different proposals. Why many? Because I realized my audience would be varied. Even so, I began to sense failure early on, but I did not want to believe it, that I would not be able to find a pivot. I kept thinking: I'll figure it out. Bottom line, for several reasons, I let myself become too ambitious without understanding the difficulties of the task. But I was stubborn or obsessed or embarrassed—however you want to call it—so I kept pushing and finagling, hoping for clarity. Like many folks who make things, I learned as I went. Initially I believed I could actually make a work that could speak to people, different people across a wide spectrum and geography. And speak to them in layers. I gradually realized this was a fantasy—maybe a very American one? And even if I could speak in such a way, what was I really saying? Finally, I realized that no matter what I said, I'd never be able to say enough or the right thing at the right time. Sound works temporally. You only have the hearing-time someone is willing to give. And my awareness, as the instigator of the encounter, is always delimited by what I can know or offer at any one time. So—what is this about, this conjunction of time and knowledge? In what space do they meet? They meet in the space or architecture of ignorance. The construction of what we do not know. Or do not want to know. Or know but do not want to know. It's a constructed space made of mechanisms of obscuring, removal, disavowal, and disassociation. I realized that my pivot was ignorance and went on from there.

ZC: It is so easy to bring a personal story to the topic of immigration, and those personal stories can be so strong and overwhelming that they can stymie the conversation.... How can you possibly argue about somebody else's personal story? Put in another way still: to say that "we are all immigrants," while magnanimous, tends to flatten experience when we are talking about immigration exactly at a time when such distinctions seem to matter more than ever. We may, in fact, all be immigrants, but not "all of us" are subject to deportation, racial profiling, and detention. Is it possible to talk about the politics of immigration without personalizing it? Is that even advisable?

Pope.L: Zach, I am not sure that, for the person telling it, it's ever "easy" to tell their personal story of trauma, whether it is about rape or racism or immigration. These tellings can come off very raw, hot, and blunt—seemingly unintellectual and messy. To those hearing the stories, the stories may sound careless, embarrassing, lacking in grace, possibly even irritating—that someone could expose themselves so thoughtlessly. The intellect in these stories is in the feeling. The heat in these tellings is real and may need many retellings to find a cooler translation. If these stories stymie "conversation," what do we mean by "stymie"? What do we mean by "conversation"? What is so great about "conversation"? Who is to say what constitutes a "good conversation"?

In fact, I find the type of conversation you speak of—the type that is stymied by personal stories of trauma—is typically, though not always, the intellectual, more distant, so-called dispassionate type. The personal turns the dispassionate to stone. Trauma can be threatening, and, in order to remain unmarked by it, maybe we dispassionate folk have to distance ourselves. But the cost might be that we become judges instead witnesses. And maybe we are not as innocent as we think we are. Yes, the statement "we are all immigrants" may flatten and reduce the complexity of the issues surrounding immigration today, but what description of its complexity would not do this? It would be a rare bunch of words that could accomplish this. And while we are waiting for the perfect description, what is one to do? We must do the imperfect, say the imperfect, be the imperfect. I prefer to engage in the imperfect rather than not engage at all. Indeed, sure! The phrase "we are all immigrants" can be a way of absolving ourselves from any responsibility for what is happening with immigration—or it could serve as a rallying cry to remember a common heritage we all in this country inevitably share. For me, the cry best means who I want to call family and align with politically and materially as equals.

ZC: You are co-teaching a course titled "Art and Knowledge"—two intertwined subjects that have generated mountains of discourse and theoretical material. Without wanting to sound sneaky or cheeky: what exactly constitutes the "and" in your minds as you navigate this conjunctive project?

DR: Twelve years or so ago, I was involved in the founding, in Amsterdam, of a journal called *F. R. David*; it was named after a French singer from the 1980s best remembered today for releasing a hit single titled "Words (Don't Come Easy)," which over time became the journal's informal motto: in art, "words don't come easy." (It still says today that "*F. R. David* focuses on the status of writing in contemporary art.") In the case of a journal like *F .R. David*, in other words, the question concerns art "and" language (a nod, obviously, to the British conceptual art collective Art and Language that I was enamored with as a philosophy student getting into art so many years ago), much like the question of our course, which concerns the status of art's relationship to knowledge. There's art, and then there's knowledge, and countless variations can be dreamed up as to how they relate. Perhaps art *is* knowledge, pure and simple. Or perhaps art merely poses *as* knowledge. (This is a very popular position to take right now, and the course is inspired in part by a desire to better understand the entanglement of art in what has been called the "knowledge industry"—indeed, what is art even *doing* in the academic realm?) Can there be art *without* knowledge? Does art come *before* knowledge? Can there be art *after* knowledge? Et cetera. But the bluntest variant is perhaps this: do I choose art *or* knowledge? Now, the shape that this "and" takes as we navigate the art-and-knowledge nexus changes over time, and I find myself vacillating as always. (Art "question mark" knowledge?) One day I find myself on the side of the art-as-knowledge equation; the next day I find myself returned to a more oppositional understanding of that relationship: art *instead of* knowledge. Of course, as a curator and writer, I have been associated for some time with the promotion (so to speak) of artistic practices tending toward a closer alignment of art and knowledge: research-based art practices, art as type of intellectual labor first and foremost, the artist as a knowledge worker, the exhibition as essay, art as a form of critical inquiry, etc. So, in the context of this course, my very presence evidently represents the historical rapprochement of art and "knowing"—but in teaching this course, with a practicing artist, to art students, taking recourse to historical examples of particular art practices that we believe to either complicate or enrich the conception of art as a form of knowledge, I am constantly reminded of the limitations of this paradigm. Art is a form of knowing, sure—and then some. So if you'd ask me where this course will lead to in my own understanding of the art-and-knowledge complex, I'd say I would probably be tempted to conclude that art should properly be understood to exist somewhere *after* knowledge, *beyond* knowledge. Art *exceeds* knowledge. Does that make sense?

POPE.L: Our discussions in the "Art and Knowledge" class usually involved a version where some part of art intruded into knowledge, not the reverse. I was the most skeptical. Dieter is definitely a believer. The students were more attracted to his version, I think. Even I was attracted but not convinced. I do not believe art needs knowledge to be interesting, useful, or to justify itself. I do believe the two, art/knowledge, inflect each other, but I also believe that art inflects pudding. For some, the desire to annex art with knowledge is a matter of status-building—for example, to raise their status within the knowledge economy of education or the conceptual art mafia. Some folks believe they need to protect art from its own uselessness. What if the art/knowledge "smoosh" creates the total opposite and art becomes indistinguishable from knowledge in a world dominated by corporate info-oligarchies: what would this mean? And why smoosh with knowledge? Maybe there are better or interesting things to smoosh with?

ZC: OK, I need to ask you this: who is the conceptual art mafia??

POPE.L: I don't mind naming a few names. Whether I like it or not, I am perceived as a member, I think. And you and Dieter are perceived this way also. We may not see ourselves as such but I think other folks do.

ZC: Dieter, perhaps I have skewed the question of immigration slightly toward the American context, but it is obviously a major discussion in Europe right now as well. You have commented on the form of Pope.L's project above, how, as a sound piece, it had this large looming presence yet nonetheless remained utterly immaterial. I wonder if you could speak to the work's content or what it was about. Did you feel that Pope.L's project hinged on the question of the stranger and/or the thing that is unknown and therefore makes us anxious and enervates us? Or did it move much more along the lines of what we think of as a whispering campaign—the spreading of disinformation and lies? What does it mean to enact a whispering campaign that calls into question knowledge itself?

DR: Well, there were many ways in which I think the Whispering Campaign managed to speak to many of the simmering fears and anxieties that subtend the so-called “immigration crisis” in Germany, in particular, in varying degrees of directness. Firstly, there’s the work’s very nature of sonic scattering—an *infestation* of sound: as if the entire urban fabric of Kassel had been invaded, infiltrated, contaminated, indeed “polluted” with certain phrases in particular—and the fact that they were whispered rather than shouted out made them feel all the more omnipresent and pervasive, *invasive* even. And I’m consciously marshaling the pathologizing language of certain political responses to the migrant crisis here—the old fear-mongering chestnut of xenophobic discourse: cast the alien, the foreigner, the other as an invasive species, as an infection or contagion. The work consisted of sound bites that seemed to spread like *viruses*—up to and including among the airwaves of local radio stations and the like. Diasporic or “migrant sound,” if you want. And then there’s the actual spoken content, of course, with its occasional testimonial shards of refugee life, which often sounded especially poignant in war-ravaged, jittery, self-doubting Athens.... (The “war” in question being an economic or monetary one, the self-doubt that of the so-called cradle of European civilization shut out of Europe’s economic comfort zone.) I lived in Kassel for the entire duration of documenta 14 and heard this one phrase whispered just about *everywhere*, at all times (most notably broadcast from a car parked outside my home): “ignorance is a virtue”—a regular earworm, that one. But of the most unsettling kind, of course: who wants to preach the virtue of ignorance in this year, 2017, of all years? Isn't ignorance the root of all evil? Unknowingly the most vicious of all vices? I distinctly remember having to coach a small troupe of performers—young people tasked with going around Kassel muttering "ignorance is a virtue" under their amplified breaths—through a bad patch of existential doubt halfway through the exhibition's run.... And how the more challenging neighborhoods to navigate bandying that phrase about were indeed often Kassel's immigrant quarters—parts of town that had never figured much, historically speaking, in documenta psychogeography as it was. (This was a hugely important facet of documenta 14's *genius loci*.) The whispering of "ignorance is a virtue" became something like an official soundtrack to the summer of 2017 there—a provocative, unnerving rallying cry, to say the least! Anyway, I think that the genius of the project was compressed in the contrarian gnomic wisdom of that very phrase's collapsing of fear, knowledge, and otherness. It seems to answer so many questions that probe the very essence of so many of our current predicaments: do we not crave the lost comfort and bliss of *not* knowing? Doesn't knowledge by its very definition imply exposing ourselves to the unknown alien, other, and stranger? Have we reached a point where we effectively dread the prospect of knowing more? And this, in conclusion, reminds me of the best three-word definition of ethics that I know of, courtesy of Terry Eagleton: ethics is "trouble with strangers"—a problem of *knowing*.

ZC: We've been discussing a series of collaborative projects, and so far I have tended—wrongly, I now think—to bracket the project's permutations (documenta 14, the exhibition at the Logan Center, and the class) off from one another. Yet I am starting to see some clear throughlines. There is something happening in your work that concerns disrupting the institutions of knowledge, and perhaps trying to alter their configuration—or at least call it into question. So I guess the jokey questions stand: Who is the conceptual art mafia? What kind of knowledge do you associate them with? And how does that knowledge relate to the academy? And if we were to change the balance from focusing on a knowledge economy to, let's say, an *ignorance* economy.... Well, what might that actually look like?

DR: If you ask *me* who's at the helm of the intertwining of art and knowledge economies within the academy—and this is a crucial qualification—I'd say we're talking *neo*-conceptual art mafias rather than the original late-1960s, New York Seth Siegelaub-led cabal of Robert Barry, Dan Graham, Lawrence Weiner, et al. An artist like Liam Gillick is probably a paradigmatic figure in this regard. In truth, if you'd ask me who are some of the artists most closely aligned (whether rightly so or not, doesn't even matter here) with a certain academization or trend toward academicism in art-making that defines the very confluence of art and the knowledge economy, I'd probably have to name some of the artists I've worked with on more than one occasion, and who've been instrumental to the formation of my curatorial philosophy, so to speak—people like Mark Dion, Joachim Koester, Goshka Macuga, Simon Starling, et al. In other words: I'm probably part of that particular neo-conceptual art mafia! I'm fully aware of my share in this process of academization, and of all the problems inherent in the half-willed, half-forced rapprochement between these two worlds: "art" and "knowledge"—but so, of course, are all of the artists I just mentioned. And we should, of course, note that this rapprochement was initiated in no small part by artists keen to challenge the academy's monopolizing of certain notions of knowledge by mobilizing a particular paradigm of art making that sought to propose other forms of knowing and other knowledges. And this is very much the position I will continue to defend: that art produces a "brand" of knowing and knowledge that *rivals* the standard model of science, the academy, the market, and other epistemic citadels precisely by remaining "other"—though *not* ignorant. I appreciate your coining the tantalizing term of an "ignorance economy," but I'm not sure if I can go there.... Do you know the medieval mystical treatise titled *The Cloud of Unknowing*? Not a plea for ignorance by any means, but more of a meditation on life *after* and *beyond* knowing and knowledge. Perhaps that's where I see art take place in the future, so inevitably and irreversibly subsumed in the knowledge economy or the academy: on a plane past plain knowing.

Pope.L: I have already claimed membership in this group—the art mafia—in this interview. Or at least my perceived connection. I am not sure that this group creates knowledge or is even interested in knowledge, per se. I think if this group is interested in knowledge at all, it is intimately connected to self-interest and power. Like most groups, maybe in spite of our most positive intentions, we cannot help but to want to preserve ourselves. So maybe what an ignorance economy might look like is to divest ourselves of that kind of safety. It's funny—we in the art world talk about the disappearance of art, but for a lot of people on the planet, art doesn't even exist.

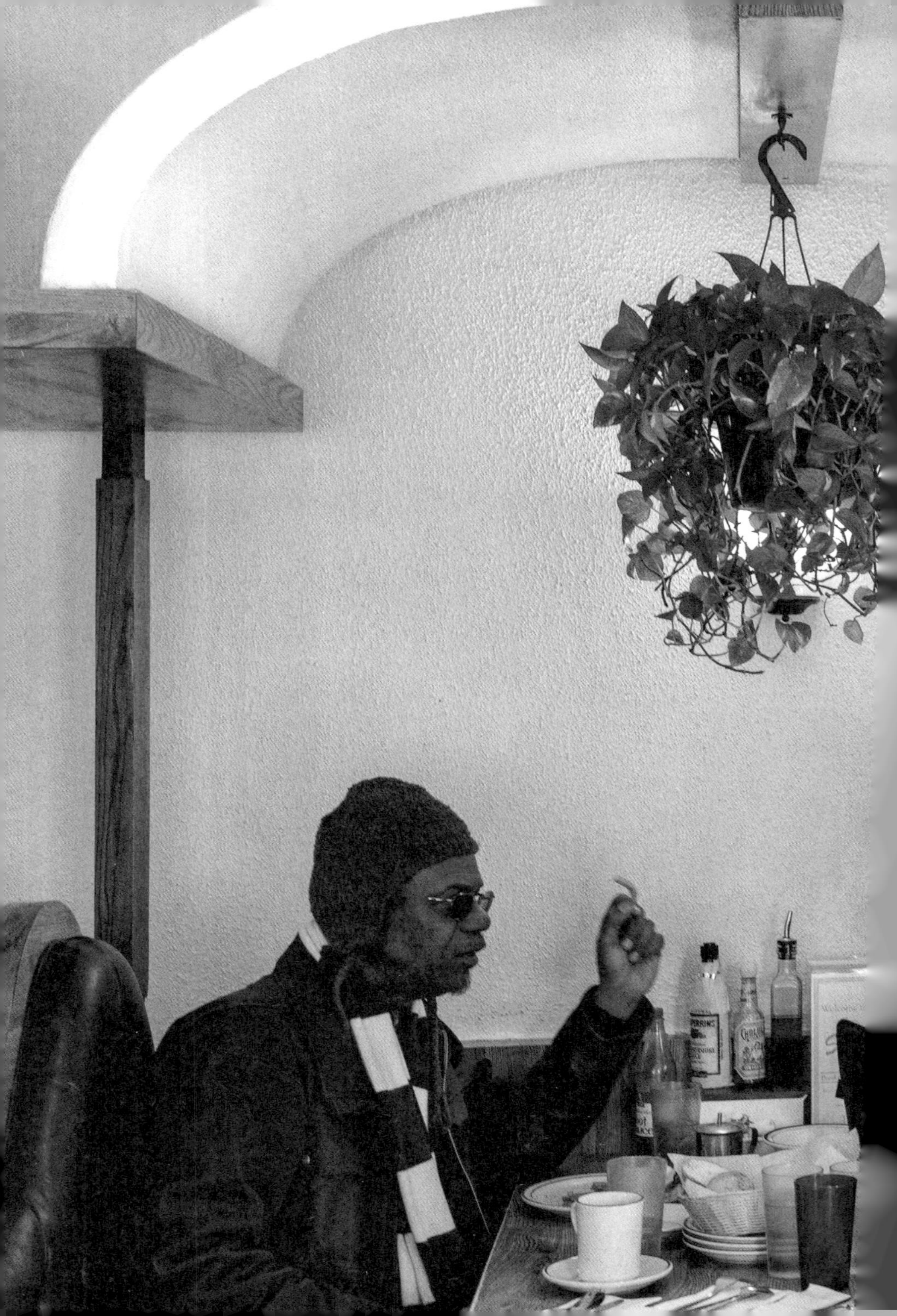
PERRINS

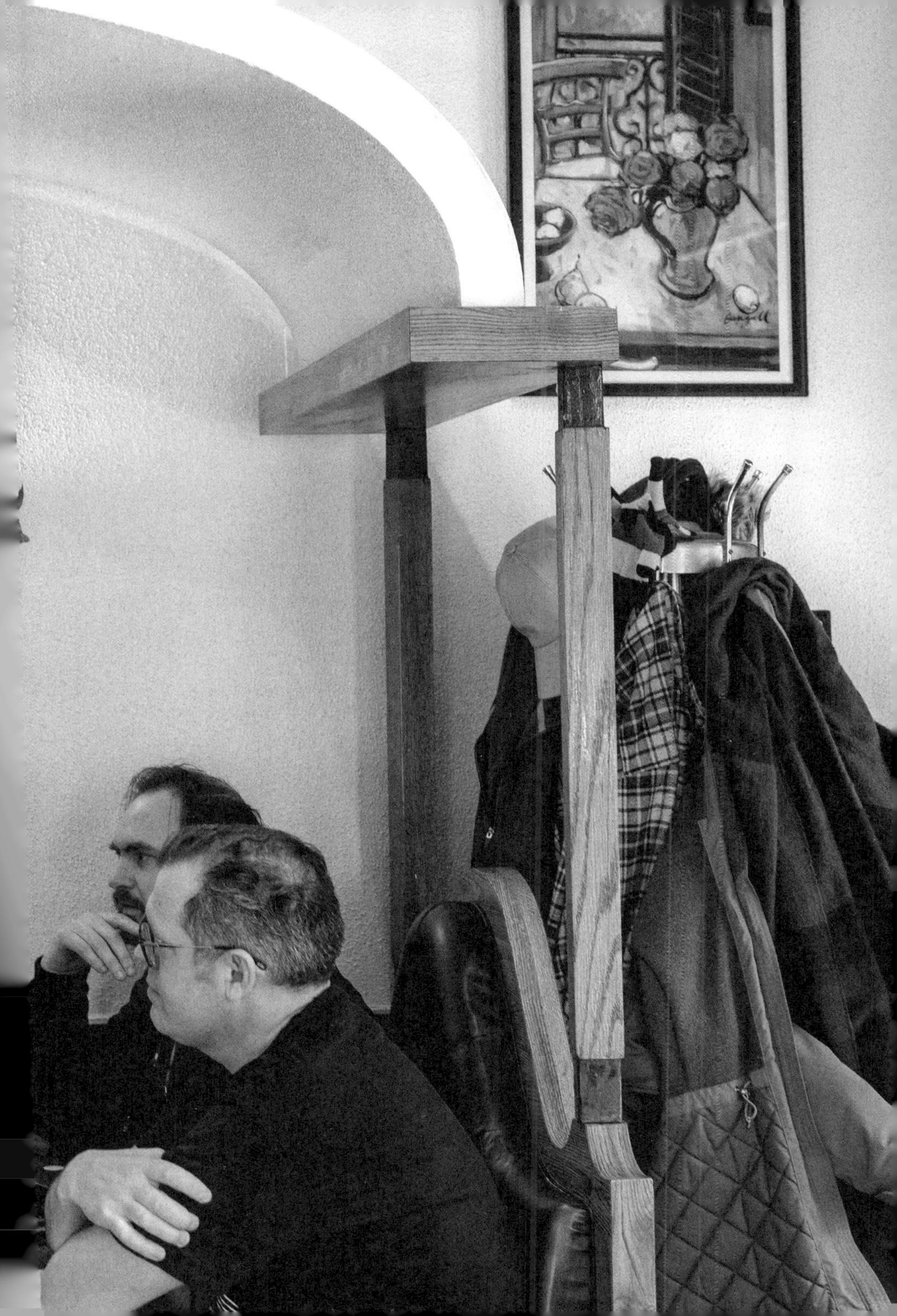

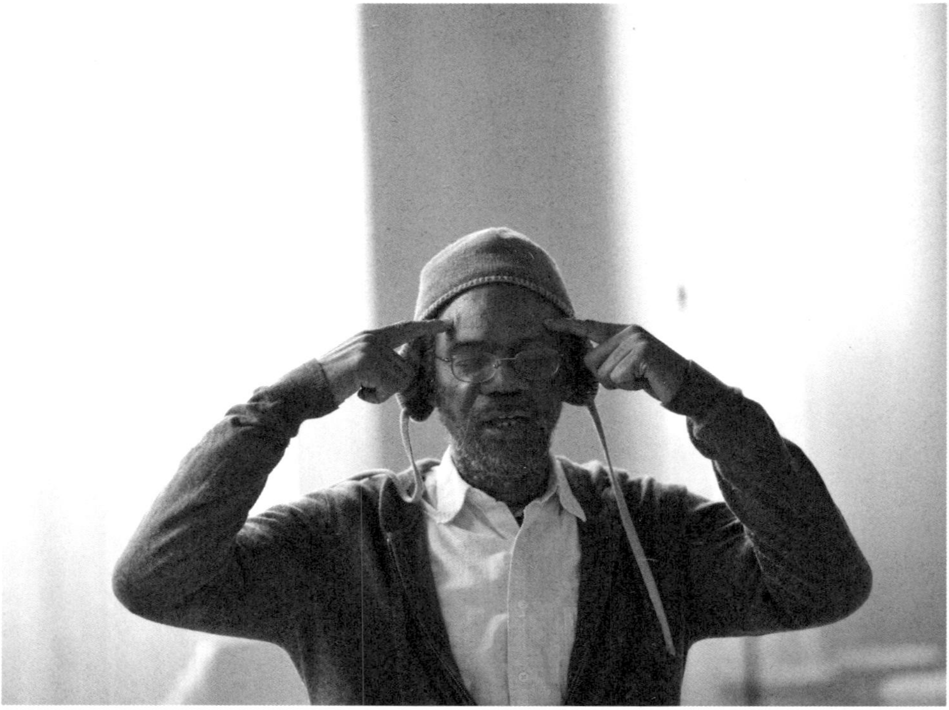

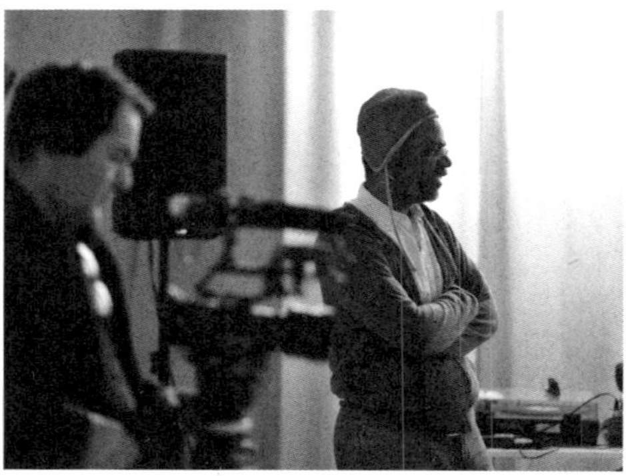

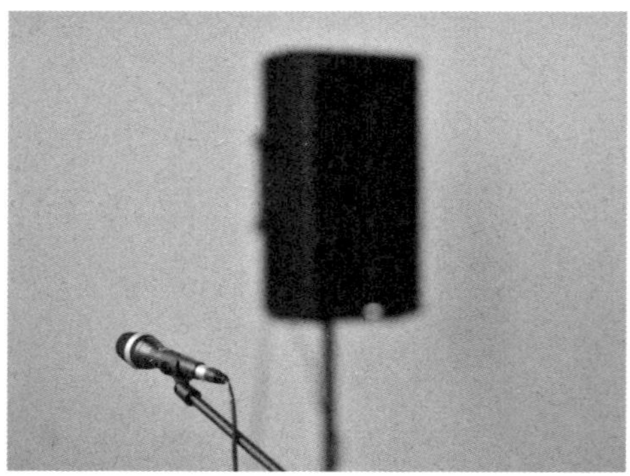

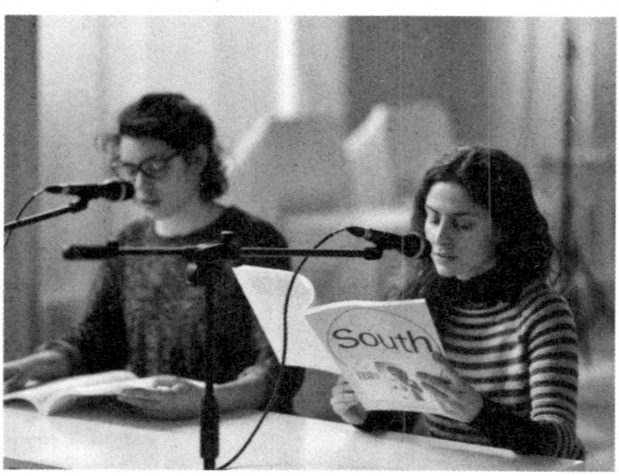
South

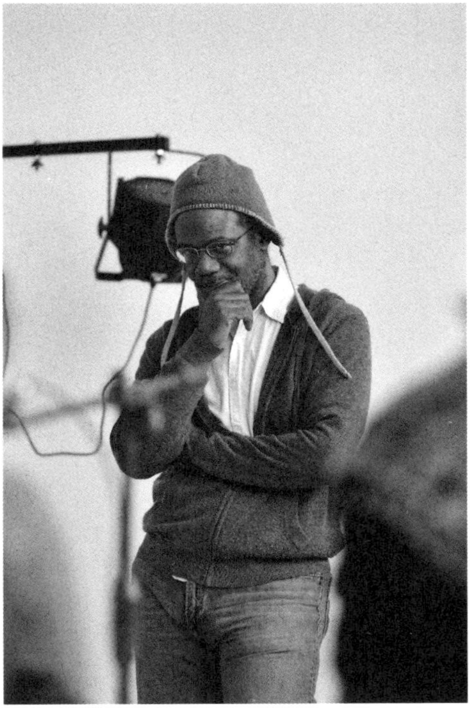
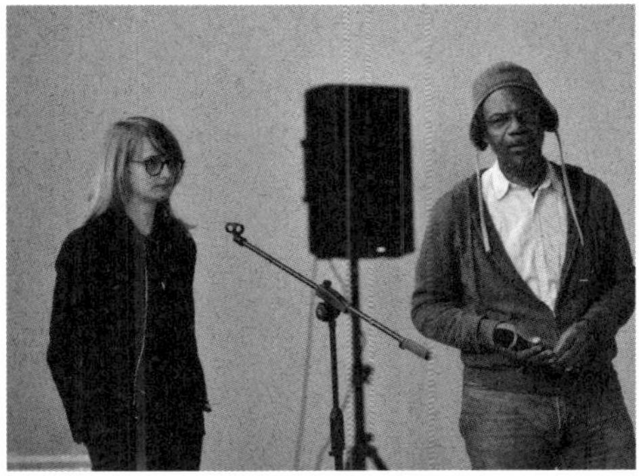
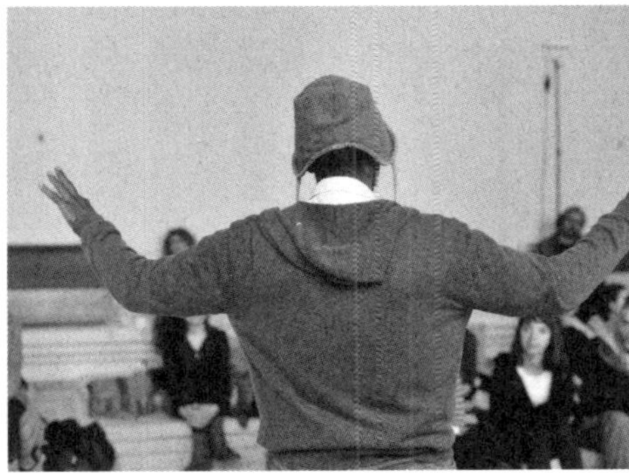
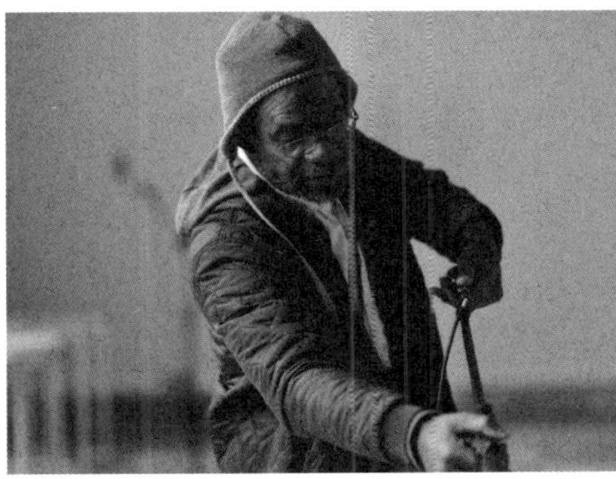
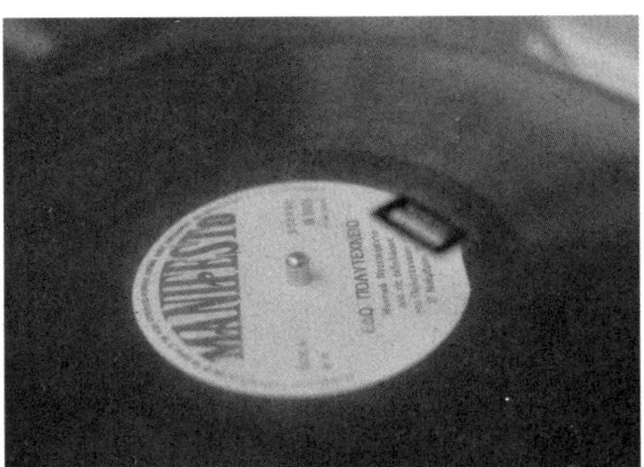
MANIFESTO
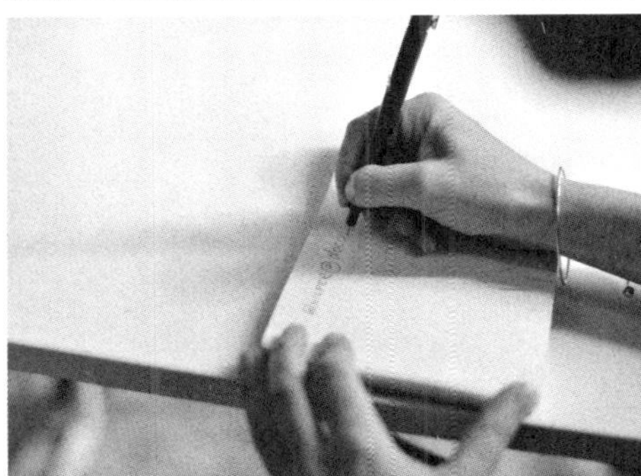

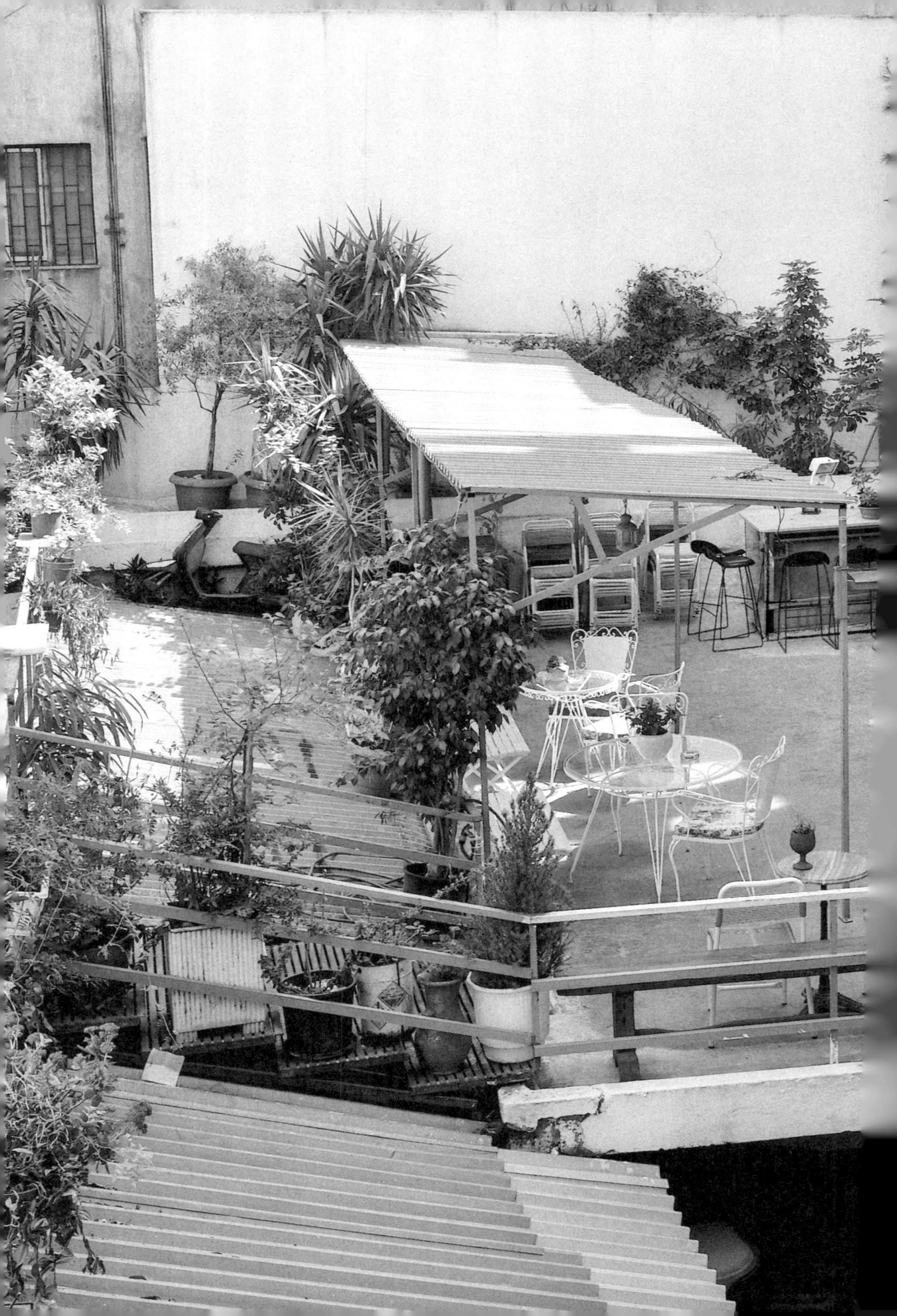

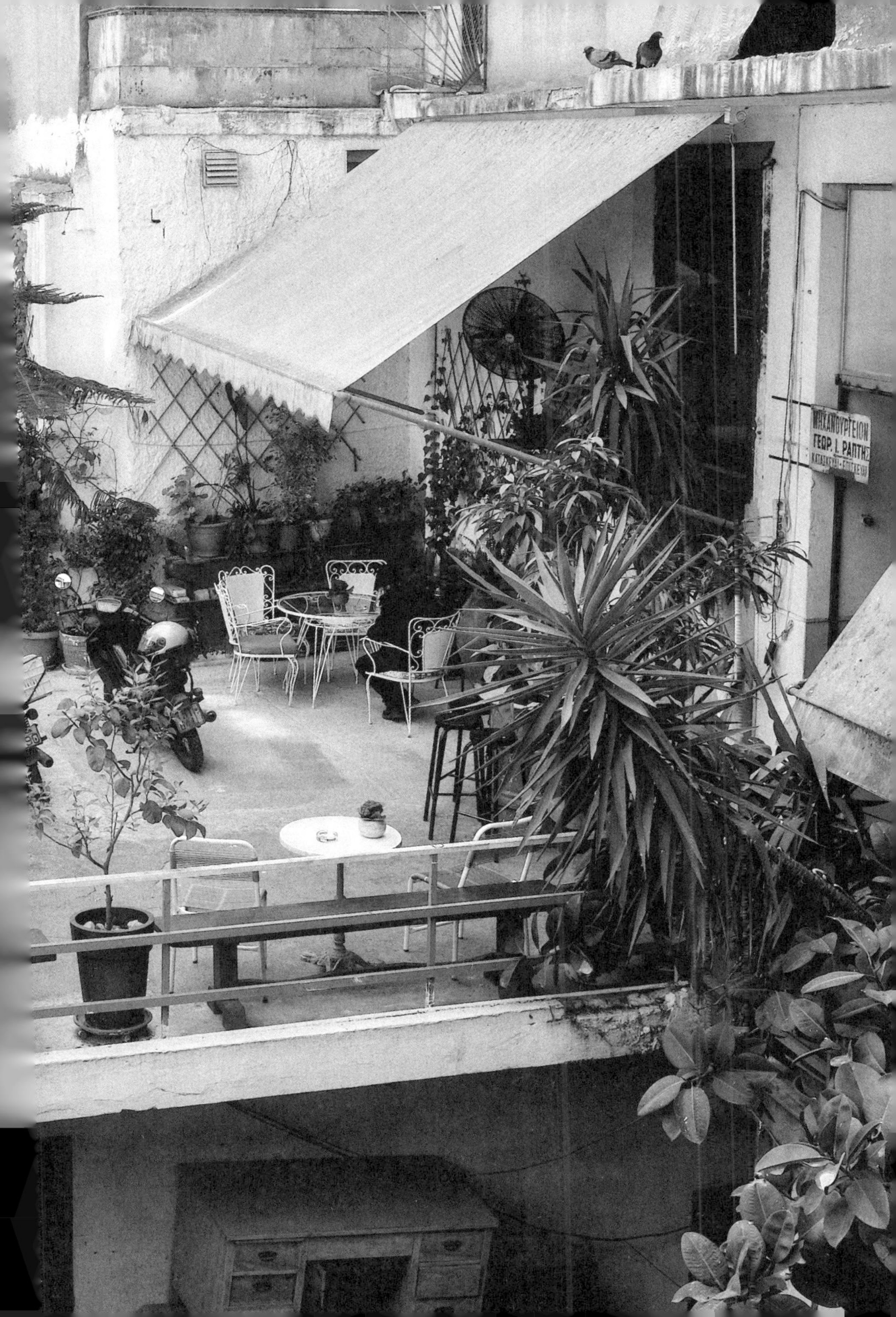
ΜΗΧΑΝΟΥΡΓΕΙΟΝ
ΓΕΩΡ. Ι. ΡΑΠΤΗΣ

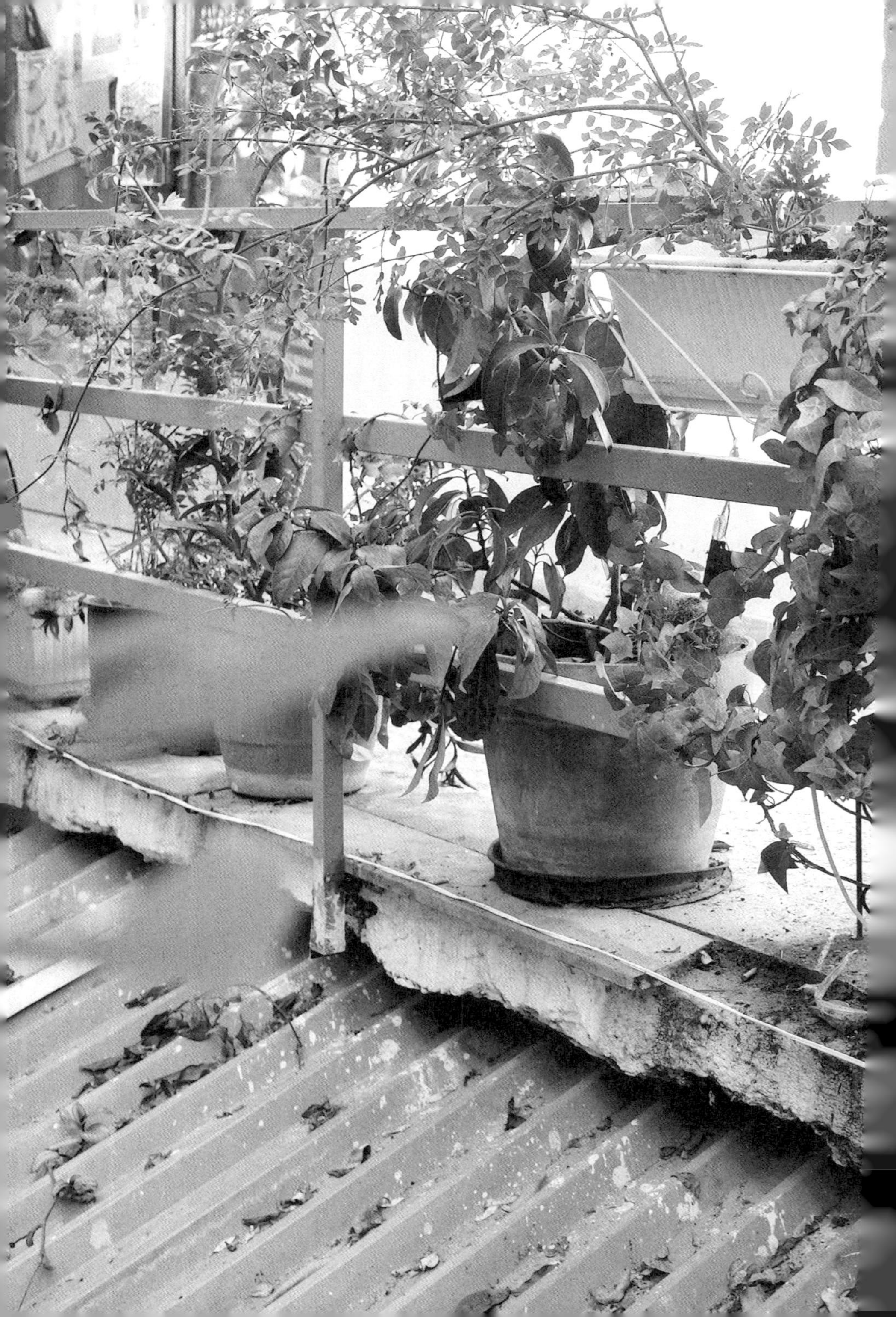

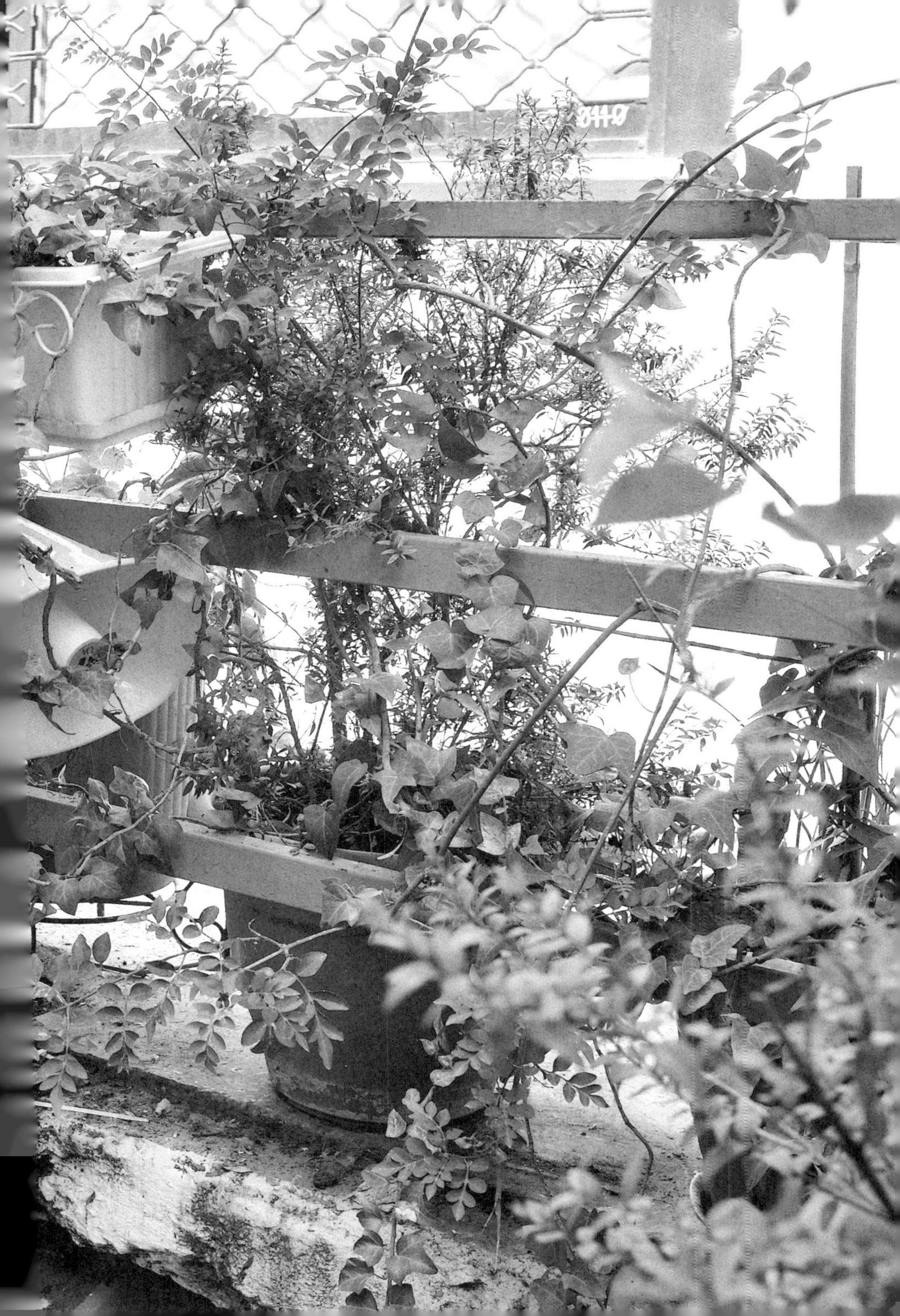

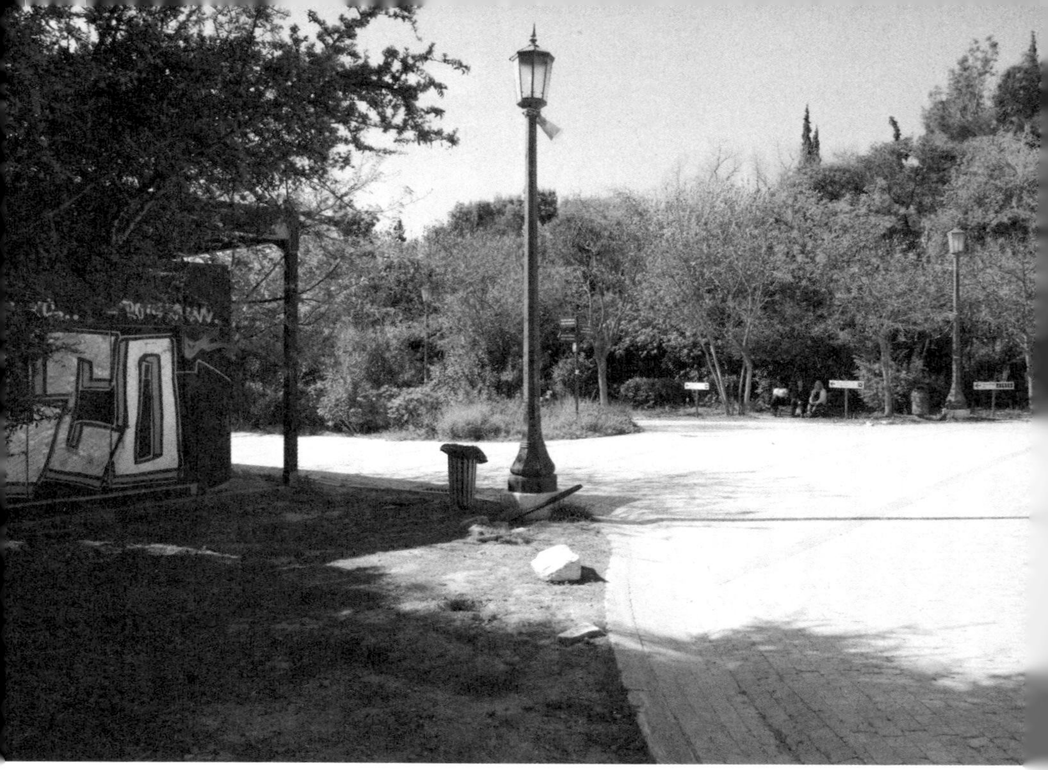

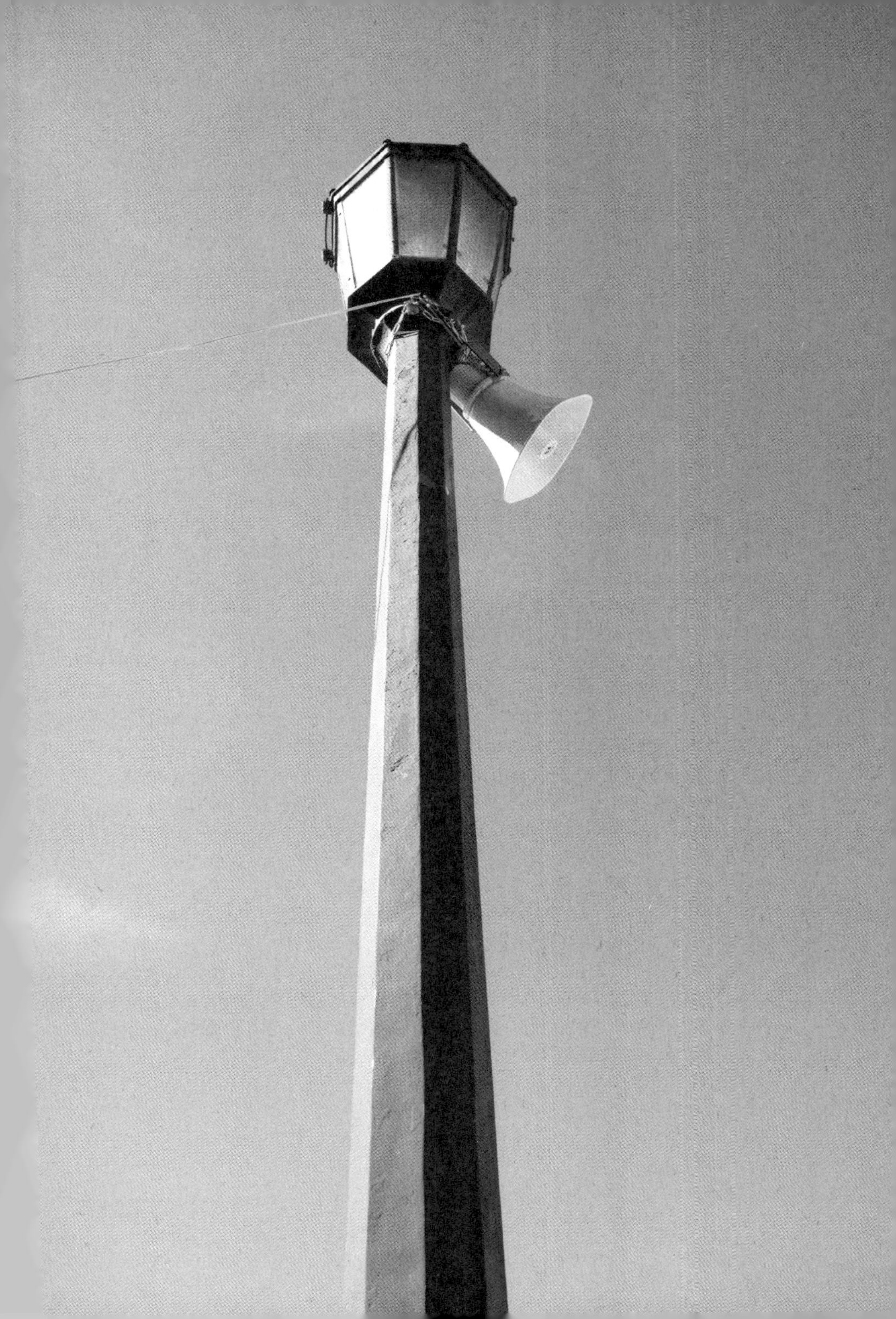

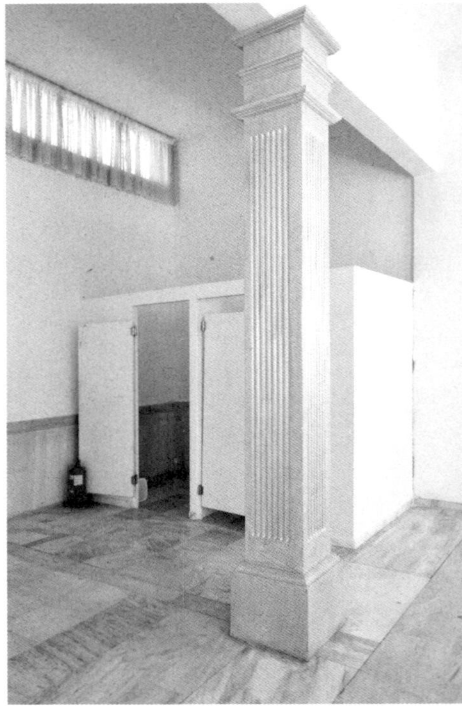

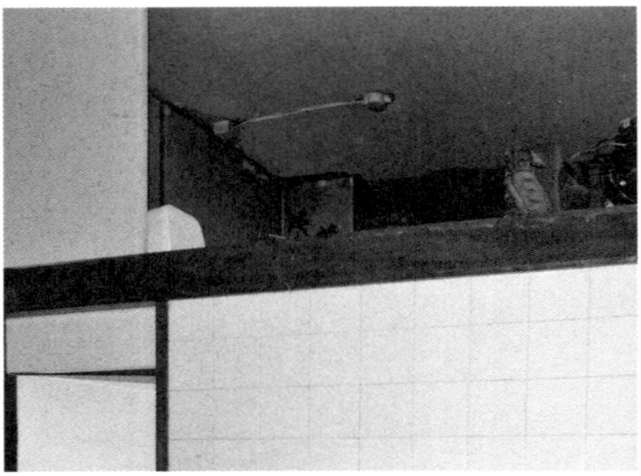

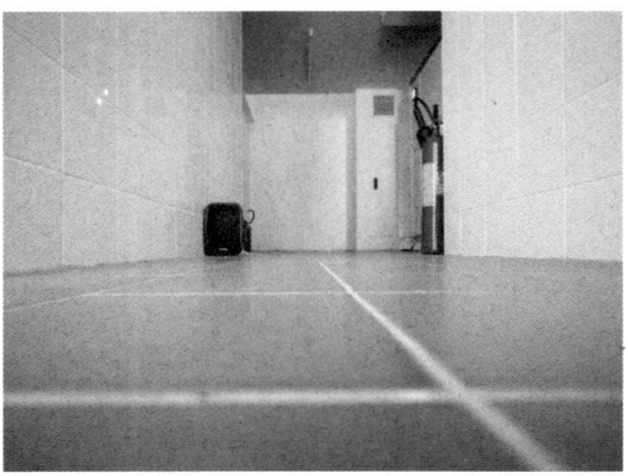

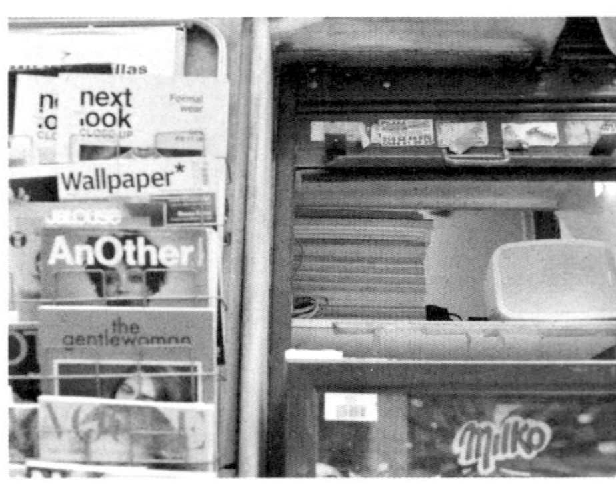
next look
Wallpaper*
AnOther
the gentlewoman

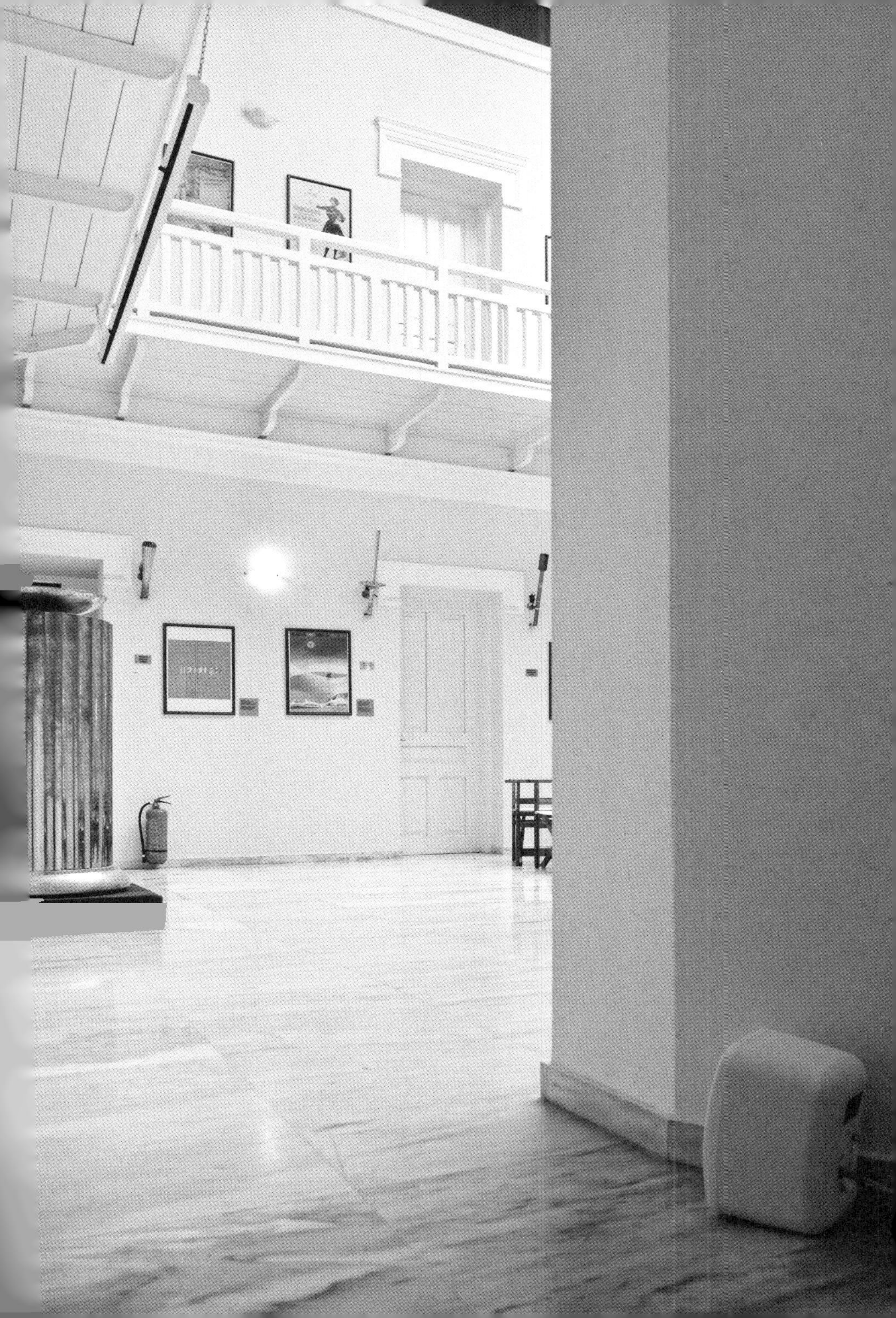

Diary of a Whispering Campaign

Klea Charitou

The whisper comes and goes. The whisper never knows.

1.

Occasionally visitors are surprised to learn that the myths of ancient Greece took place in sites whose names have remained unchanged for millennia. Megara, Thebes, Delphi, Corinth, Sparta, and Eleusis are all still there—dusty, windswept towns with an archaeological museum that may or may not be closed. Sometimes these visitors will detect, also, a similar pattern in the names of the people around them: Electra, Demetra, Calliope, Athena, Penelope, Antigone, Eurydice, and so forth. The point being that in certain societies, the presence of myth is no mere remnant of archaic times; it continues to inform many aspects of contemporary life and remains central to our understanding of its culture.

Spring 2016. We met the artist Pope.L in the lobby of the Radisson Blu Park Hotel, located on busy Alexandras Avenue in central Athens. Its Oak Room cafe was decorated in the usual international style, with hollow oak logs scattered here and there in a likely gesture toward the Pedion Tou Areos, or the Field of Ares, as the city park opposite the hotel is named. This early in the morning, people were still asleep in their rooms inside the luxury hotel. In the park, people, too, were sleeping out in the open. The winners and losers of the game of capital accumulation, divided not just by a roof over their heads but by the very condition of their bodies. The sight of the wasted figures of the broken, the consumed, the sick, the addicted, and those simply hanging by a thread told its own mordant story of the ongoing economic catastrophe.

Welcome, then, to Athens, the newly adopted home of documenta 14, where the banks had recently been shuttered and the gears of international finance had ground abruptly to a halt. It had not always been this way, of course: the city's largest public park was built to commemorate the heroes of the Greek Revolution of 1821, whose marble busts still stand scattered within. But as the park entered its wilderness years due to lack of public funds, the heroes' tranquil expressions seemed to have acquired a cast of doubt alongside the usual pigeon droppings, graffiti, and vandalism that are a hero's lot nowadays. Dressed in jeans and black sneakers, Pope.L gave us a quick look, raising his eyes beneath his baseball cap. A rental car parked across the street was waiting for him.

Our destination was the ancient city of Mycenae, hundreds kilometers to the south, once a hegemonic power when Athens was little more than a crossing point for sheep and goats. Our aim was to find sites with particular acoustic qualities that might act as echo chambers for the artist's *Whispering Campaign*, his proposed contribution to documenta 14. Pope.L's emailed instructions in this regard were rather laconic, indeed pleasingly cryptic: "Imagine a set of whisperers who whisper twenty-four hours a day for one hundred days—what are they whispering? Secrets."

Together we approached the Tomb of Agamemnon (or Treasury of Atreus, as Pausanias named it), a beehive-shaped building that once functioned as a royal burial site and exchequer. Alongside the Lion Gate, that last surviving piece of in situ Mycenaean sculpture, the Treasury of Atreus had come to symbolize a Bronze Age civilization that once dominated Mediterranean trade routes by force of arms. The tomb's decorated marble columns, friezes, and capitals had long since been pillaged, first by Lord Elgin and then by Heinrich Schliemann, destined for state collections in London and Berlin, respectively. Its vast door, too, had disappeared. Now only the heavy smell of animal dung made us hover at the entrance. The buzzing of a swarm of bees, too, started ringing in our ears. The queen bee was making her presence felt, controlling the colony with her reveille, while the pulse of the male drones merged with the female workers returning with pollen from the thyme and oregano scattered across the ruins: a reminder of life's cycle passing from heyday to decay, from princely gold to animal shit, from splendor to ruin.

On our first day roaming the ancient stones of the Mycenaean acropolis—so vast that later generations believed they were lifted there by Cyclopean giants—the documenta 14 curators could not yet intuit the comparison to the beehive, but that was what the team of fifty-something people driving *Whispering Campaign* would soon amount to. For the aim of this project was to produce, in less than one year, 9,438 hours' worth of audio work, whose sound was to flicker back and forth between Athens and Kassel for the entire 143-day duration of the exhibition, guided by a score that identified the elements of "nation, people, sentiment, language, and time" as the work's base materials.

2.

A few months later, we met again in the same hotel. Pope.L was suffering from a sore throat, and the plan was to spend the day at a workshop in the recording studio. On the way there, we picked up a bottle of propolis—another manifestation of apian energy. The artist drank the concoction reluctantly, listening closely as an actor whispered into the microphone, releasing the first rumor into an unsuspecting world: "The sound of the skateboard's wheels is the hum of bees or the grind of history's teeth or the whispers of fabulists lost in a forest...." Pope.L's narrative was at once aphoristic, prophetic, minatory, contradictory, rhadamanthine, darkly tragic yet filled with sharp humor and coruscating sarcasm. The characters were drawn from every period of history—Agamemnon, Spyros Louis, the Brothers Grimm, Rashel the Bangladeshi migrant, Anwar the Syrian refugee, Laskarina Bouboulina, Sappho—their disparate voices woven into a whispered chorus. As though summoned by an acoustic force, the protagonists seemed to have stepped from the darkness at long last—a forest of desperation, so to speak. They were on their way to Germany, perhaps Kassel even, or if not there, then some other land or shore that might offer a moment's shelter. From what? The mighty blows of fate. "By following a trail of bread crumbs, XXX each crumb in the shape of Europe."

We had stumbled across the first protagonist as he waited on Stournari Street, just outside the gates of the Athens Polytechnic. It happened to be the exact spot where the colonels' tanks had massacred student demonstrators some four decades earlier. Now the pavement was occupied for purely commercial purposes by Mondol Rashel, an optimistic thirty-year-old from Sylhet in northeastern Bangladesh. In the interview that provided the background for Pope.L's score, Rashel explained how he made a living selling tax-free cigarettes for twelve euros a carton. We learned that he had left his family to live in a single room he shared with other migrants; how he had risked his life to cross the river Evros into Greece; how he sent half of his income back home to support his family. More than anything, Rashel explained that he wanted to obtain legal papers that might offer a degree of protection from the police and allow him to return home one day to marry and live a normal life. In the meantime, he remained cheerful, acknowledging that the process might take some time. And by "some time," it is left to the audience to infer that Rashel may mean the remainder of his life.

Pope.L wove Rashel's story together with that of Agamemnon, the Mycenaean king who sacrificed his daughter Iphigenia so that the Greek fleet could set sail for Troy. The whispers align ancient myths with contemporary trials, the continuity of Agamemnon and Rashel bound in cryptic, dark connections, uncovering truths of sacrifice and migration, of survival and vengeance—all themes that push toward a futile and tragic teleology. The hitherto anonymous migrant Rashel is transformed by Pope.L into a contemporary Homeric hero whose dreams of a better life are cloaked in sadness. "All for a linen undulation, a filmy cloud, / a butterfly's flicker, a wisp of swan's down, / an empty tunic—all for a Helen,"[1] the Greek poet George Seferis wrote, as if precisely for this moment. A reminder, also, of the poetic quality that runs through Pope.L's score. The words evoke an immediacy reminiscent of Allen Ginsberg and, within their seeming chaos, an element of compassion we may recognize in William Blake.

1. George Seferis, "Helen," in *Collected Poems*, trans. Edmund Keeley and Philip Sherrard (London: Anvil Press, 1986), 359.

Following a similarly haphazard trajectory, we encounter our next protagonist, Anwar, a forty-three-year-old lawyer and father of seven from Al Harak, near the city of Daraa in southern Syria. "I am forty-three years old. I am slender and tall. I've lost my hair. I am sunburnt almost all the year, for there is no shade here in the camp to take shelter from the sun. I have lots of wrinkles all over my face, which I acquired since the war began. I like them. They are the signs of what I suffered, they are reminders of my personal history and of the history of my family, my country." In his interview, Anwar described how the revolution broke out among a handful of idealistic school kids in Daraa who had watched images of the Arab Spring on their color TVs. Within weeks the city was turned into a battleground, and his mother and brother's family were killed by Assad's army. Anwar fled for his life with his children, walking for twenty-four hours through the snow to reach safety in the Zaatari refugee camp in Jordan. His testimony entered Pope.L's text virtually unadorned. "Some children from five months to twelve years old had lost hands and eyes, had burns on their legs, and you could see their bones. But nobody could do anything to relieve them. I kept talking to them, as a means to keep them alive. 'Do something,' I yelled to the doctor. 'With what?' he replied tearfully.... Outside, the streets were deserted, and bombs were continuing to fall. If you got out into the street, you were lost.... I remember life before the war. I remember life before the war. I remember life before the war."

Pope.L's intent in broadcasting these fragments so barren and bald remains disguised. The audience is left with an unsettling feeling of profound disquiet. And the realization, too, perhaps, that everyday xenophobia becomes much more difficult to stomach when the humanity of each individual is made known. Though there are no answers here, only questions: "Is Greece now the nigger of Europe? Is Greece? Is Greece? Is Greece now the nigger of Europe... Europe is a very dark place. Europe is a very dark place. Europe is a very dark place. Europe is a very dark place."

3.

A more traditional type of hero emerged in the form of Spyros Louis, the twenty-one-year-old water carrier who won the first modern Olympic marathon in 1896, after running for two hours, fifty-eight minutes, and fifty seconds (including a pit stop for half an orange and a glass of cognac). Pope.L mysteriously greets the national hero wandering the same Panathenaic Stadium a century later. It seems that Louis has returned to his old profession of selling water on the streets of his native city. The narrative was broadcast inside the Gallery of Torches, a room filled with the twenty-nine torches of past Olympiads—one for every city that has hosted the modern games. Symbols of civilization and peace, and yet, as Louis reminds us, it was only in antiquity that the Olympic truce was ever granted.

Less than a kilometer south of the Panathenaic Stadium, at the end of Anapafseos Street, lies the next location of this strange campaign. At the First Cemetery, the whispers broadcast a mournful list of calamities to have befallen us from antiquity onward: a catalogue of diseases and pandemics, assassinations and disasters. "Pavlos Bakoyannis, New Democracy politician, shot outside his office in Athens by members of the revolutionary organization 'November 17,' on September 26, 1989." The coffee shop inside the cemetery was closed, waiting to be auctioned to new lessees—which should not present a problem since death remains a steady business even in these lean years. After the ceremony, or "last voyage of the deceased" as they say in Greece, the relatives still gather to remember and speak about their loved one's past—a funereal custom that has changed little since antiquity.

In ancient Greek mythology, Pheme was the goddess who personified the transmission of speech, traditions, insights, and victories. Her favor was the origin of the word "fame," her wrath a reputation destroyed by scandal and rumors. Nowadays, of course, Pheme is the goddess of advertising, public relations, and "fake news." The Greek word for advertisement, διαφήμιση, derives from the goddess. Then the thought occurs that when myth forms the very origin of language, it becomes impossible to escape. Thus the river of the Underworld, the Lethe, is not only the river of forgetting. It also informs the Greek word for truth, αλήθεια, which literally means "an absence of forgetting." By aligning the contemporary "heroes" alongside their ancient counterparts, this is precisely the space Pope.L contrives for his audience to enter—an absence of forgetting, or utopia of memory, if you will, where all human life is rendered indivisible in word as well as deed.

Pope.L's score, meanwhile, follows its own course, interrupted occasionally by long sequences of numbers. Their significance, or lack thereof, is left unexplained. The audience can only make an educated guess inspired by the spirit of the text. Counting for safety? Counting because otherwise people will be left uncounted? Counting because, as the text itself tells us, "dyslexia rules"? We do not know if the numbers are even mechanisms for counting or recollection, for the numbering of the dead, or the digital traces of stacks of hidden cash, the final panacea for our crisis-riven age, when currency controls are in full effect and half the country is haunted by the prospect of a ruinous devaluation. Perhaps the young can bear it, but the old suffer most acutely the humiliation of insecurity. On the TV news, another pensioner has committed suicide in despair. "One four nine nine three one one three." And then silence.

Was all this a hallucination, an incantation, a tragic fantasy masquerading as economic farce? The thought occurred on the day the next speaker was installed in a safe in an empty room at the Athens Conservatory of Music. The building itself is a Bauhaus modernist jewel on Rigilis Street, an exclusive neighborhood of central Athens overlooking Aristotle's Lyceum. Outside, along the main marble corridor, adolescent skateboarders blew off steam on an improvised ramp, and graffiti covered the surface of the white Pentelic marble. Most of the space inside had been left unused for years because the government can afford to keep the conservatory only on fiscal life support. For the skating teenagers, the meandering fortunes of economy and capital were no longer of any real concern—maybe because half their lives had been nurtured at the dry teat of unemployment and austerity. Perhaps here, then, was the best answer to the riddle of Pope.L's numbers in *Whispering Campaign*—as mocking echoes of the labyrinthine systems of exchange, which share a mythic or fantastical quality and yet no longer bear any relationship to the welfare of the nation's citizens. To the extent that the graffiti disfigures the marble with the scabrous tropes of anticapitalism, we witness the slow and painful death of modernism. Civilization ebbing gently backward with the rattle of the neon paint cans and the whirr of the skaters' wheels.

4.

In the wood-paneled Galaxy Bar off Stadiou Street, the well-off locals sat drinking dry martinis and whiskey sours. In their drunken state, they have convinced themselves that if all else collapses, the bronze sculpture of the freedom fighter Kolokotronis will remain astride his horse outside the old Parliament with his raised hand pointing no longer to Constantinople but to their favorite bar. Down in the basement, next to the toilets and the cracking sounds of the ice machine, Pope.L has added his own translucent whispers to the ambience. "Greek themes being this and that Germany. Being this and that king. This and that war. This and that god. This and that beehive. This and that fate. DARK. This and that austerity measure."

In an attempt to lure the Chicago-based artist into Athens's peculiarly decadent nightlife, we wandered the streets of the "historic triangle"—which is how Athenians refer to the city center, reducing layers of history to mundane geometry. The drunken revelers on their hands and knees offered an unwitting reminder of Pope.L's own crawling performances along the pavements of New York City. In an empty alley between the tall buildings surrounding the Cantina Social, an island utopia lay hidden for those cut adrift in the night, where the beer came from Russia and time seemed to vanish into a black hole right before the break of dawn. The stencil of a raven watched from the back of the courtyard—a friendly omen, perhaps, or otherwise. Inside a flowerpot, the soil had been replaced by another speaker—the whispers masquerading now as botanical decoration inside a space where a porn movie from the 1970s is played in an endless loop. Only its audio track had been replaced by a disconcerting new score. "But also an actual place because I am somehow in it right now, this is proof! This is proof! This is Proof! ... Language, though spoken by all, remains a mystery." Pope.L whispered goodnight. It was already very late, time to go.

The next day we met for the last time at the Radisson Blu Park Hotel. We needed to make some last-minute adjustments to the various speakers before documenta 14's grand opening. For the occasion, Pope.L's gallery had sent a large black limousine. The driver opened the doors for us, bracing himself for the infernal task of covering thirty-five kilometers' worth of urban gridlock in pursuit of *Whispering Campaign*. Unraveled by traffic, the thought emerged that Pope.L's narrative may constitute a new geography of time evoked by this most ancient of cities. The first of twelve stops was at the School of Fine Arts, a former shoe factory in the city's industrialized zone. Halfway down Piraeus Street, the Parthenon can still be seen here amid the abandoned factories and stray dogs roaming the scrap metal yards. Over the art school's entrance gate, someone has placed a reminder: Ενας Στο ΜοΜa, Χιλιάδες Στον Αγώνα (One in MoMA, thousands on the battlefield). Only in Greece, it seems, can a rhyming couplet serve to tranquilize the expectations of the students. But we had already entered the old library, now stripped of its books and renamed the "Empty University." At the right-hand corner entrance, Pope.L listened carefully and adjusted the volume of the speaker installed there. "Ignorance is a virtue," it whispered. He winked at us on our way out.

The day's final destination was the National Museum of Contemporary Art. The Greek version of MoMA has remained closed for years now, since long before the crisis even started. We passed quickly through the entire chapter of documenta 14 now housed here to reach the top floor. The empty café had not yet opened to the crowd of journalists and art world professionals intent on drinking iced cappuccinos and discussing monumentality in contemporary art while enjoying the glorious view of the Parthenon opposite. Inspired by Pope.L's whispers, to us it suddenly felt easy to ascribe agency or consciousness to the sacred rock, seemingly asking its goddess Athena for protection from the chattering newcomers. *Whispering Campaign*, after all, is nothing if not animistic in its state of mind. Perhaps the rock will agree that an artwork can be monumental today without being large in size, solid, or permanent. Perhaps, too, it had grown more confident in its own presence, we thought, having read Don DeLillo's multinational executive protagonist confess the following, three decades earlier: "For a long time I stayed away from the Acropolis. It daunted me, that somber rock. I preferred to wander in the modern city, imperfect, blaring. The weight and moment of those worked stones promised to make the business of seeing them a complicated one. So much converges there. It's what we've rescued from the madness. Beauty, dignity, order, proportion."[2]

Going bankrupt, Ernest Hemingway once wrote, happens gradually, then suddenly. The recognition of a contemporary masterpiece may follow a similar trajectory. Its reputation builds, unaware of its own renown. Long after all the visitors have gone, Pope.L's whispers echoed in the same silent room above: "a chunky superannuated Greece composed of glitchy neoclassical columns of gray plus black plus more gray plus maybe bits of blanched white that is today's dark dark Europe.... Is it a fragment of the Parthenon? A neoclassical poltergeist?" We stood there, smiled, and renewed our appointment, one hundred days later, in Kassel.

2. Don DeLillo, *The Names* (New York: Knopf, 1982), 9.

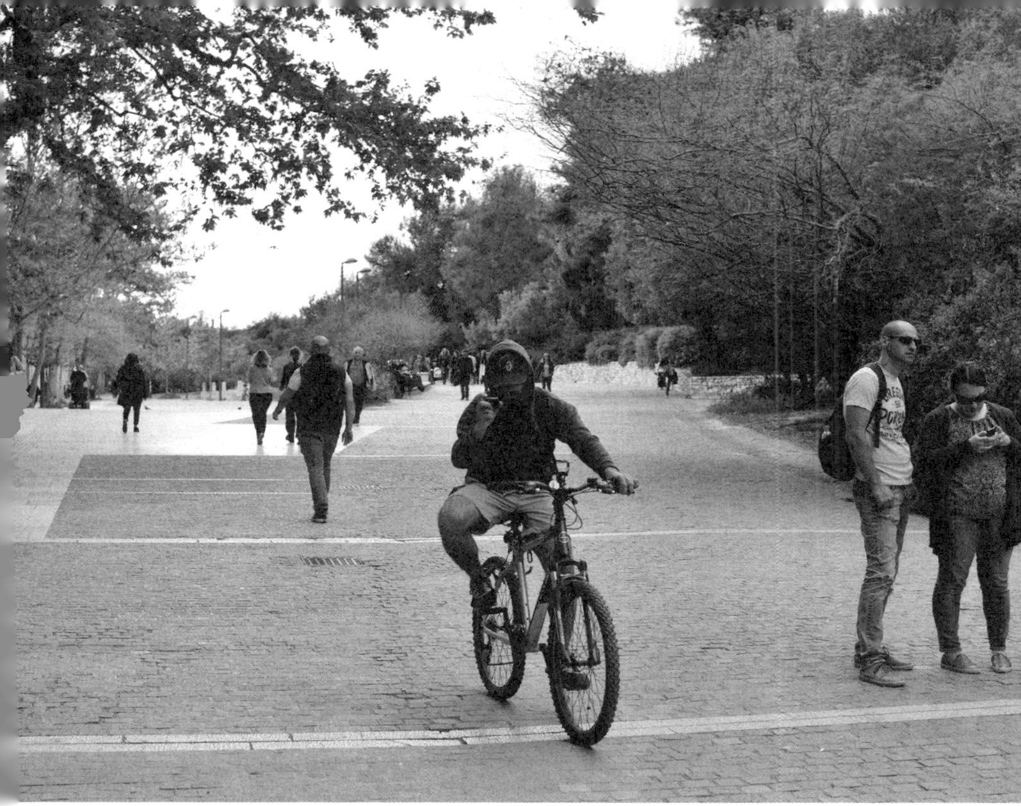

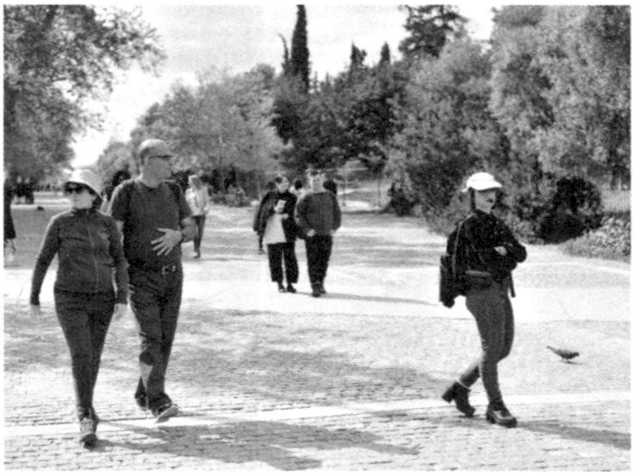
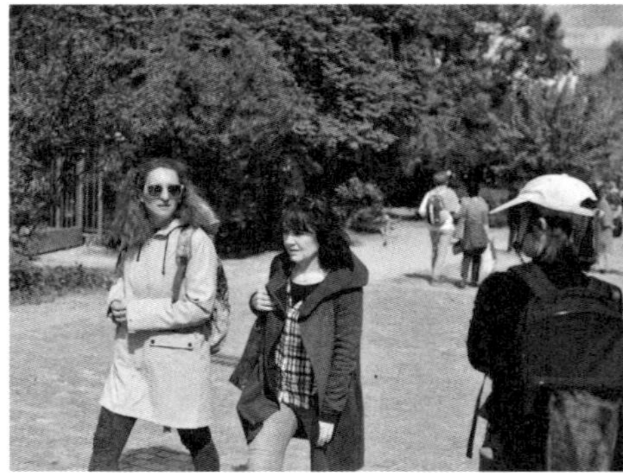
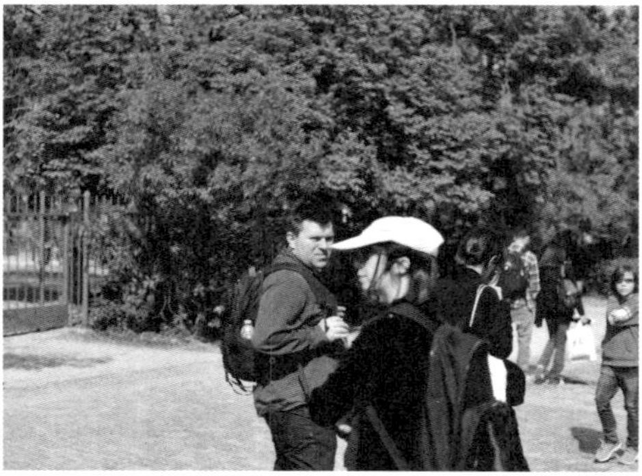
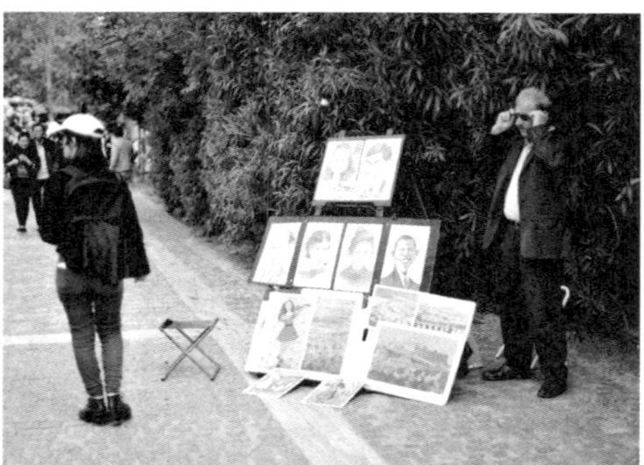
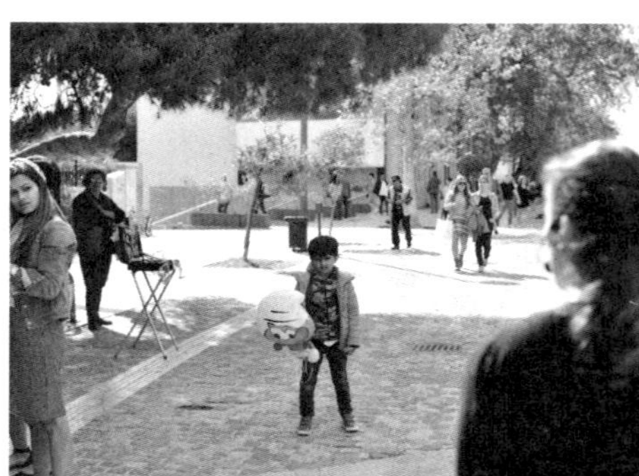

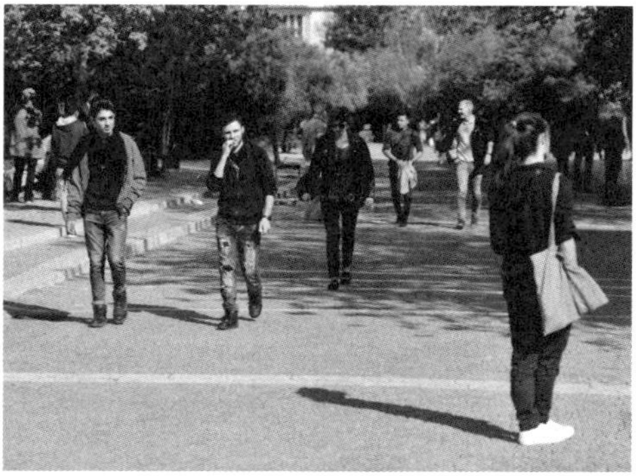

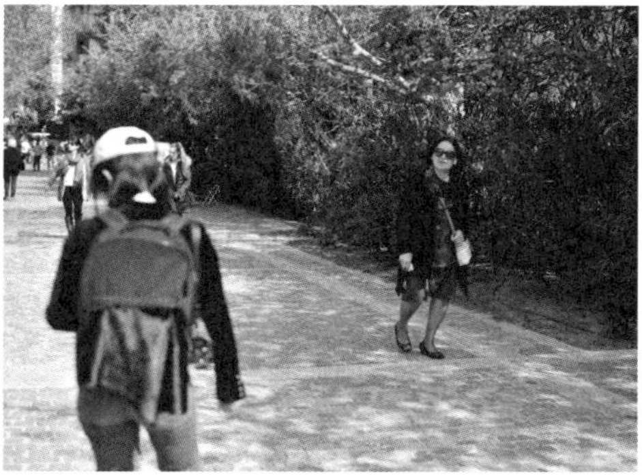

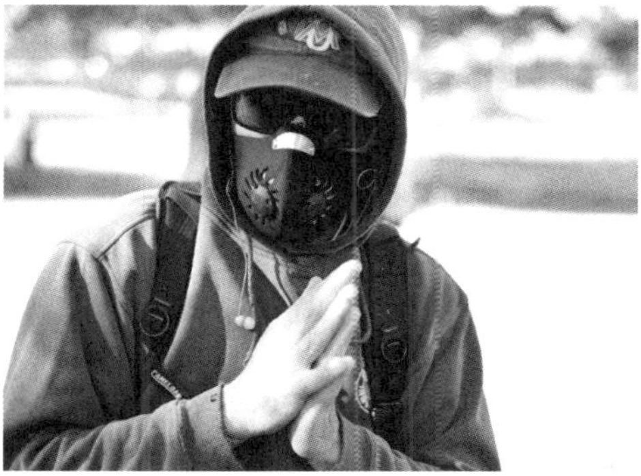

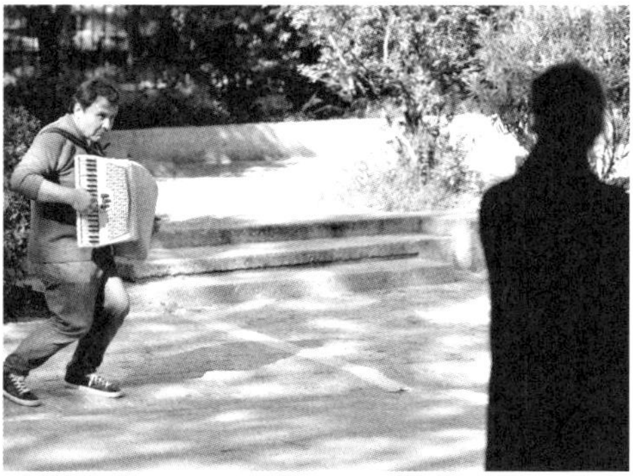

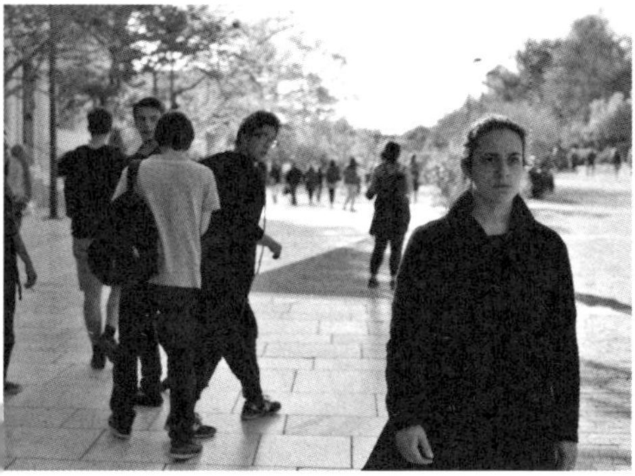

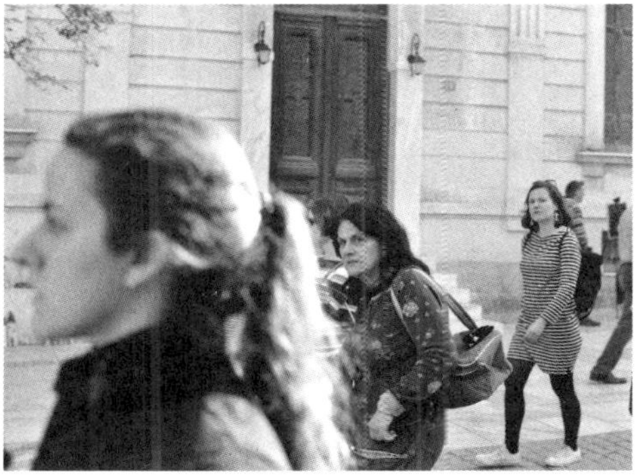

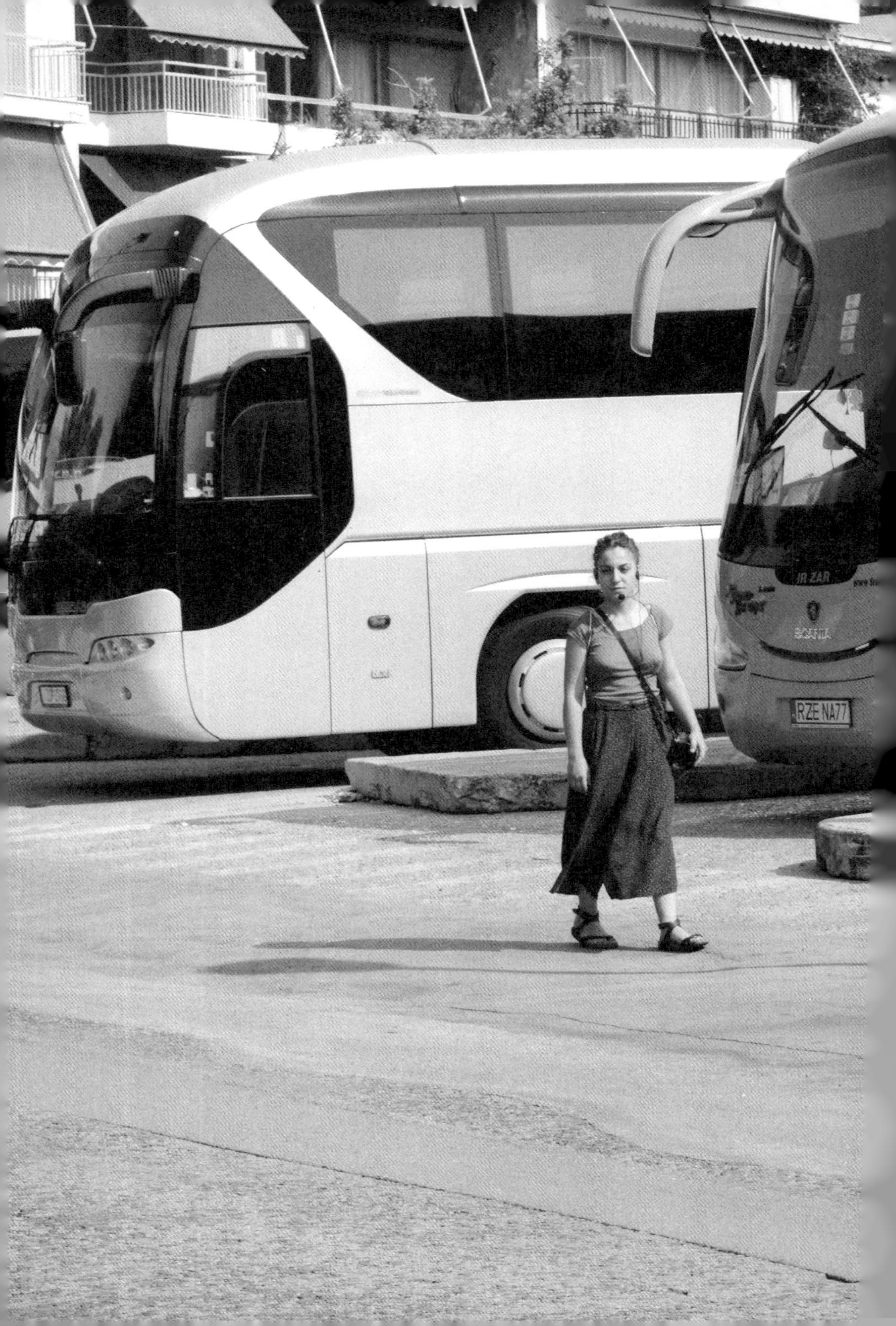
SCANIA
RZE NA77

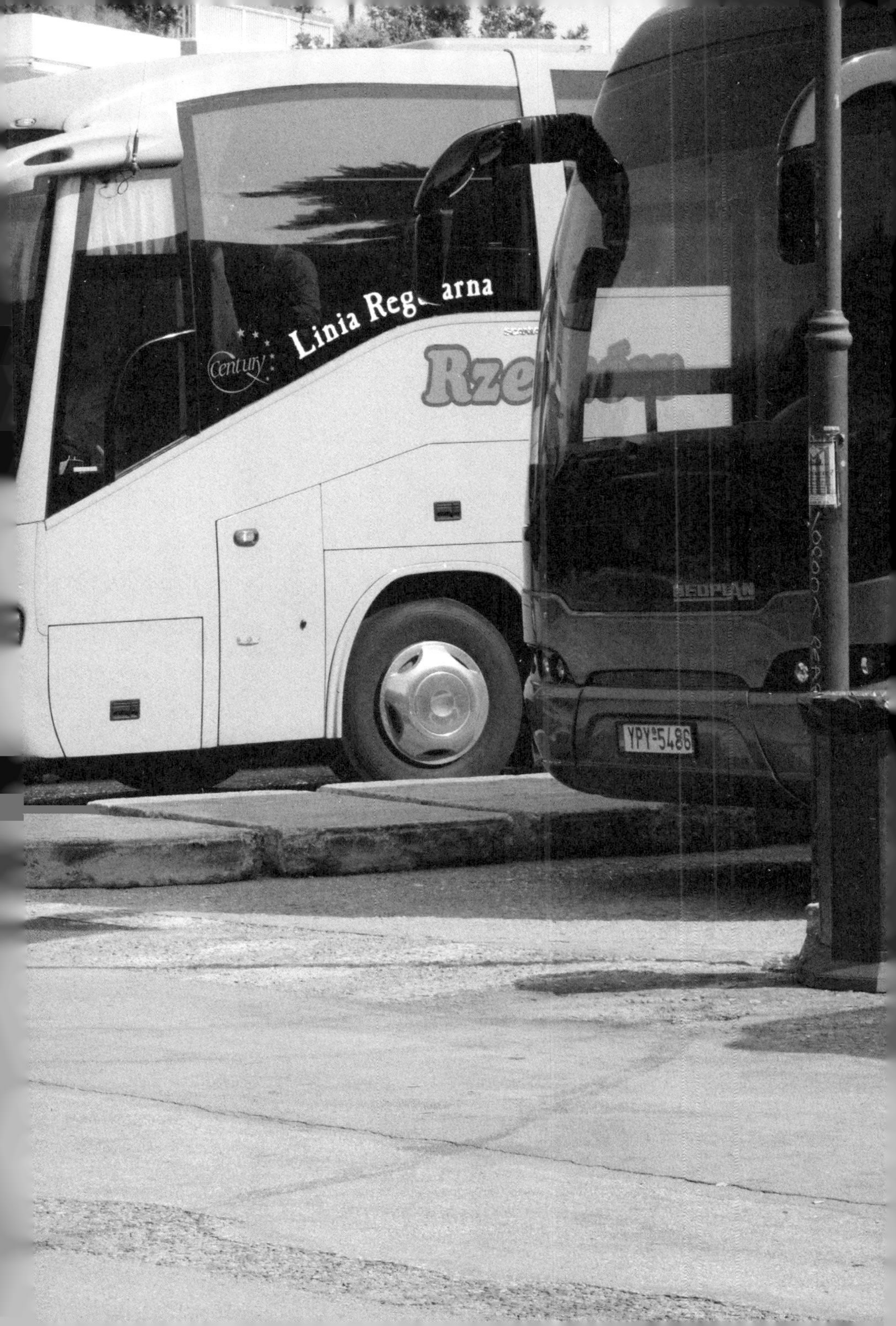
Century
Linia Reg
arna
Rze
YPY-5486

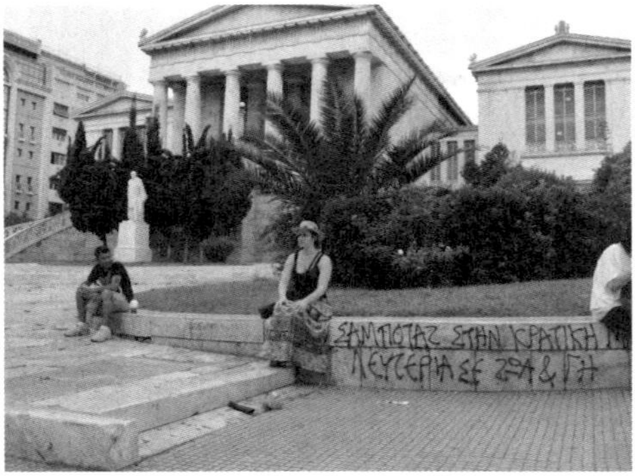

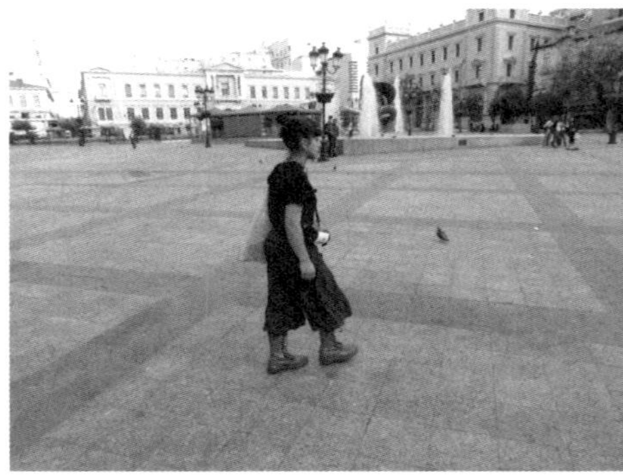

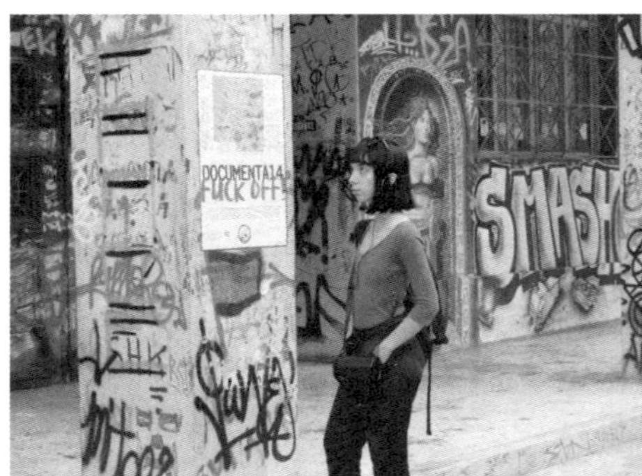
DOCUMENTA14
FUCK OFF
SMASH

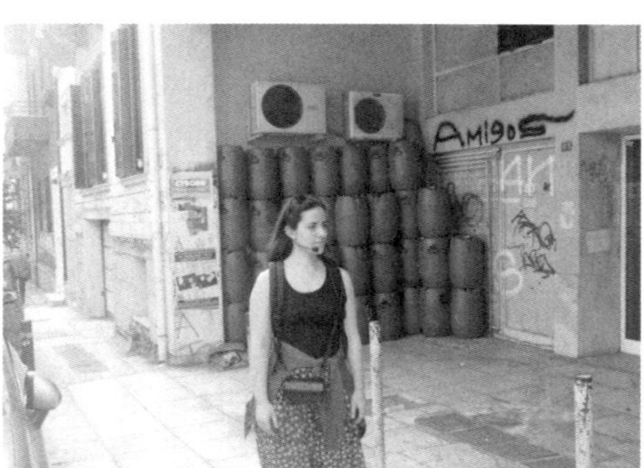

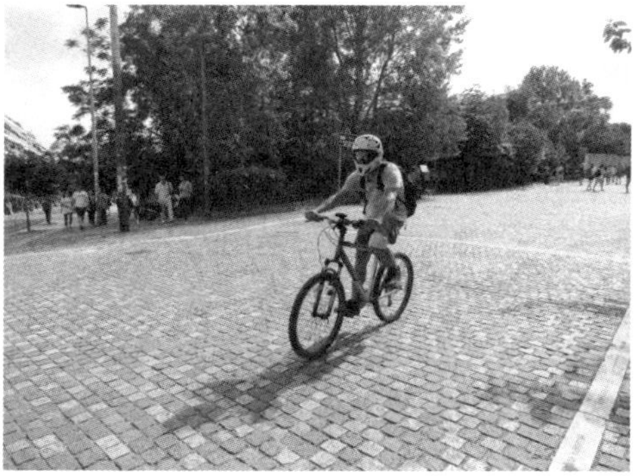
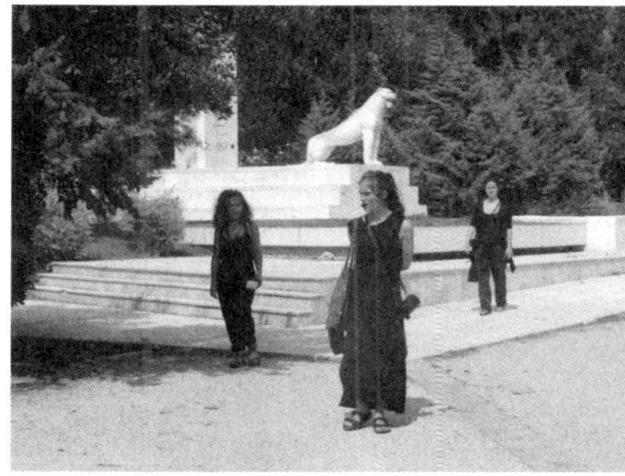
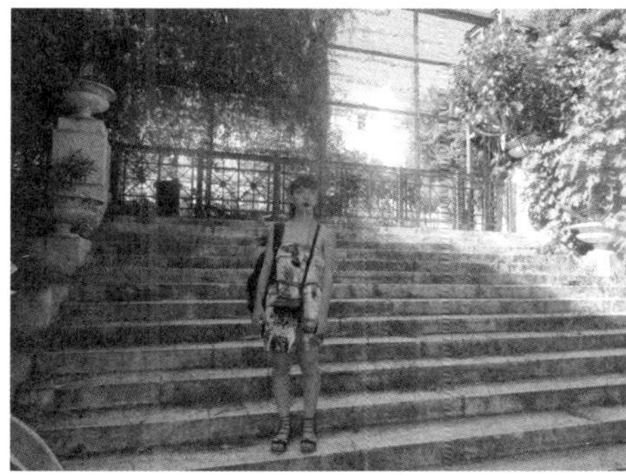
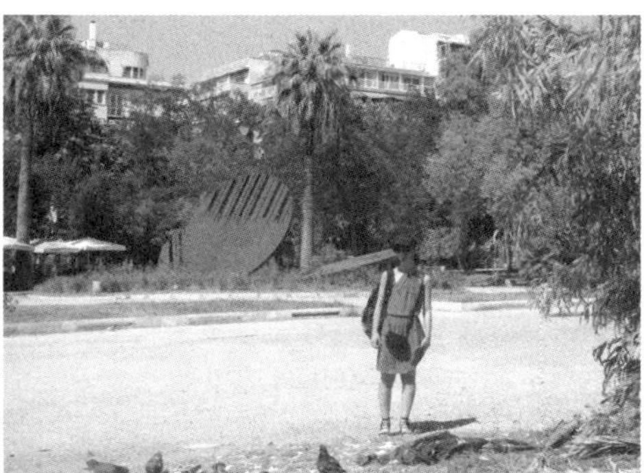
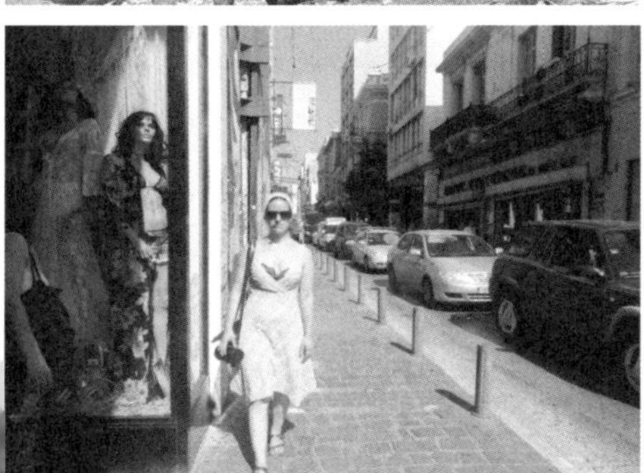
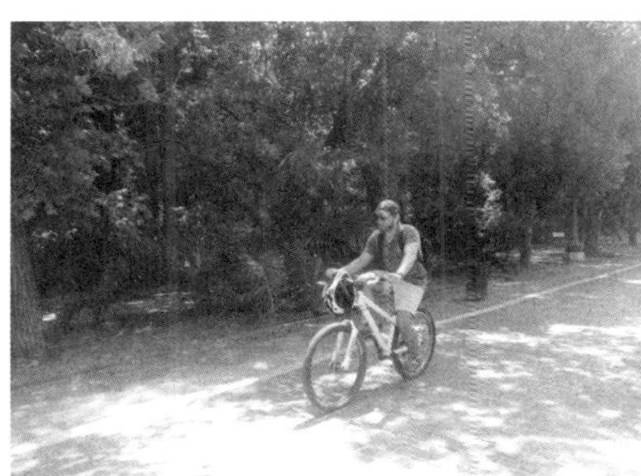

Pope.L, Aprophet
Monika Szewczyk

I know that I know nothing.
—Socratic paradox (hearsay)

The year 2016 turned out to be one of wild speculations, burning insults, half-lies, and post-truth—the Oxford Dictionaries' Word of the Year. But even before the Brexit referendum with its demonized immigrant laborers or the US presidential election with its (at first only muffled)[1] accusations of Russian interference, Pope.L thought to make his contribution to documenta 14 a whispering campaign. On February 20 of that year, I received an email summarizing the artist's meeting with my colleague on the case, Dieter Roelstraete, in Chicago:

> My meeting with dieter was short but full. We discussed a whispering campaign project--i am still working on more specifics--but imagine a set of whisperers who whisper 24 hours a day for 100 days--what are they whispering? Secrets. A history of the world. Directions to the on ramp of possibility.
>
> What is the relationship between the whisperers in the two cities? Well, they influence each other--somehow--not sure how--it would be interesting for them to echo, pirate and conflate each other--whispering is a musical form of identity. making via sound--

In March 2016, during Pope.L's first visit to Athens, we organized a workshop in the studio environment of Prevelakis Hall at the Athens National Technical University, or Polytechnion.[2] Students from the Athens

1. Jane Mayer, "Russia Won," *New Yorker*, October 1, 2018, 18–26. As noted in Mayer's article, "at 12:40 p.m. [on October 7, 2016] the Obama Administration released a stunning statement, by the Department of Homeland Security and the director of National Intelligence, accusing the Russian government of interfering in the election through hacking. This seemed certain to dominate the weekend news but at 4:03 P.M. the *Washington Post* published a report, by David Fahrenthold, on an "Access Hollywood" tape that captured Trump, on a hot mike, boasting about grabbing women "by the pussy." Then, less than half an hour later, WikiLeaks released its first tranche of e-mails that Russian hackers had stolen from [Clinton's campaign chairman John] Podesta's account." In the same article, the following detail: "The Blacktivist ruse was part of a larger Russian plot to divide Americans, according to Senator Mark Warner, the vice-chair of the Senate Intelligence Committee. An expert told the committee that automated accounts typically push extremist views twenty-five to thirty times more often than authentic American social-media users do. 'It blew my mind,' he told me. 'It was an OMG moment. *The extremes are screaming while the majority whispers.*'" (My italics.)
2. The space was refurbished for documenta 14 by the Athens- and Berlin-based architect Aristide Antonas.

Academy of Fine Arts and documenta 14 staff gathered to hear the artist's first thoughts on the form his participation in the bilocated quinquennial would take. He was after a tone. Some volunteers began to improvise, speaking immediate observations, freestyle speculations, riffs on one-word prompts (like "debt" or "colonialism"), in ones, twos, and more together, through mics or a handheld loudspeaker recognizable from street demonstrations. Pope.L noted how a lo-fi filter amplified the whispers but also degraded them, gave them some texture, made it feel like the truth was struggling to get out.

At the time, an anarchist group was housing some one hundred refugees in one of the buildings on the gated campus. Unlike the heavily and privately policed University of Chicago, where Pope.L works as a professor of fine arts, all Greek universities have been off-limits to police since 1982, when the university asylum law went into effect following the killing of at least twenty-seven people and the rounding up for torture of many others during the 1973 Polytechnic uprising. That event marked the beginning of the end of the seven-year "dictatorship of the colonels," which lasted from 1967 until 1974. The old gate mangled by the junta's tanks is still lying just outside the graffitied neoclassical entrance of Prevelakis Hall. The new gates are transaction zones—and they are exactly where we would later meet a man who traded his story of arrival in Greece via Syria, Turkey, and the sea. But first, we toured resonant sites where speakers could be tucked away or performers could whisper in an unsuspecting crowd. Pope.L kept an eye out for PA systems already burrowed into the city's infrastructure. This work was half-blind as—especially in Athens—we were not sure what places could be secured for the public exhibition set to open in just over one year. Unlike in its birthplace in Kassel, documenta 14 was a recent immigrant in Athens, arousing suspicions.

On May 15, several major news outlets ran stories headlined "Ignorance is not a virtue," quoting then president of the United States Barack Obama during a commencement address at Rutgers University. His advice was read as a thinly veiled critique of the candidate who would become his successor: "It's not cool to not know what you're talking about. That's not keeping it real or telling it like it is. That's not challenging political correctness. That's just not knowing what you're talking about."[3] The president never named a single ignoramus, but the next day, just ten days shy of receiving the Republican nomination, @realDonaldTrump tweeted: "'In politics, and in life, ignorance is not a virtue.' This is a primary reason that President Obama is the worst president in US history!" In the next months, Trump's campaign of slander mounted as major news outlets amplified whatever he published on Twitter or spoke into a mike.

At some point during the scripting of his *Whispering Campaign*, Pope.L introduced the German and English phrases "Ignoranz ist eine Tugend" and "Ignorance is a virtue." These appear amid a vast array of texts whispered by hired voices, recorded in studios in Athens, Kassel, and Chicago, and emitted from speakers installed in fifteen locations in Athens and nineteen in Kassel, including live transmissions on the streets and through the radio waves. There were other isolated phrases such as "A dearth swept across the land" (the first line of *Hansel and Gretel* as recorded by the Brothers Grimm)[4] and "Europe is a very dark place" ("Η Ευρώπη είναι ένα πολύ σκοτεινό μέρος" in Greek, "Europa ist ein sehr dunkler Ort" in German), as well as fragments of stories procured the old way (via live oral testimony), summaries of local myths, biographies of figures surviving in stone, and lists of numbers that *sounded* random—though we will never know whether they really were.

3. See: "Barack Obama mocks Donald Trump: 'Ignorance is not a virtue'," *The Telegraph*, May 15, 2016. www.telegraph.co.uk/news/2016/05/15/barack-obama-mocks-donald-trump-ignorance-is-not-a-virtue

4. The Brothers Grimm recorded their now famous fairy tales from less credited storytellers who were working orally, such as Dorothea Viehmann, whose biography Pope.L studied for his *Whispering Campaign*. He had already amassed five years of experience staging *Hansel and Gretel* with MFA students at the University of Chicago prior to documenta 14, rewriting the script each year, a method addressed in "H+G: An Introduction," the artist's contribution to *South As a State of Mind* magazine no. 8 (documenta 14, no. 3), accessible online at https://www.documenta14.de/en/south/1525_h_g_an_introduction. The magazine also published the script to "H+G" by Pope.L's students Elizabeth Allen-Cannon, Vidura Jang Bahadur, Andrew Bearnot, Jan Brugger, Evan Carter, Kyle Hossli, Ben Nicholson, and Shanna Zentner. See: www.documenta14.de/en/south/898_h_g

Now, just over a year after the conclusion of documenta 14 and well into the forty-fifth presidency, the campaign has become a shared memory, told from various viewpoints, much like *Rashomon*, the New Testament, or the news. Newsprint handouts prepared for Athens and Kassel with Pope.L's frequent graphic design collaborator, the artist David Khan-Giordano, are just about the only material remnant of this vast undertaking. (The audio files exist in a digital format and, while still held on memory devices, their physical substance is inherently unstable and susceptible to unforeseeable change.) These folded A1 sheets, printed on both sides, carry scores of details—including city maps, schedules, credits, fragments of the whisperers' scripts or prompts, and a facsimile of a typed out and hand-edited page titled "(Unclassified) I love Europe Text" and subtitled "Question: How should I classify this text?"

At the top left of the drawn page facsimile, a postage-stamp-sized frame contains the following stacked words, scribbled in capitals: "BROWN / PEOPLE / ARE / THERE / IS NO / EU / IN / HEAVEN," connecting one vast incremental endeavor to another, namely *Whispering Campaign* to Pope.L's *Skin Set Drawings*, a work in progress begun in 1992. A small selection of that vast accumulation of mostly letter-sized works on paper was installed throughout Kassel's documenta-Halle, some prominently, others tucked away, much like the speakers of *Whispering Campaign* strewn across both documenta 14 cities. The invocation of *Skin Set Drawings* inside *Whispering Campaign*'s maps of Athens and Kassel brought into focus a continuum of coded messaging in Pope.L's work, much of it touching on the matter of living inside Europe's empire on this earth.[5]

And there are bugs. Oversized, realistically rendered bookworms—each over an inch in length—are distributed

5. The selection for documenta 14 included *Black People Are the Wet Grass at Morning* (2001–02); *Black People Are the Silence They Cannot Understand* (2001–02); *White People Are the Cliff and What Comes After* (2001–02); *Green People Are a Recent Invention* (2011); *Orange People Are the Way Things Used to Be When They Were in Power* (2012); *Red People Are My Mother When She Sick and Visiting Me in the Hospital* (2010); *White People Are God's Way of Saying I'm Sorry* (2010); and *Yellow People Are the Dog's Seed* (2010). While these titles are already telling—and it should be noted here that, in preparing this selection for placement inside the documenta-Halle, Pope.L's only rule was to not limit ourselves to the *Black People* and *White People* sets—the reader must imagine varied scribbles and embellishments: schoolbook doodling with hints of the depths and illuminations offered by medieval marginalia, adding layers of meaning and feeling to each iteration.

to look like they are crawling in space and time, over map and schedule, with a one-foot-long, ghostlike watermark of these grotesque insects spread diagonally across the page composed of English, German, and Greek text fragments. Unfolding the newsprint for the first time put me in mind of Manny Farber's 1962 essay "White Elephant Art and Termite Art"; this critique of the pretentions of certain European art-house films then being screened in the United States can also be read as a treatise on broader aesthetic tendencies still playing out today. For instance, Farber found key examples of "termite art" in popular forms such as political campaign coverage:

> The best examples of termite art appear in places other than films, where the spotlight of culture is nowhere in evidence, so that the craftsman can be ornery, wasteful, stubbornly self-involved, doing go-for-broke art and not caring what comes of it. The occasional newspaper column by a hard-work specialist caught up by an exciting event (Joe Alsop or Ted Lewis, during a presidential election), or a fireball technician reawakened during a pennant playoff that brings on stage his favorite villains (Dick Young); the TV production of *The Iceman Cometh*, with its great examples of slothful-buzzing acting by Myron McCormack, Jason Robards, et al.; the last few detective novels of Ross Macdonald and most of Raymond Chandler's ant-crawling verbosity and sober fact-pointing in the letters compiled years back in a slightly noticed book that is a fine running example of popular criticism; the TV debating of William Buckley, before he relinquished his tangential, counterattacking skill and took to flying into propeller blades of issues, like James Meredith's Ole Miss-adventures.[6]

Read the fragmented map-script-schedule of *Whispering Campaign*, and you might get a sense of how the project spread through Athens and Kassel. Perhaps the bookworms—a late addition to the design that was never

6. Manny Farber, "White Elephant Art and Termite Art," *Film Culture* no. 27 (Winter 1962–63): 243.

discussed overtly—are there to remind us that the work was calibrated to burrow, permeate, seep into the infrastructure, eating away at any sense of stable power to which a monument could be raised. (As "vermin," they also recall the slurs directed at immigrants and minorities by the Nazis—among many others.) One of the most quoted summary sentences from Farber's essay captures something of the condition of Pope.L's work, which is epic without being visibly announced as such: "A peculiar fact about termite-tapeworm-fungus-moss art is that it goes always forward, eating its own boundaries, and, likely as not, leaves nothing in its path other than the signs of eager, industrious, unkempt activity."[7] The invisibility of Pope.L's *Whispering Campaign* brings to the fore many associations—with invisible people, invisible struggles, slow or hardly discernible incremental progress—none of which figure much in Europe's well-lit metaphors of virtuous knowing.

*

Then again, like the glasses I cannot see on my nose when I am busy looking for my glasses, the invisible artwork may also be a lens. Through *Whispering Campaign*, it is possible to speak more cogently about certain necessarily nebulous features of the vast, complex, and unruly space-time continuum called documenta 14. Dimitris Athiridis, the Greek filmmaker who, at the time of writing, is still in the process of editing a feature film about the making of documenta 14, currently thinks to open with a shot of Pope.L's makeshift stand for a loudspeaker placed in front of Kassel's Fridericianum and programmed to emit the whispered motto "Ignoranz ist eine Tugend." (A roughly fifteen-minute teaser screened at the 2018 Cannes Film Festival begins with this very shot.) Above this scene, another paradoxical message could be read for the duration of the hundred-day public exhibition: *BEINGSAFEISSCARY*. The sign was placed on the portico of documenta's traditional main venue after the artist Banu Cennetoğlu removed the letters that normally spell

7. Farber, "White Elephant Art and Termite Art," 242.
8. Cennetoğlu's work quotes a shard of graffiti found on the walls of the Polytechnic in Athens: a sly transposition of Technicolor defiance to the white marble purity of the Hellenist mirage—that white elephant erected by German idealists and their acolytes in an attempt to give their supremacist fantasies and attendant suppressive tactics a solid base in ancient art and architecture.

out FRIDERICIANUM.[8] In front of the building (Europe's oldest purpose-built gallery, which also became a parliament and a library), Marta Minujín's *Parthenon of Books*, a 1:1 scaled copy of Athena's temple on the Acropolis of Athens, made up of thousands of censored volumes gathered in Kassel, in Athens, and at the Frankfurt Book Fair, conflated the white elephant and the termite (or bookworm). Its siting on the Friedrichsplatz conjured memories of the Nazi book-burning campaigns of the 1930s.

Elsewhere, Amar Kanwar's film *Early One Morning* extended the sense of what I will call endarkment, played out in so many works across documenta 14. Kanwar's portrayal of a mysteriously reclusive mathematician slowly divulges the nature of the man's scholarly eminence: the ability to account for forty-nine distinct forms of darkness, that very phenomenon to which Europe returns, again and again, as a cipher of ignorance. It is often forgotten that one of the continent's most celebrated ancients, Socrates, is rumored to have said, through that transhistorical whispering campaign propagated by Plato and his Latin-speaking followers, "I know that I know nothing." Socrates's intellectual courage was apparently rewarded by Pythia, the oracle at Delphi, who called him "the wisest"—but this did not save him from banishment from the *polis* for allegedly corrupting its youth.

If an expressed need to learn, from Athens and elsewhere, spurred documenta 14 on, this learning progressed with a sense of unfamiliarity, adjusting positions, multiplying perspectives, making room in space and time for varied artworks and other social phenomena that themselves dramatized the limits of knowing and dispelled the false security of surveillance. In his initial proposal for the exhibition, the subsequently elected artistic director Adam Szymczyk had written of the choice to work both in Athens and in documenta's traditional hometown of Kassel:

> These two projects, realized in different ways while learning from their respective places and from each other, will form two pictures that could

never be superimposed to form a single image. Nor will the two shows be possible to be grasp from a one vantage point. By asking documenta visitors to take a similar route as its makers, the exhibition would also ask them to take their time, allowing a break in visibility while journeying between the two locations. My hope is that the exhibition will thus become an agent of change and a transformative experience for its audience and participants in both cities.[9]

Needless to say, it was not simple to sell the bilocated project politically or to give clear prescriptions on how people taking part might best navigate this amorphous "it." The curators, artists, and extended team of documenta 14 proceeded in proverbial darkness, incrementally eating away at the borders of our ignorance, trying to make things happen within various degrees of hospitality. In the preparatory years of the exhibition, with the growing influx of different people whom the news abstracted as "migrants" into Europe, encounters with strangers, with strangeness, were increasingly mediated as threats. Many works or gestures comprising documenta 14 were the works or gestures of artists with lived experience of migration; of crossing continents in a state of danger, loss, and grief; of becoming strangers in strange lands. Others either had or got a sense of what it means to descend from colonial encounters, wherein uneven firepower (also from psychological and economic weapons), uneven defenses (including physical immunity), and, perhaps most importantly, differing attitudes to difference all contributed to the killing or serious maiming of equal and therefore truly free relations.

When Elephants Fight, It Is the Frogs That Suffer, Benjamin Patterson's "sonic graffiti" from 2017, composed of field recordings and human simulations that were disseminated on speakers tucked away in the gardens of the Byzantine and Christian Museum in Athens and the Karlsaue park in Kassel, carried the Fluxus artist's characteristic "high-silliness" but also his clear sense of social justice. Sadly, Patterson passed away as documenta 14 was

9. Internal document produced by the Communications Department of documenta 14, spring–summer 2017.

taking shape—though luckily he got his chance to visit Athens, the home of Aristophanes, the comic playwright whose *The Frogs* of 405 BCE had been the inspiration for his proposal. With his work as well as Postcommodity's sound installations *The Ears of the World Are Always Speaking* (2017) in Aristotle's Lyceum in Athens and *Blind/Curtain* (2017) at the entrance of Kassel's Neue Gallery, or the production and world premiere of Joaquin Mejía Orellana's *Symphony from the Third World* (2017), not to mention *The School of Listening* devised by curator Candice Hopkins, the Listening Space curated in Athens by music advisor Paolo Thorsten-Nagel, and the entire public radio program *Every Time I Ear di Soun*, organized by curator-at-large Bonaventure Soh Bejeng Ndikung along with his colleagues at SAVVY in Berlin, "making via sound" emerged as a central feature of the fourteenth edition of documenta. Amid this rich sonic field, Pope.L's campaign became even more pronounced *as whispers*—that strangely conspiratorial, subconscious, open-secret, fugitive-truth register of speech—rather than as a singular sound work in a predominantly visual art exhibition. Widening the spectrum of darkness begat a wider spectrum of listening, begat a wider spectrum of learning.

Around 4 a.m. on October 3, 2018, the twenty-ninth anniversary of German reunification, the Monument for strangers and refugees (Das Fremdlinge und Flüchtlinge Monument), a sixteen-meters concrete obelisk erected on Kassel's Königsplatz and inscribed with the phrase from St. Matthew's Gospel "I was a stranger and you took me in" in English, German, Arabic, and Turkish—the contribution to documenta 14 of Olu Oguibe, a survivor of the Biafran War of 1967–70—was secretly dismantled by municipal workers, even as deliberations continued about its possible adoption by the city as one of the public works that would remain from documenta's fraught fourteenth edition. (About one week later, it was announced, just as unexpectedly, that the obelisk would be reinstalled in another location, at the top of the Treppenstraße in the city center.) Formally, Oguibe's monument is just about the opposite of the horizontally dispersed, quasi-invisible yet all the more oddly audible *Whispering Campaign*. In sharing the same field, however, they may perhaps be understood to act as foils for each other. The dimensions of Pope.L's *Whispering Campaign* are truly sublime—that is, quite literally ungraspable. Within the exhibition materials, in print and online, the duration and materials of the work were stated as "Nation, people, sentiment, language, time, 9.438 hours." That is more than all the hours making up the one hundred days of documenta 14 in Athens and those making up the one hundred days of documenta 14 in Kassel combined. Reasoning through the work's duration is like trying to grasp it from the outside, dismember it or carry it away. This cannot be done. The whispered narrations constitute an atmosphere. And amid much speculation, in this *cloud of unknowing*, there is no desire to soothe the audience (literally "those who hear") with a prediction of what is to come.

Pope.L is no prophet. Consider again the often-repeated phrases:

> Europe is a very dark place.
>
> Ignorance is a virtue.
>
> Sprache bleibt ein Rätsel, auch wenn sie von allen gesprochen wird.

In Greek: "Η γλώσσα παρότι ομιλείται από όλους παραμένει ένα μυστήριο." In English: "Language, though spoken by all, is a mystery." Language is like love—also a mystery. When you love someone, you don't necessarily *know* them. But you certainly know that you want to *get to know them*. You might keep getting to know them your entire life. Love is not, therefore, some kind of blissful ignorance. Nor is it a stagnant oblivion. It could be a chewing or a nibbling. Or kissing. Or editing—like the scribbles scrawled across Pope.L's "(Unclassified) I love Europe Text." Thinking

10. Thank you to Darby English for generously sharing a version of the manuscript for his book, *To Describe a Life: Notes from the Intersection of Art and Race Terror* (New Haven, CT: Yale University Press, forthcoming 2019), 42–85, based on his 2016 Richard D. Cohen Lectures on African and African American Art at Harvard University. His sense of the "differing" enacted in Pope.L's *Skin Set Drawings* and broader insistence on the complexity of artistic responses to the present terror inspired this work of reflection and the initial inclusion of selected *Skin Set Drawings* within documenta-Halle on the occasion of documenta 14 in Kassel.

through Pope.L's *Skin Set Drawings*, the art historian Darby English reminds us, quoting the artist in conversation, that "There is no such thing as one drawing."[10] Of course. They are a set. But not even when looking at a single iteration in this vast set—quite literally one of many drawings—can it be understood as one. It is a bit like the mystery of the Holy Trinity, where God is *both* one *and* three. In the case of the scribbled thumbnail sketch, "BROWN PEOPLE ARE THERE IS NO EU IN HEAVEN" found in the upper left corner of the heavily edited, yet-to-be-classified document, we can see one grammatical incongruity *and* three (or more) statements flickering in and out of focus: BROWN PEOPLE ARE, THERE IS NO EU IN HEAVEN, and (if THERE IS NO EU and we mentally delete this segment) BROWN PEOPLE ARE IN HEAVEN. Taking in the particulars of "(Unclassified) I love Europe Text," we find a constant turning: "I love Europe. Europe loves me."[11] This repeated phrase is edited by hand, so, for instance, the present tense of "I love Europe" is adjusted to the past tense "I loved ~~Europe~~. *A thing. A thing called—what? What was that?*" Below, typed "I loathe Europe. I, I, I" continues in scribbles that we can make out as "*I loathe the pieces of Europe* in me." This is no sweet Valentine for Europe from the self-proclaimed "friendliest Black artist in America." There is fear, or "*that immigrant emotion*." There is a detailed breakdown of loathing: "*I loathe the Europe in me because it's his Europe. He loathes the Europe in she because it's our Europe. We loathe the Europe in ourselves because Europe has never really existed.*" And much more, as the direct reproduction on page 64 attests.

There is no foretelling what "it" all *means*. No final word.

If the "(Unclassified)" text/drawing is a key of sorts—for deciphering Pope.L's *Whispering Campaign*, and perhaps also for documenta 14 as a whole—it is because its repetitions, its absurdities, its turning of key terms continue to lock us into a kind of meditation, an active, open-ended thinking-feeling along the on-ramp of possibility.

11. Here, we hear an echo of Joseph Beuys's 1974 performance *I like America and America Likes Me*, which involved the artist being locked inside the René Block Gallery on West Broadway in Manhattan for three days with only a coyote for company—all this after having been transported there by ambulance, covered in his signature felt, and therefore never quite touching the contested soil of the island procured from locals by Dutch traders in a dubious transaction sometime in the early seventeenth century.

Τα κομμάτια της Ευρώπης σκόρπια μέσα μου. Η μπόχα από τα σπαράγματα, τις περιοχές, τις ακίδες, τα κομμένα νύχια, τα πίξελ, τα λουκάνικα, λουκάνικα, λουκάνικα, έθνη μέσα μου. Μισώ την Ευρώπη σε σένα επειδή είναι η δική του Ευρώπη! Μισούμε την την das das das das das das das das das das das das das das das das
The the the the the the the the

on their own particular analysis, ignoring those from other sources. Thus a XXXXXXXXXX goal of breaking down walls to give decision-makers a broader analysis, all easily accessible online, was completely defeated. One of the government solutions to this indiscriminate overproduction had been to create, in 2010, yet another publication, an online newspaper named XXXXXXXXXX.

generals, and infiltrate your own origi on unimportant buildings. By taking e back to your allies, you should inform the status of the enemy, and when the should kill him.

EDITED BY POPE.L
RECORDED IN CHICAGO

(Unclassified) I love Europe Text

Question: How should we classify this text?

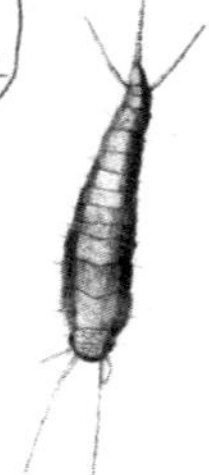

I love ~~Europe.~~

I love ~~Europe.~~

I love

I love Europe. Europe loves me.

I loathe Europe. I, I, I

~~I love~~ the ~~Europe~~ in me. The tomb in me.

I loathe the Europe in thee

~~Tears~~ Everywhere. Not here. ~~But~~ there. Not for ~~thee.~~

Me.

For me fear is ~~satisfaction~~. Fear is in the ~~air~~. Fear

is the

Europe everlasting. Everlasting. Everlasting.

~~Blind and broken.~~

~~Breaking.~~

~~Europe IS breaking.~~

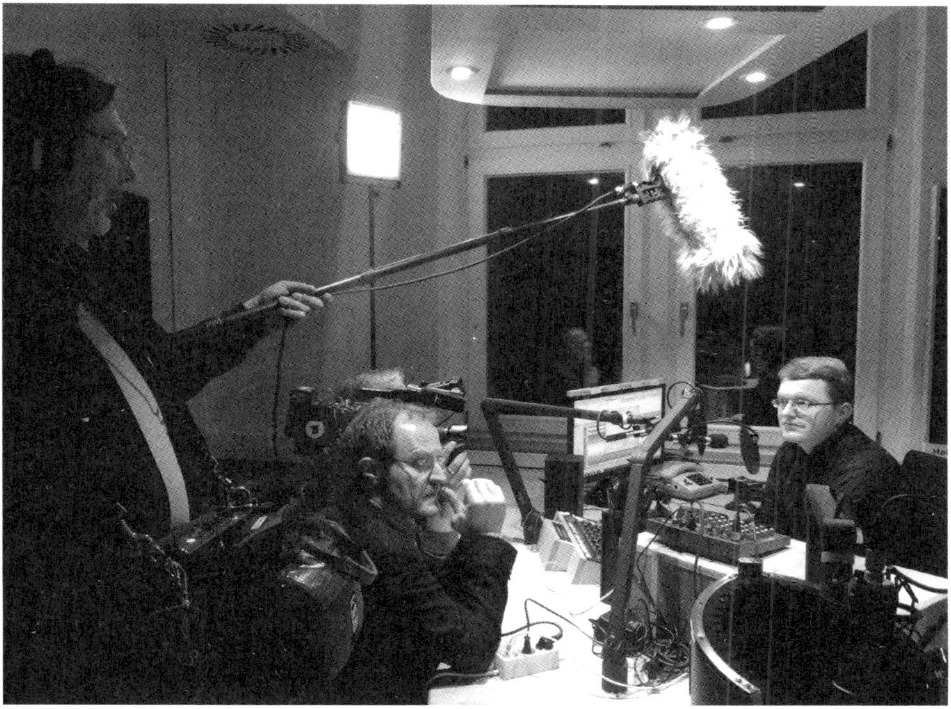

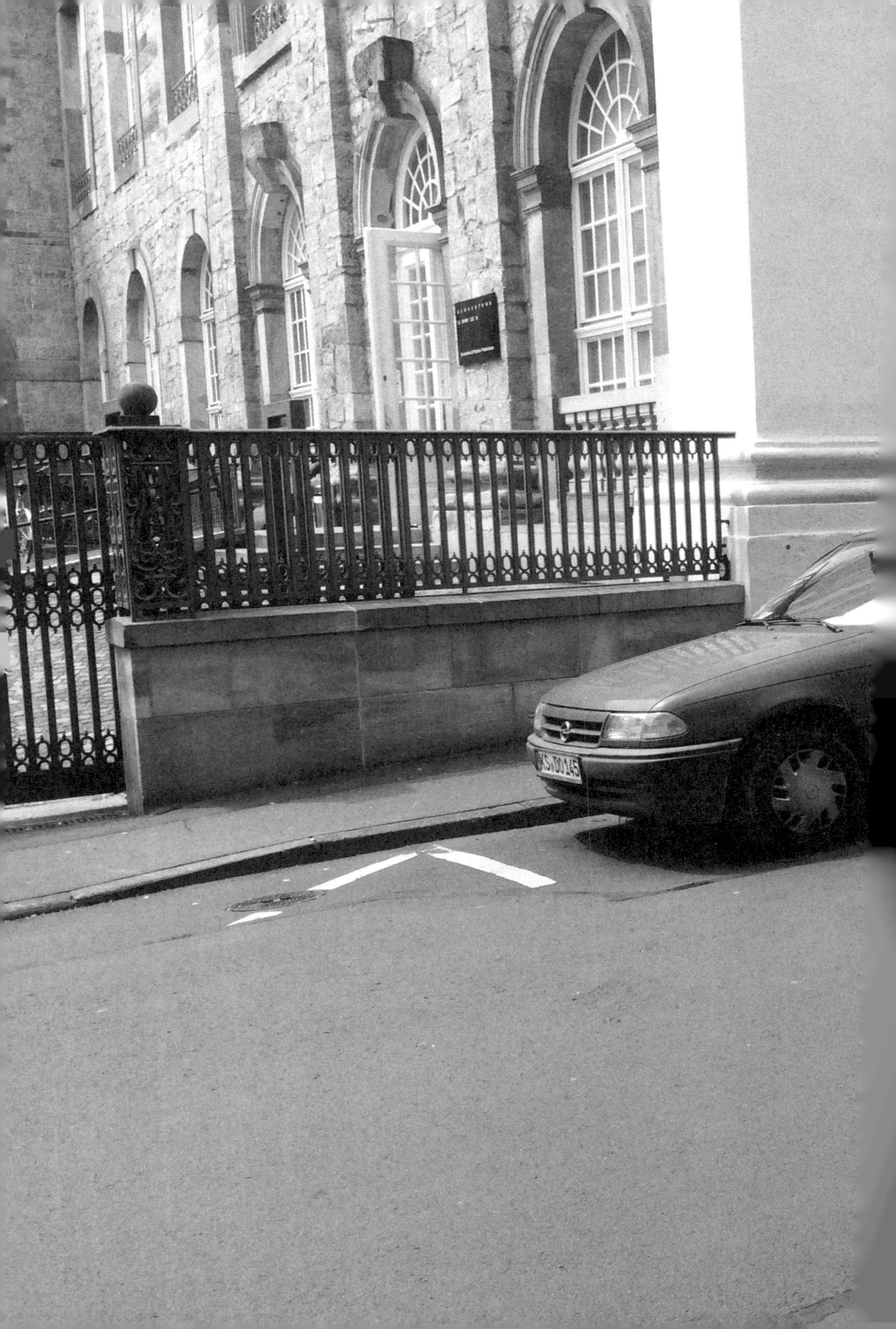
KS DO 145

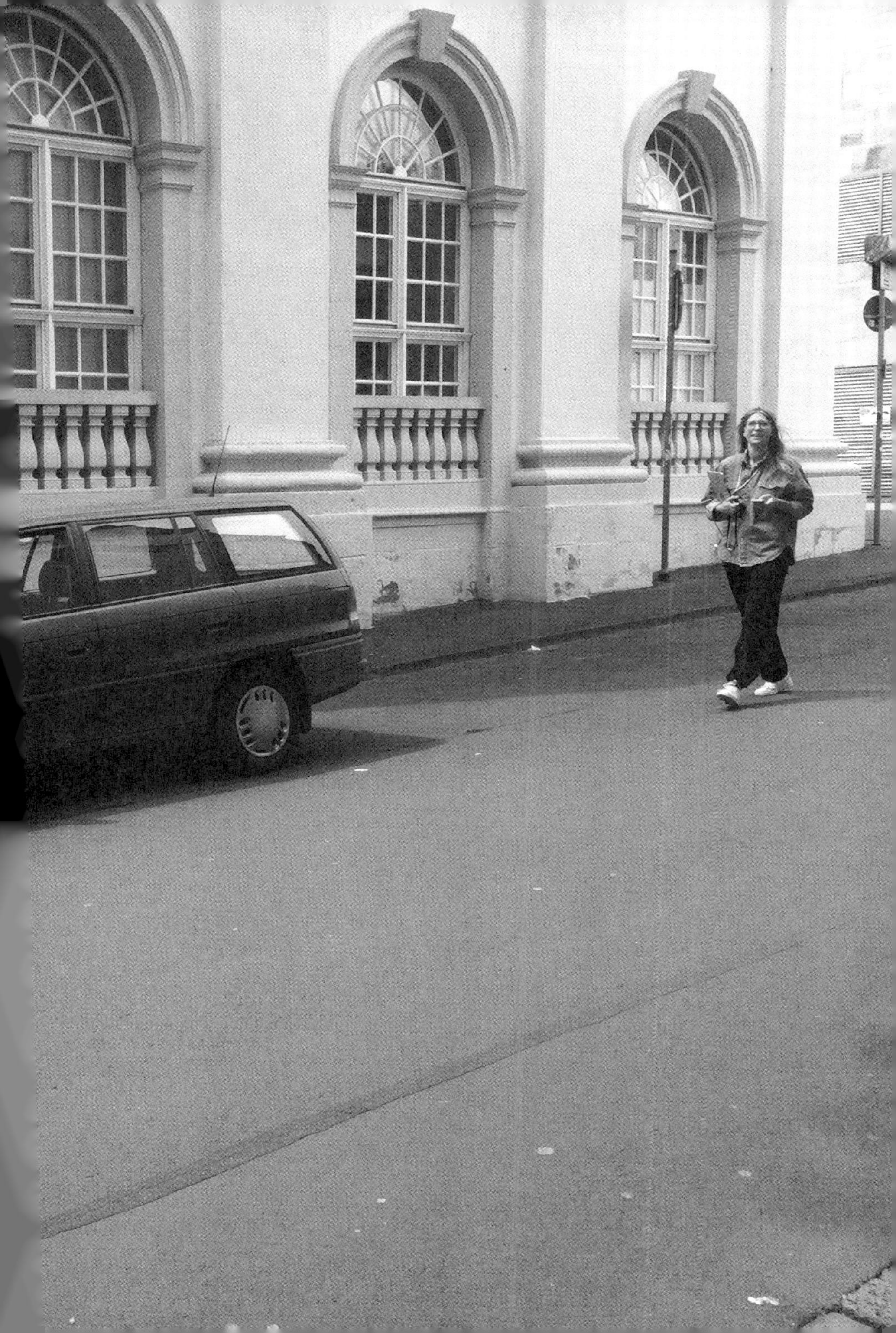

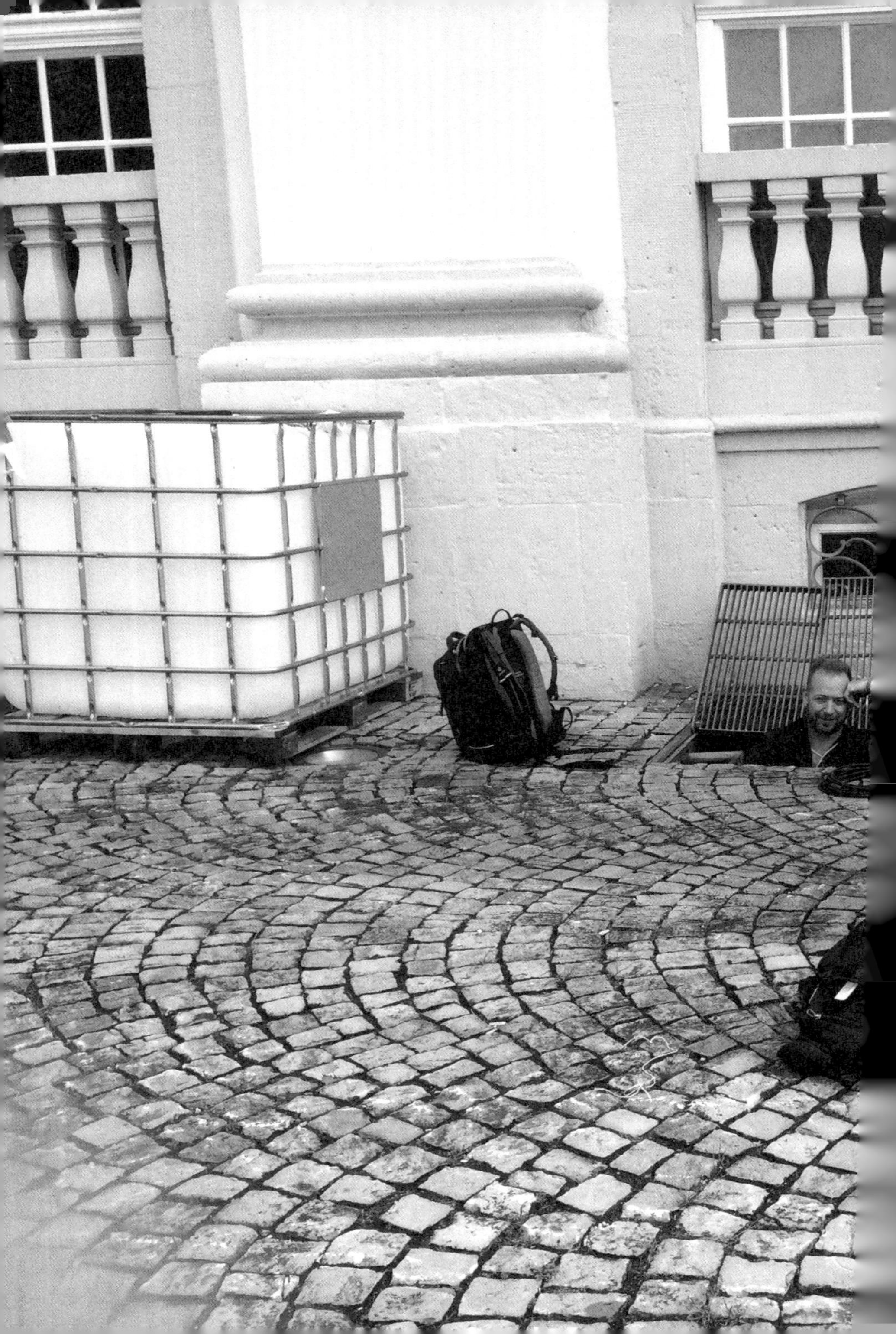

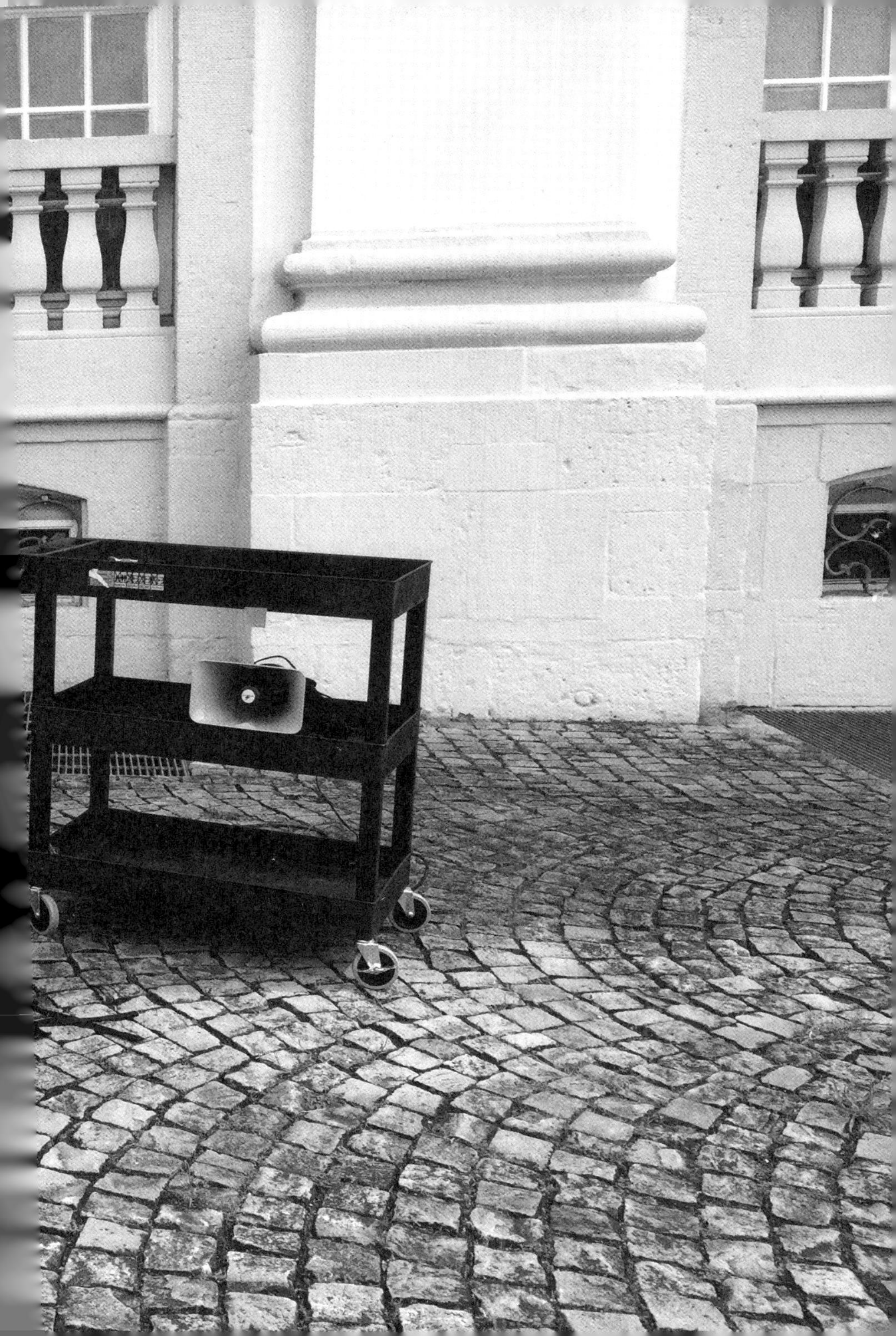

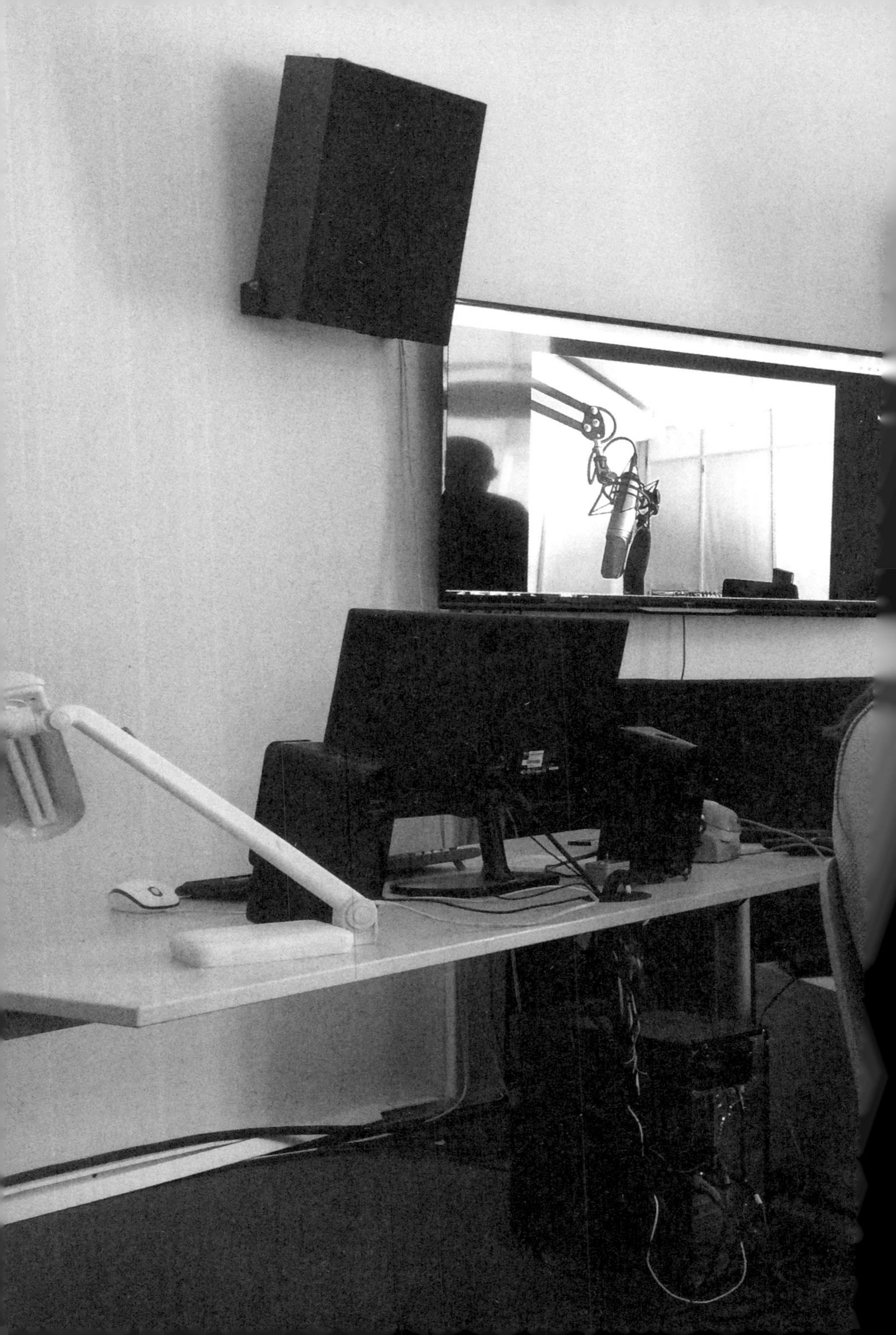

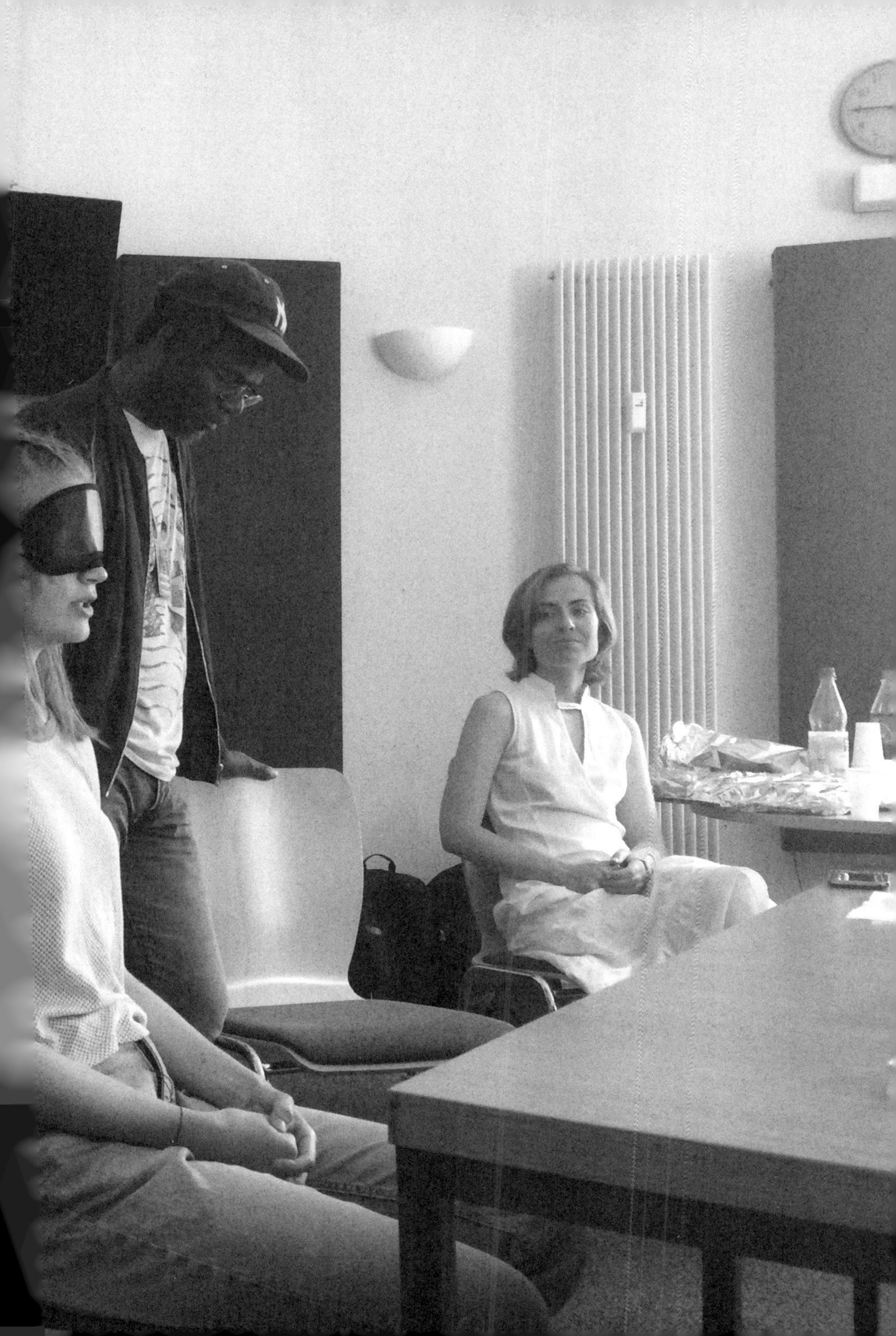

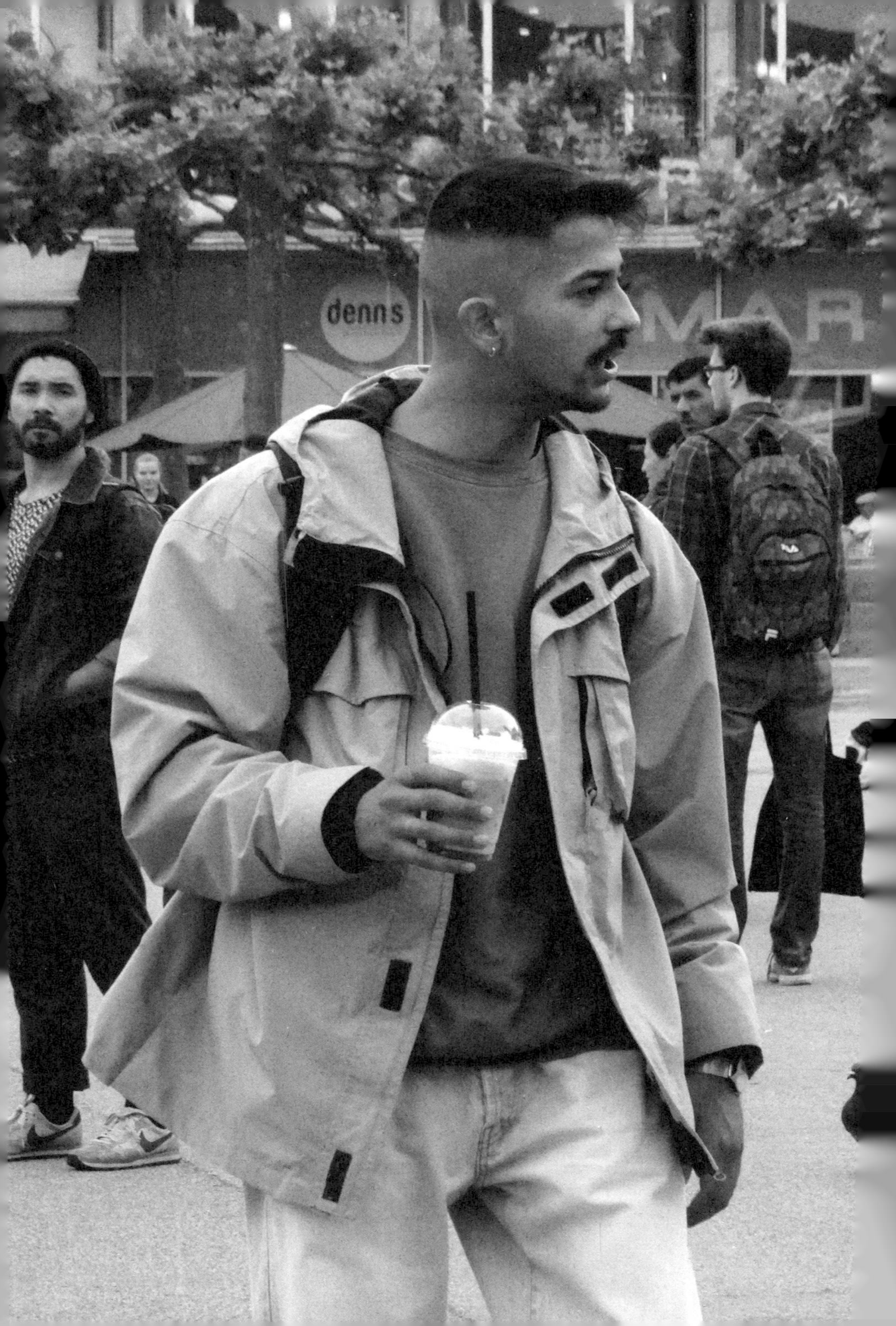
denns

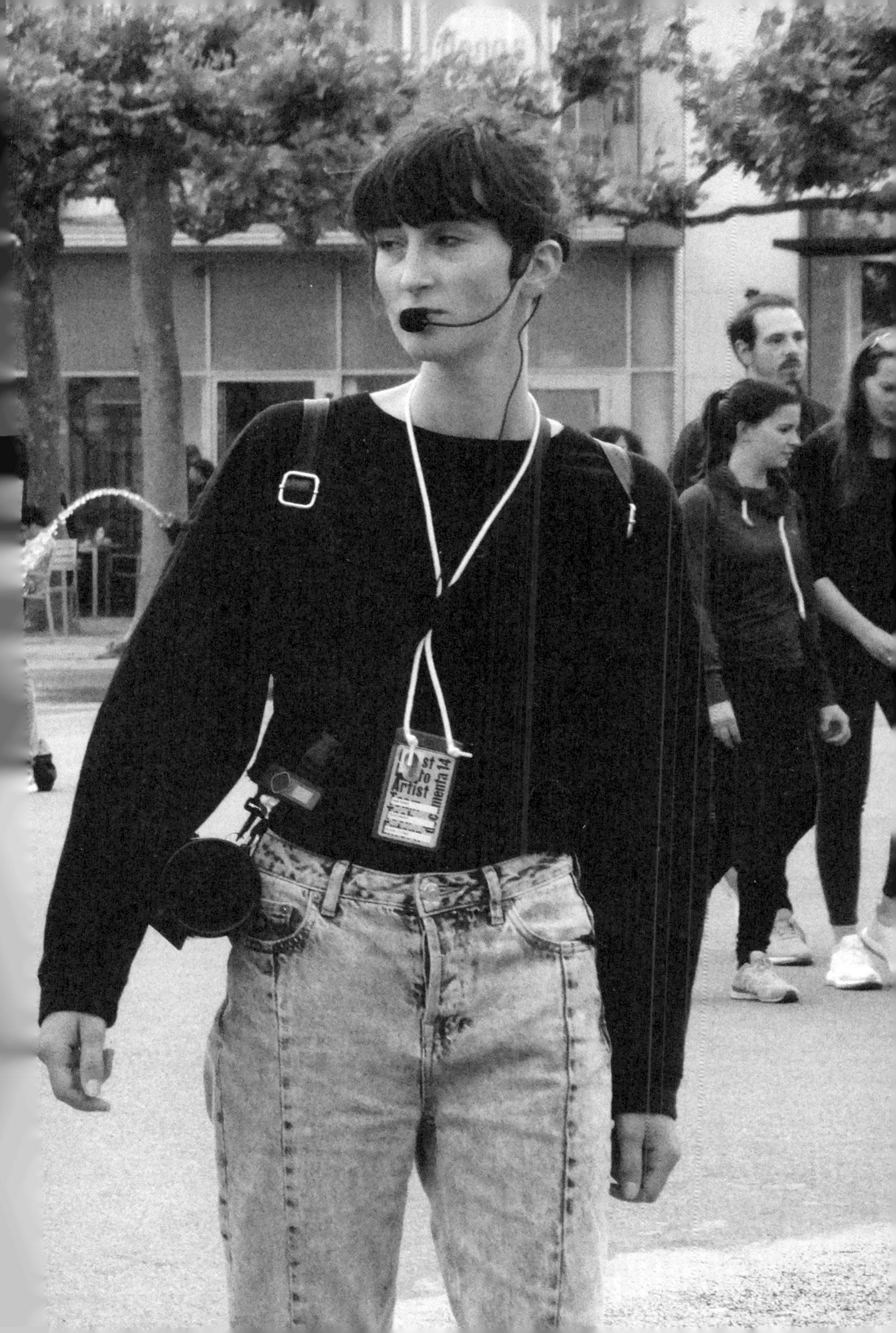

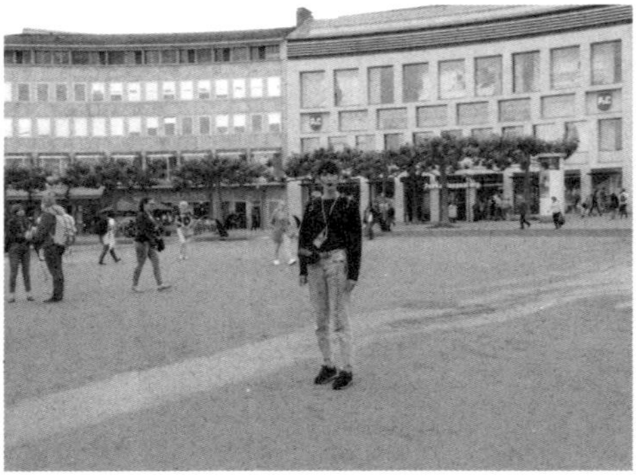

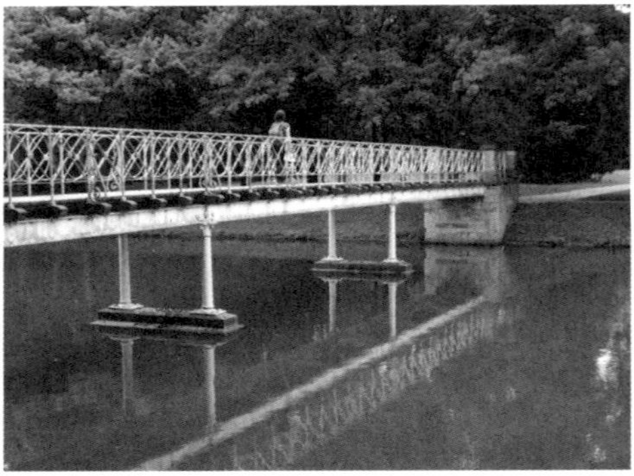

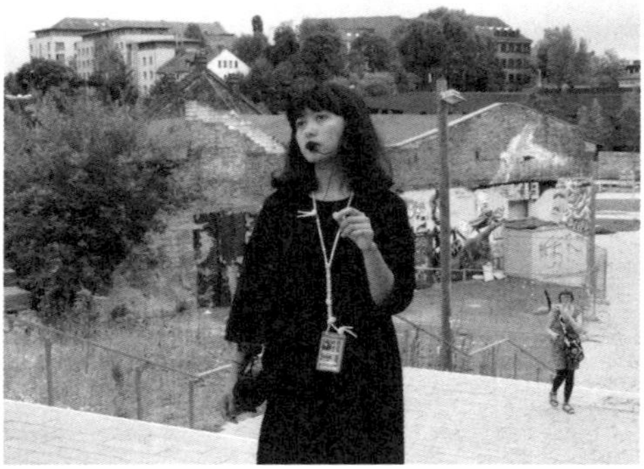

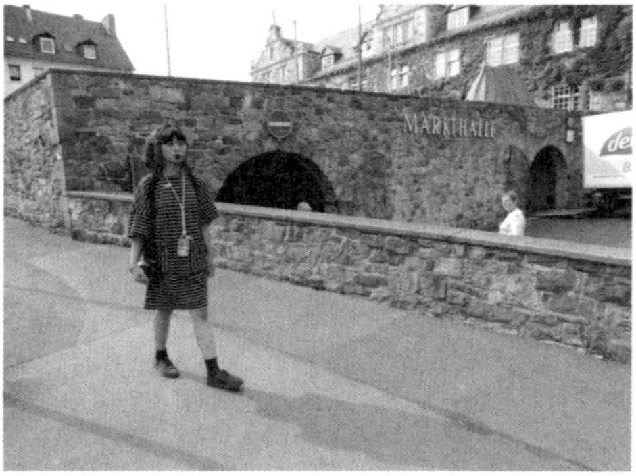
MARKTHALLE

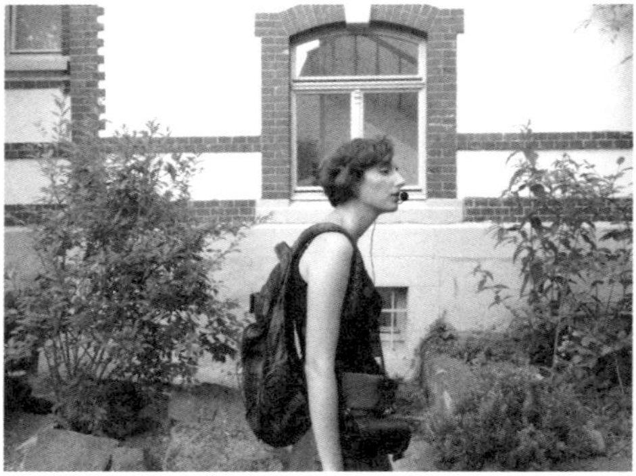

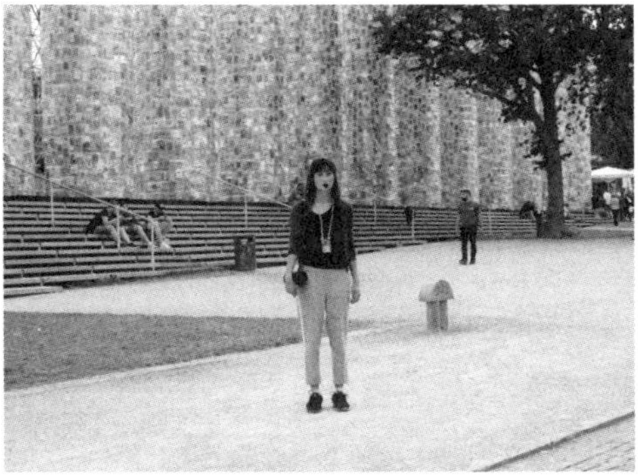
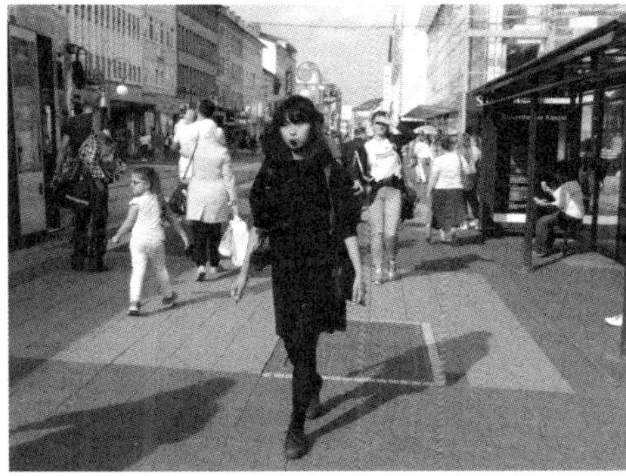
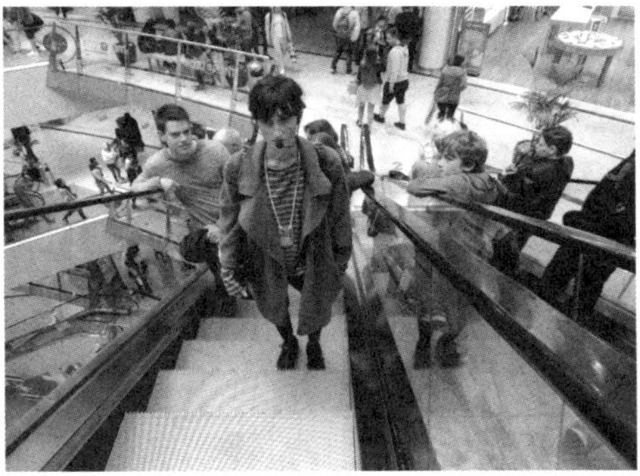
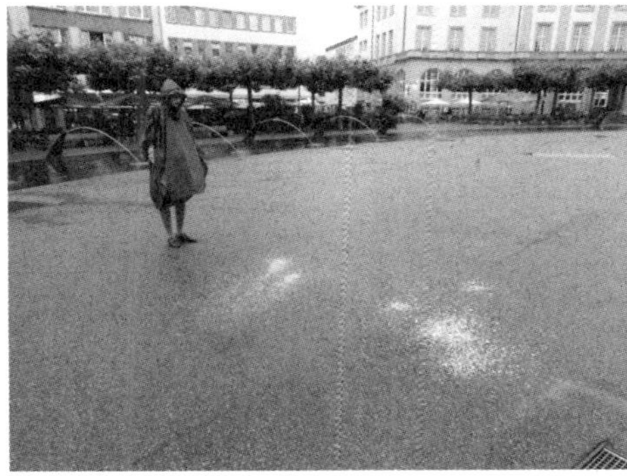
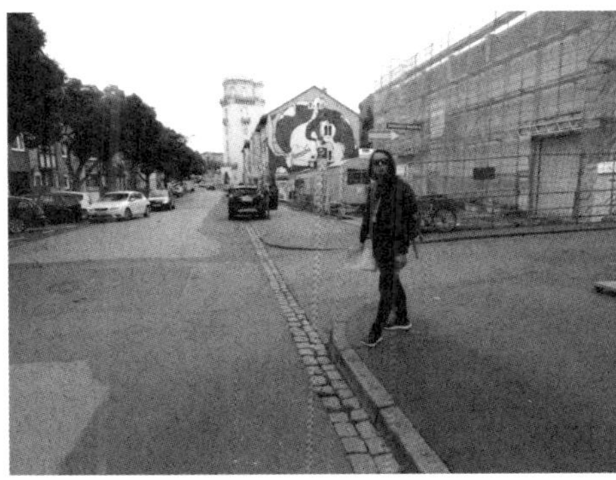
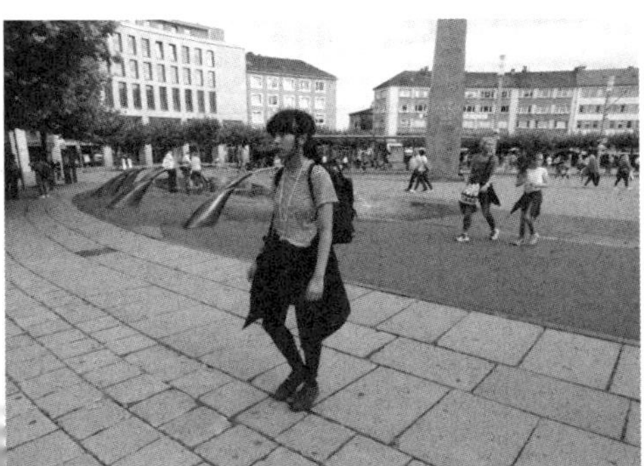
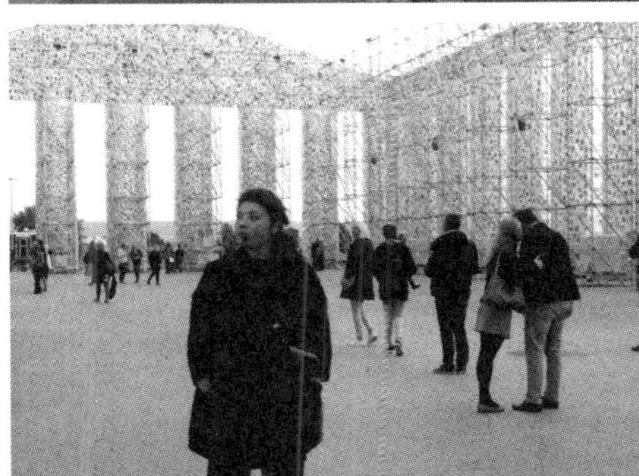

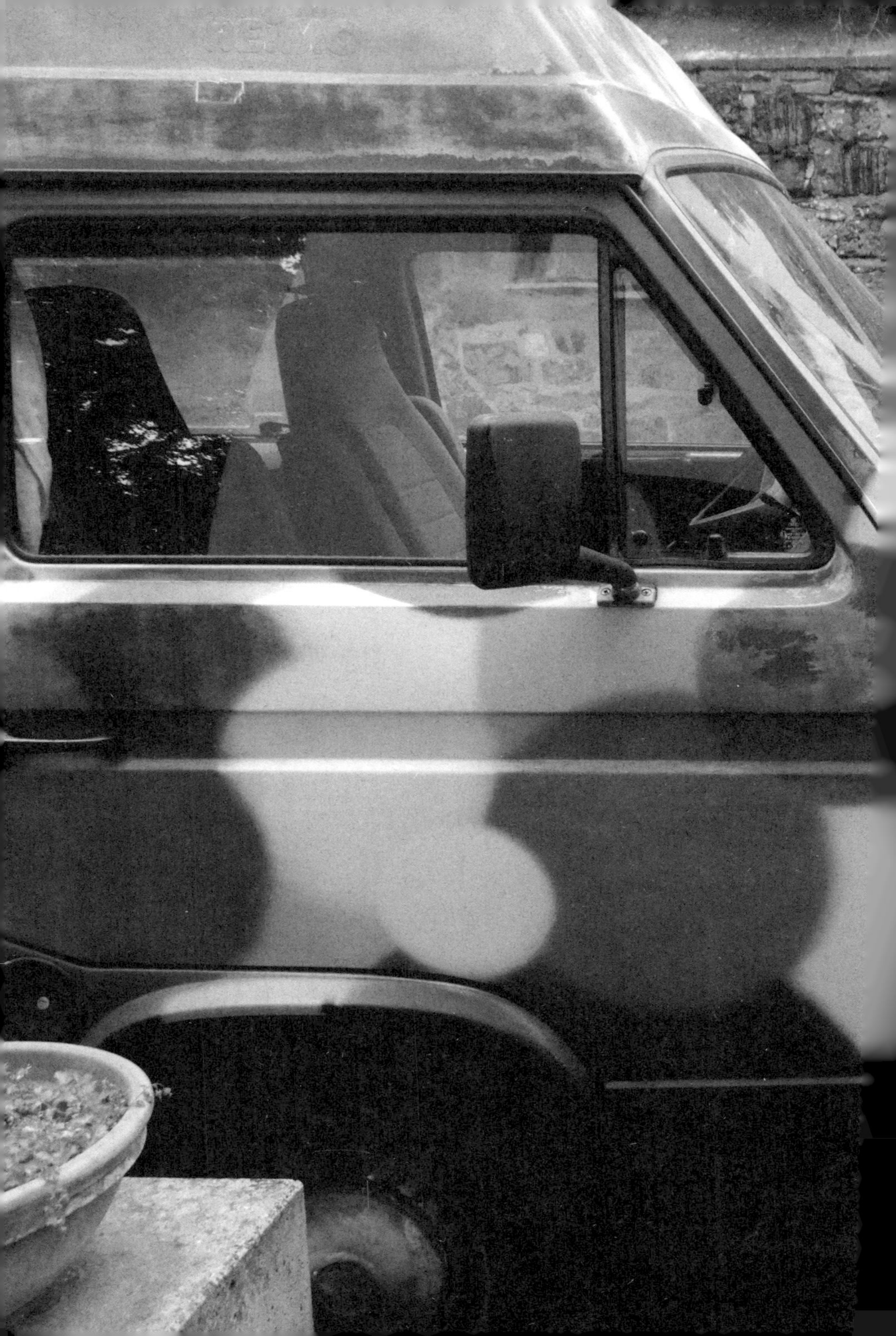

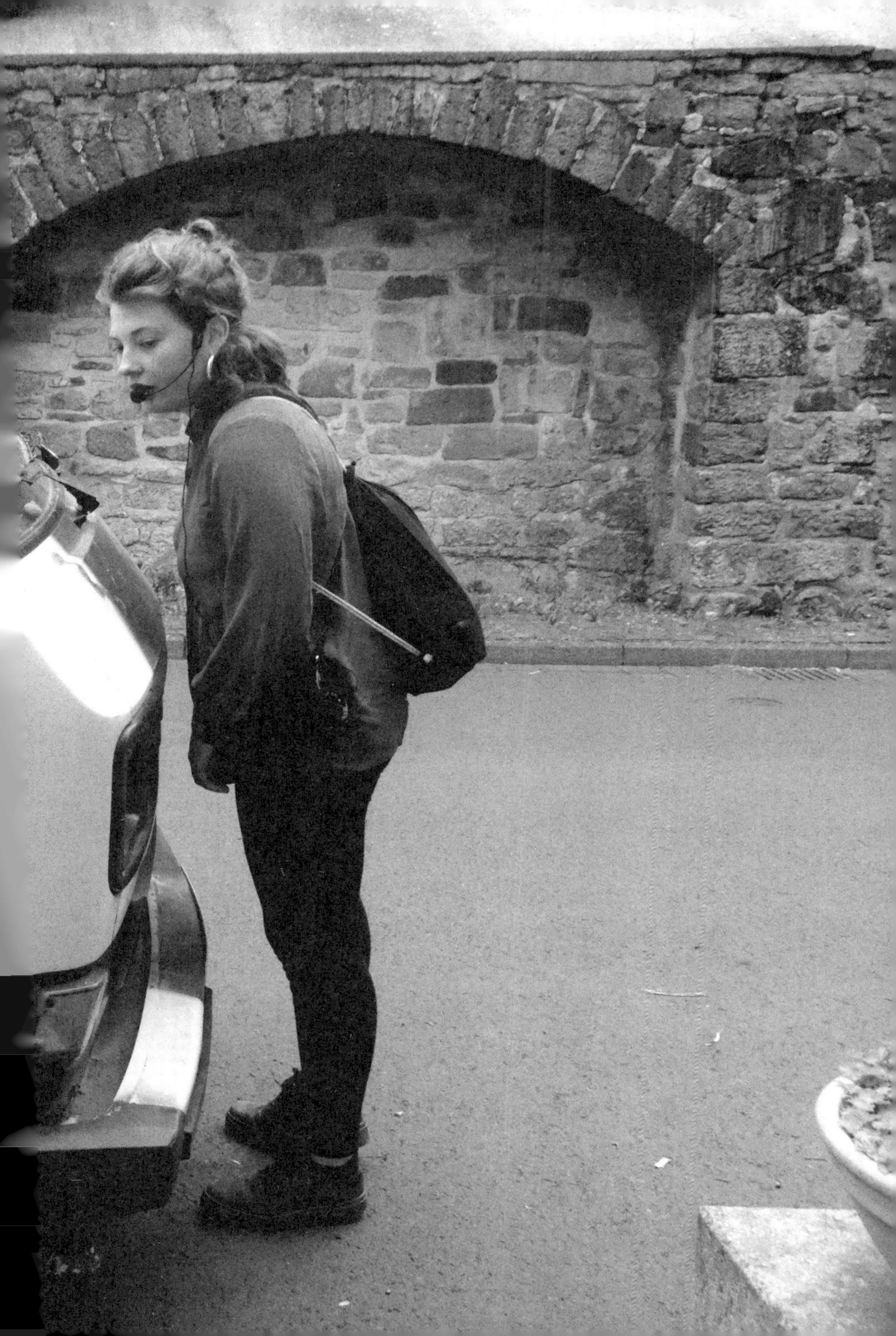

Campaigning through Kassel

Leon Hösl

> I can tell my feet are four feet from the the the the the the König's Galerie escalator because I can tell where my body is. I can even hear the mall. I can smell its moving parts.
>
> —Pope.L, *Whispering Campaign*

It is a cold morning, 8:00 a.m., in the heart of documenta-Stadt Kassel's triangle of consumerism, culture, and monarchy: Friedrichsplatz, Königsplatz, and Königs-Galerie, three sites that are marked by shopping opportunities. Hardly anything except their names reminds one of the proud royal history of the former Residenz-city of the Hessian landgraves that every five years sets the stage for documenta, often described as one of the world's most prestigious recurring art events. We are here to meet the Königs-Galerie's building manager to help us access the shopping mall's PA system in preparation for Pope.L's *Whispering Campaign*—namely, to see whether the artist's developing sound piece might be able to worm its way into this central location. It is the morning after the American elections, November 9, 2016. The curator arrives, along with the first customers getting breakfast from the bakery inside the mall as well as various office employees accessing the building from the underground parking lot.

The sound check goes swimmingly. Soon the sounds disseminated by the PA cover all four stories of the building. Human whispers, sometimes clearly audible, sometimes somewhat dull or whooshing, as good as the old loudspeakers allow the precarious sound to circulate. We follow the whispering voices that spread irregularly through the building, using stairs and escalators. The first shops start to open, by which time we've made it down to the Italian restaurant in the basement, where we come face-to-face with a flat-screen TV broadcasting the news. There is only one topic, dominating the screen with scrolling text, headlines, and footage of the president-elect's victory speech on continuous repeat. Luckily the TV is on mute, and at least this morning, Trump is silenced—Pope.L's whispering has taken over.

The customers inside the mall seem perplexed when they first notice the whispering, even more so when simultaneously looking at the news channel.

What a morning! “Haben die Amis das Radio übernommen?” (Did the Americans take over the radio?), someone asks. The bakery vendor has to explain: “No, it’s just documenta.” Don’t worry, it’s art. In Kassel, “documenta” by and large signifies immediate relief. The rhythm in which the art event evolves and changes the city every five years is well-known to its inhabitants, who have, over the decades, witnessed all kinds of public interventions, provocations, and scandals. Once its association with documenta has become clear, the early-morning whispers, so uncanny at first on this eventful day, lose their eeriness; instead, a certain sense of lightheartedness takes hold, even this early in the morning.

A little over half a year later, as documenta 14 has finally opened to the public, Pope.L’s *Whispering Campaign* has definitely managed to make people sit up and listen, through both continuous repetition and unexpected encounters, both in direct engagement and on an unconscious level. The campaign has brought stories, facts, and words to a wide range of locations across Kassel, from documenta 14 exhibition venues to public squares, parking lots, a train station, two Italian restaurants, and the aforementioned mall. Despite their particularities, these places have one thing in common: they are places of transition. Whispers appear seemingly out of nowhere in between two documenta venues, for instance, or in places that by their very nature constitute passages, such as a parking space, a bathroom, or an entrance hall. In one telling case, the sound itself seemed literally on the move, emitted, somewhat bizarrely, by an old ruby-colored Opel station wagon equipped with invisible speakers, which was driven around the city three times a day for the entire duration of the exhibition. Caught in a constant state of transit, *Whispering Campaign* strategically struck its audience unprepared. And due to its unrelenting repetition, some residents even started hearing whispers where none had been planted. This pervasiveness and ubiquity made Pope.L's whispered artwork a campaign in the true sense of the word, its intriguing core slogan a phrase that was sure to haunt both the citizens of Kassel and documenta visitors for a long time to come: "Ignorance is a virtue."

Preparations for this project started at a moment when the US presidential campaigning craze also began to keep Europe on edge. As the script for *Whispering Campaign* was cast into writing, voice actors were being recruited, and broadcasting locations were chosen, an increasing sense of disbelief took hold of us all regarding the increasingly incendiary populist rhetoric of the Trumpian moment. Indeed, it seemed as if the artist had chosen to incorporate these phenomena to kickstart his Greco-German campaign, replacing ostensible "truths" with soft but no less clear-spoken tones, and deploying whispers as a strategy to play the whole aural spectrum from seduction to poignant, alarming, or threatening sounds. This ambiguity likewise resonated in the variety of sources used by the campaign in both cities, connecting figures from the present to long-dead personages, or juxtaposing historical dates with disjointed fragments of sentences.

Although obviously differing from a political campaign in the strict sense, the number of people involved in Pope.L's *Whispering Campaign* came close to resembling staff sizes in "real" small-town politics. There were recording teams in three cities that included voice actors, sound engineers, and directors, expanded by the artist's studio team in Chicago, technicians in Athens and Kassel, two curators, two curatorial assistants, and the collaborators of the local independent radio station Freies Radio Kassel. In fact, there was even a campaign car. Yet the "staffers" who interacted most closely with the audience, doing actual street work, were the *performers*: two teams, one in each city, each consisting of three performers, a cyclist, and a stage manager. These performers were instructed to act in public space—on streets, in squares, and in parks—carrying speakers that emitted both prerecorded material and live, on-the-spot whispers. They steadily navigated the streets of Athens and Kassel at their own pace, each walking within individually prescribed areas. Occasionally they would cross paths and perform together in one spot. Physically, the performers didn't react much to their surroundings, generally avoiding direct contact with passersby but connecting to the environment in their speech acts instead. By describing what they perceived around them, they enunciated their observations in whispered monologues. At times, depending on their character and mood, performers would also comment on the people around them or engage in short conversations. They were allowed a measure of experimental freedom in mapping their territory, one day choosing residential areas where they interacted mainly with buildings, every now and then facing residents peeking out of their windows, another day walking through crowded spaces that needed to be maneuvered completely differently. For fifteen weeks they were exposed to the public, experiencing a wide variety of encounters: energizing social interactions but also total strangers yelling at them, pestering teenagers, or drunk concertgoers—a wide range of irritants and irritations. Just as in real politics, fieldwork may be the toughest test—which is why a preparatory workshop was set up in which the artist provided guidance and advice in anticipation of exactly such tricky situations. Still, a couple of weeks into *Whispering Campaign*'s disorienting success in Kassel, another meeting was called with the curatorial team in which the performers aired some of their anxieties and difficulties, primarily focused on the challenge of performing the campaign's ubiquitous core message. "Ignorance is a virtue"—really?

The performers' routes through Kassel expanded from the famous Karlsaue park across the city center and the main train station to the so-called Nordstadt, an important hub of documenta 14 activity. Walking along this south-north axis, visitors to Kassel see the city's social fabric change significantly. As if stepping over an invisible border, street life abruptly gets busier in the northern part of town: food stores, travel agencies, hairdressers, and diners primarily catering to Kassel's immigrant populations replace fashion stores and malls. Consequently, this changing environment inevitably altered the perception of the sentence "Ignorance is a virtue," not only for the ones receiving it but also (and mainly) for the performers who felt the need to share their concerns about whispering this very phrase in this socially more diverse and challenging area—concerns that had to do with issues of safety (certain "respondents" had been rather aggressive in receiving the message in question), but also with the discontent derived from having to propagate ignorance as a virtue in this precise part of the city. Where life takes place on the street to a much higher degree than elsewhere in this rather staid and stolid city, conflicts manifest themselves much more clearly. (In contrast, another performer described her relief while walking around the university campus that is part of the same neighborhood.)

Ultimately, the topics that arose during our meeting with the troubled performance troupe led to the question of the direction of the campaign at large. What are we campaigning for here? Ignorance? "Europe as a dark place"? Are we vouching for "emissaries with large black holes in their foreheads"? Or for the stumbling, puking Ferdinand, the unknown third Grimm brother? Are we promoting the dodgy "Night Time 24 Hours Bar," where the narratives seem to converge? Or is it the story of Anwar the forty-three-year-old sunburnt inhabitant of a refugee camp in Jordan, that the campaign aims to publicize? Or again Europe—though this time perhaps "the Europe in ourselves, because it never really existed"? The campaign's physical basis is the artist's score, itself a patchwork of stories and sentences, drawn from Kassel, Athens, and Europe at large. A multitude of differing perspectives, shifting between observations from afar to testimonies of the stranger within, these are not stories that can be found in a city guide or guidebook. The multiauthored, decentered knowledge that gets sent out into the streets or broadcasted on the cities' radio waves appears as scattered in content as in form. Maybe ignorance, then, is the resultant recurring posture of humility one has to assume within this maze of voices.

*

The sound check at the Königs-Galerie was a resounding success; the mall was quickly added to the list of campaign locations—a collective decision, like so many made in the process of making this work happen. One hundred days of early-morning shopping-mall whispering, from 8:30 until 10 a.m., continually accompanying the mute TV one passes on the way to the bakery downstairs. While the same familiar sentence about ignorance and virtue was being whispered again and again through the speakers every morning, the news channel scrambled to keep the viewers up-to-date about everything it knew to have happened in the world that morning. Hectic reporting all around, much of which would be forgotten soon. The whispers themselves, however, somehow remained in (and with) Kassel, as Natalia Escudero, our team's stage manager, noted: "It is as if the performers are talking to the city, leaving an awkward feeling behind. The whispers seem to belong to the city more than ever."

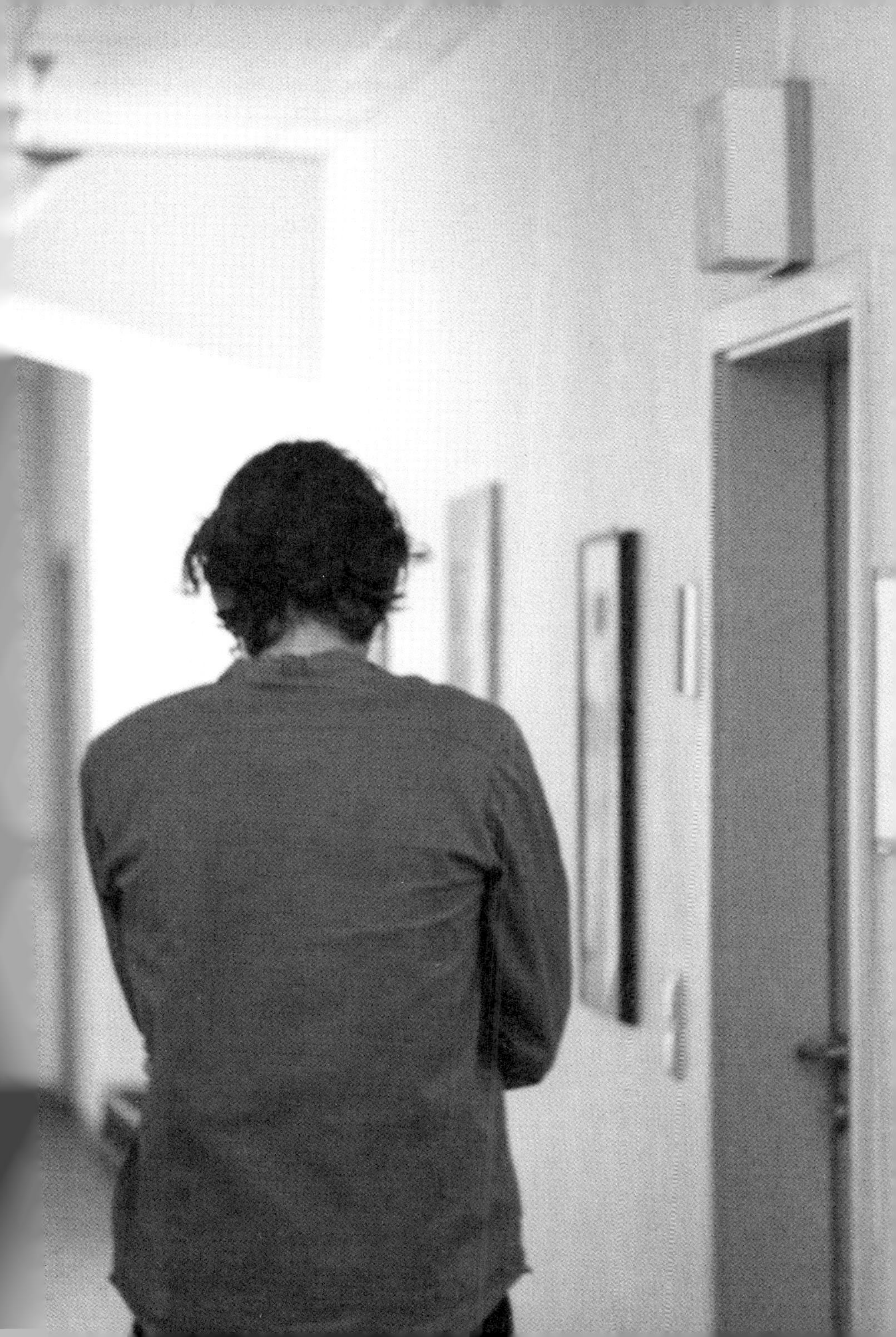

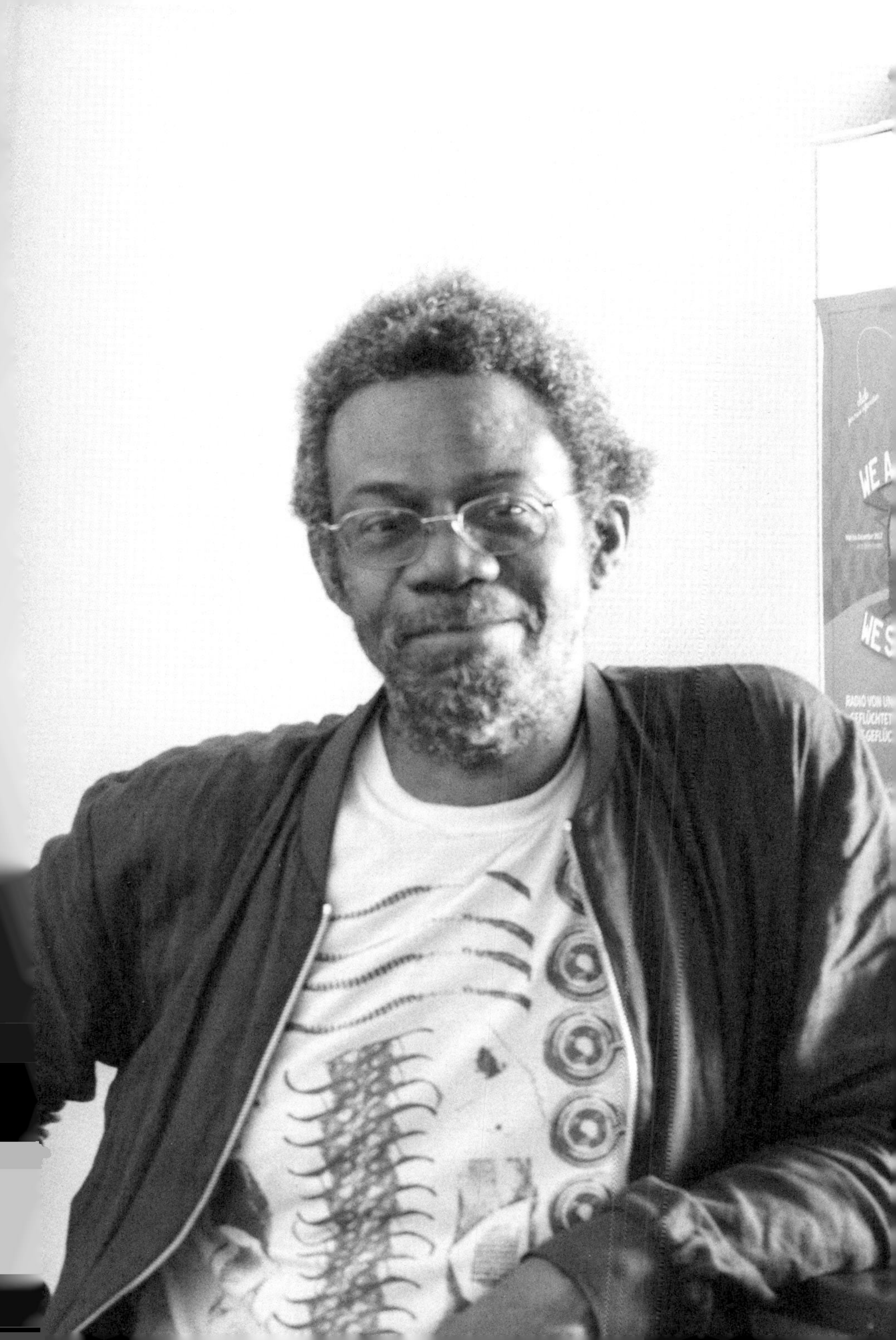

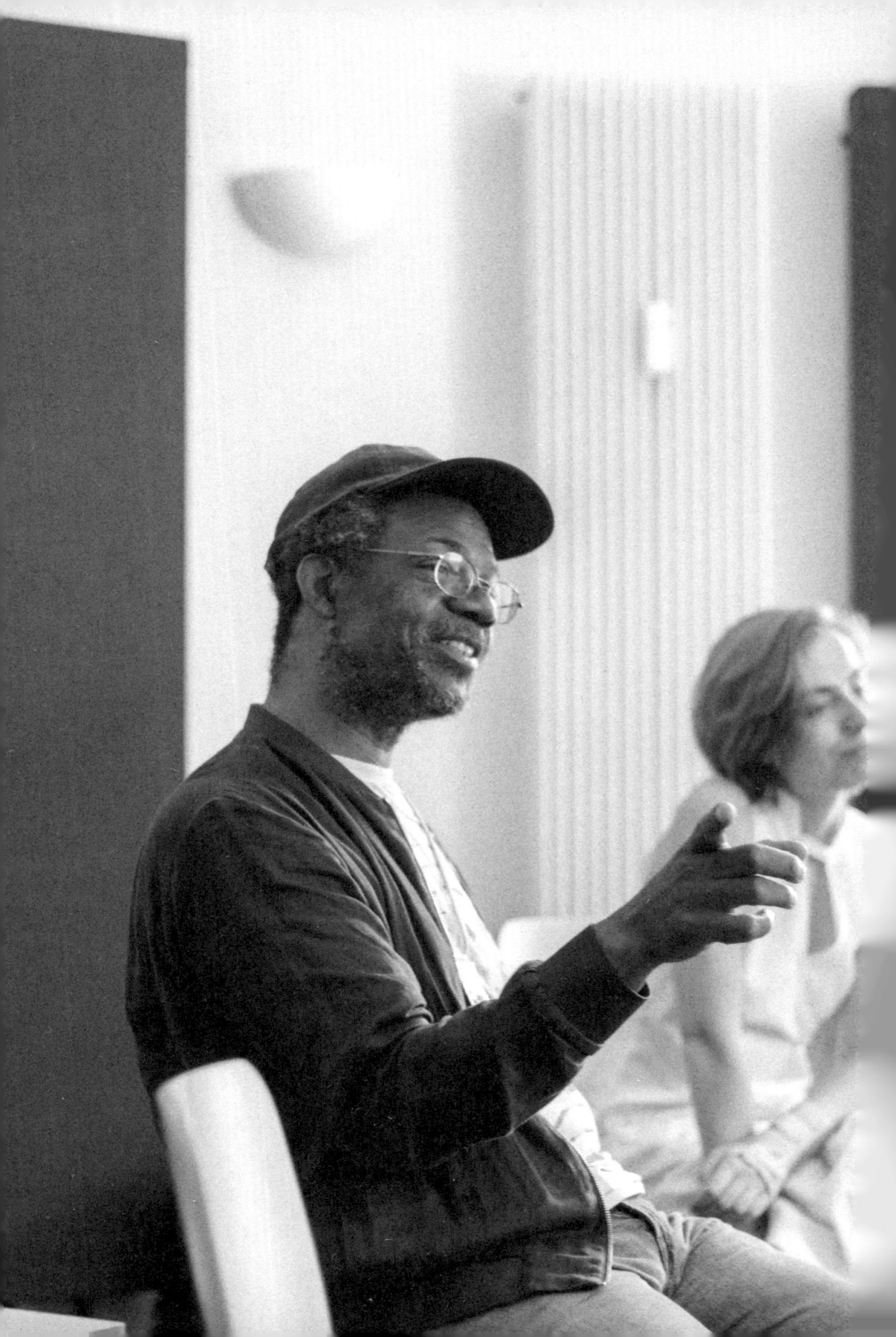

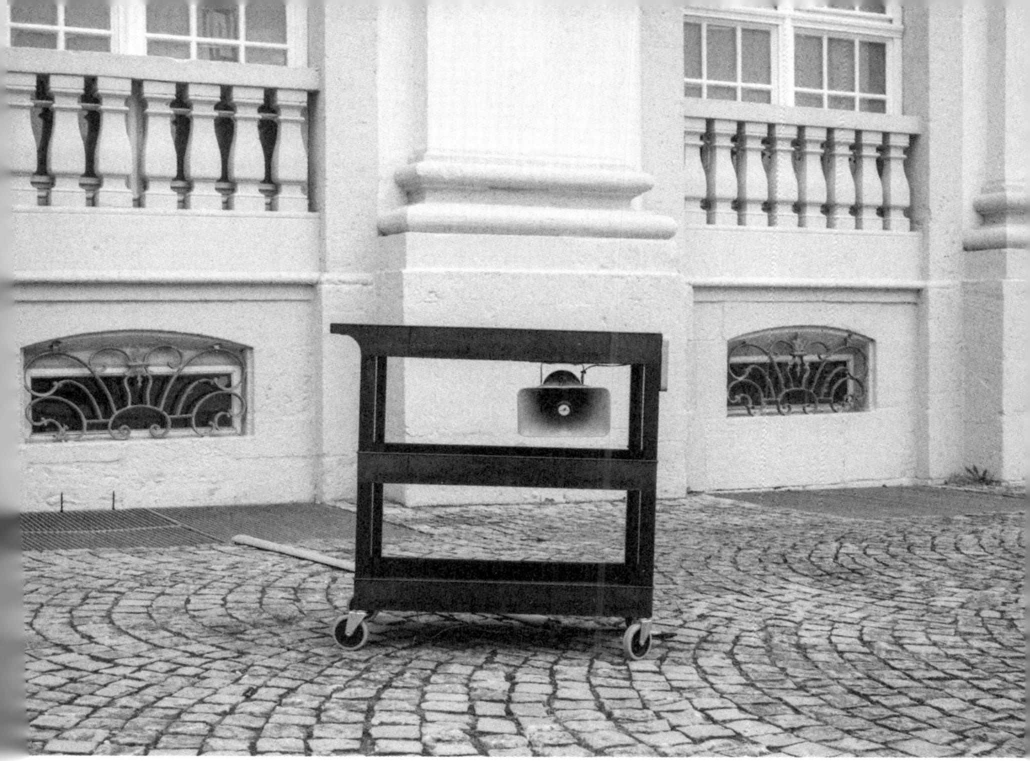

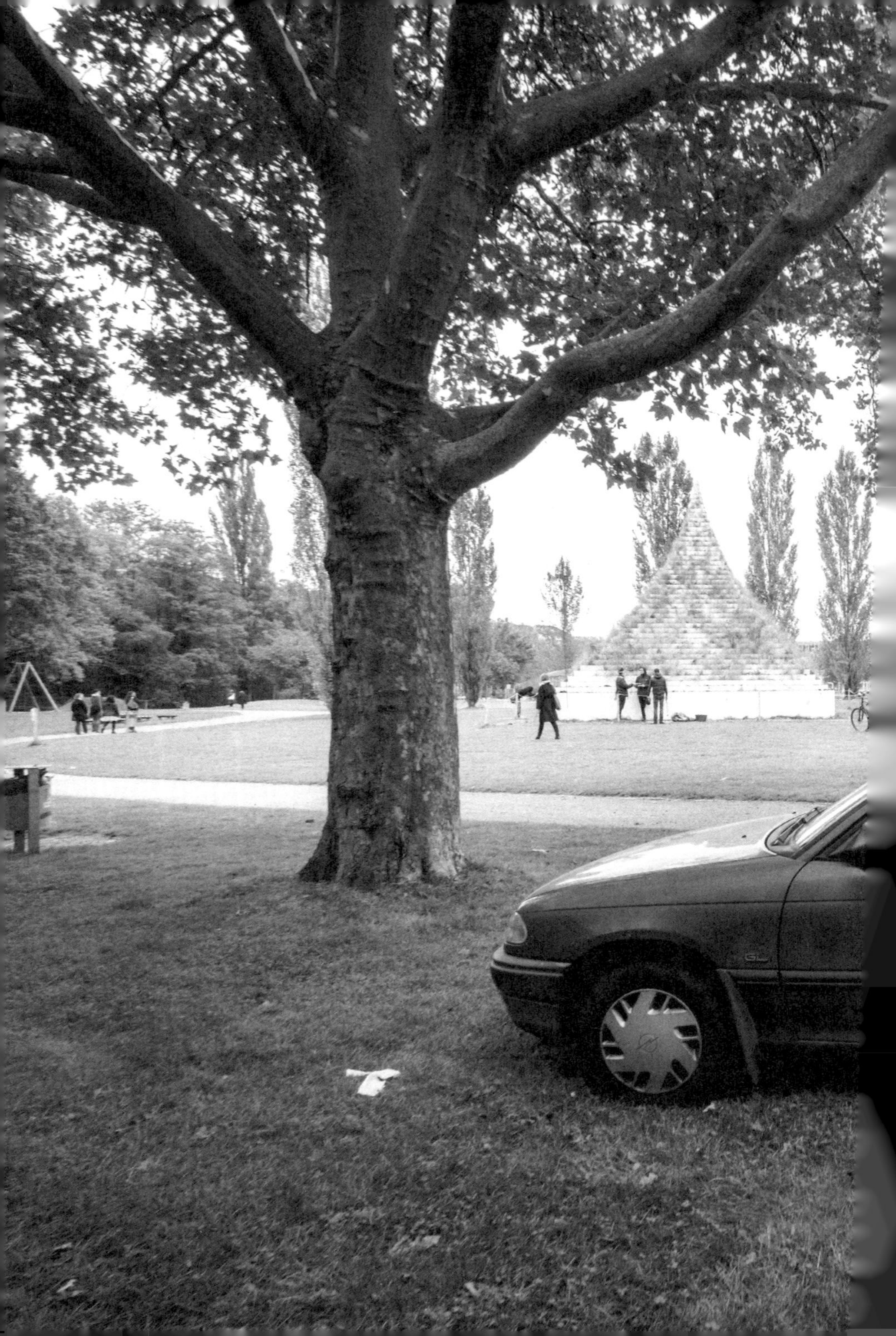
GL

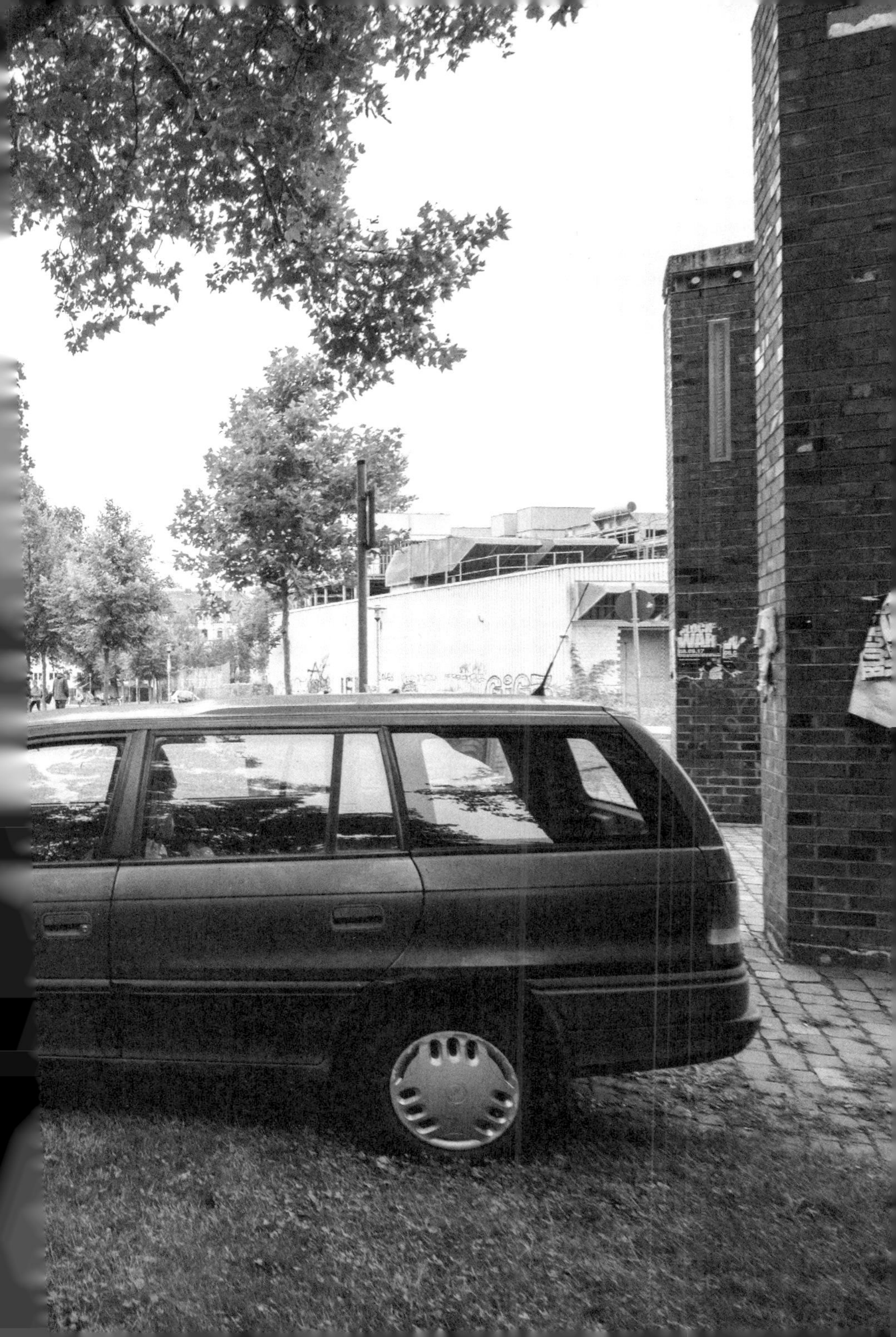

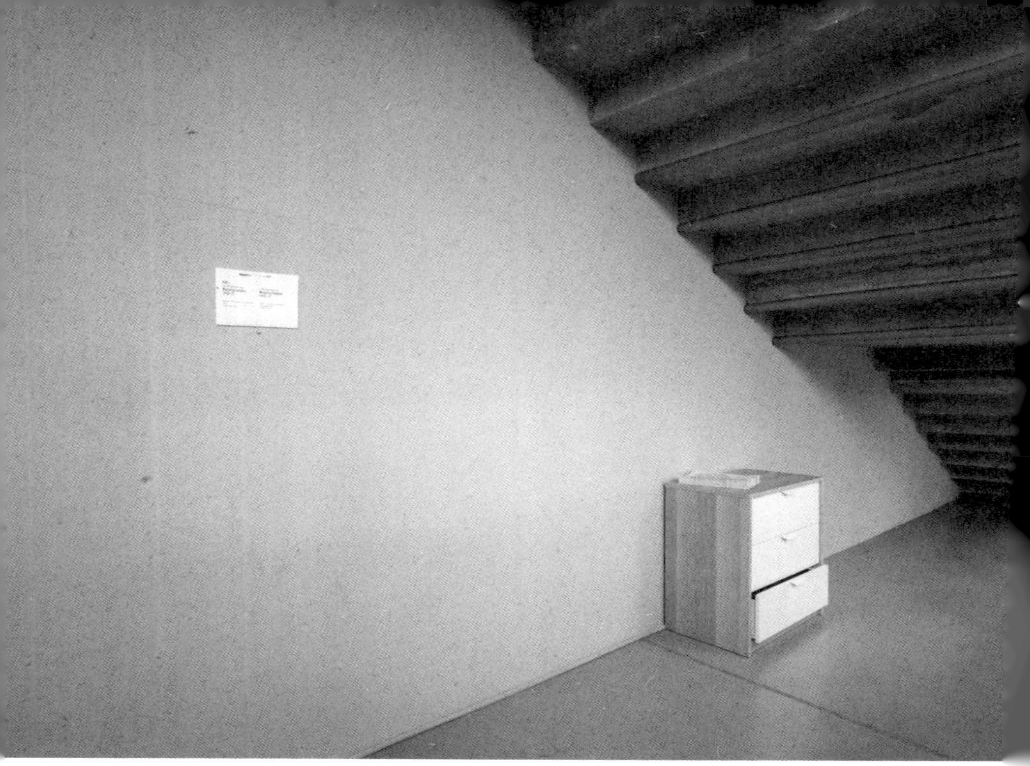

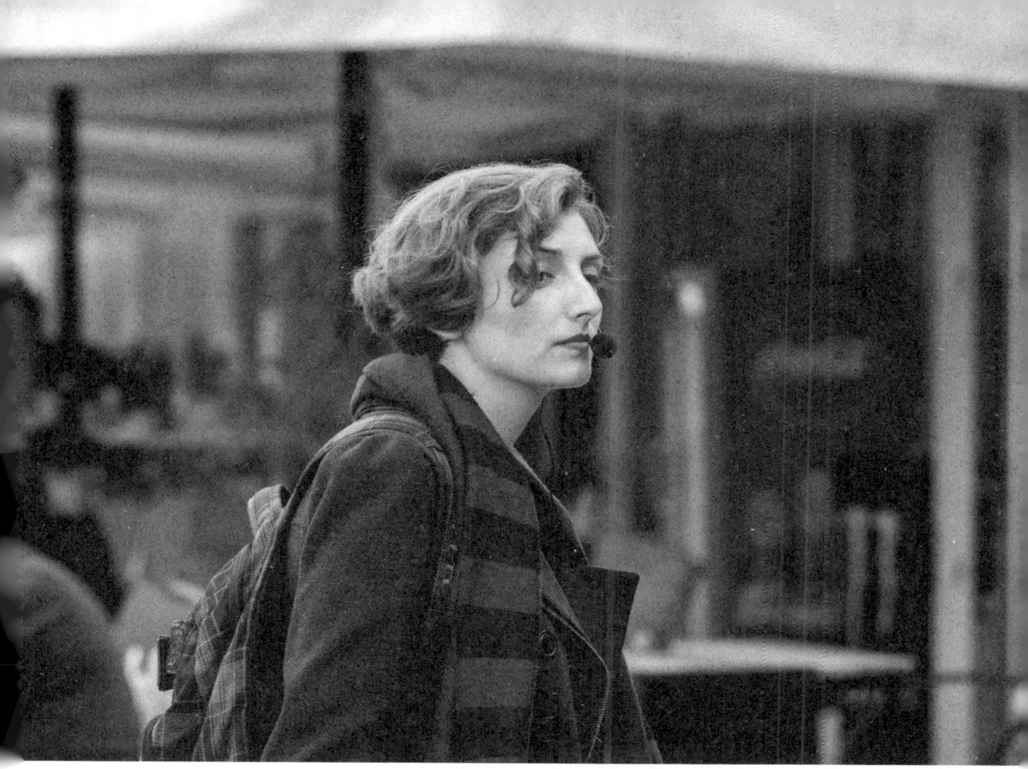

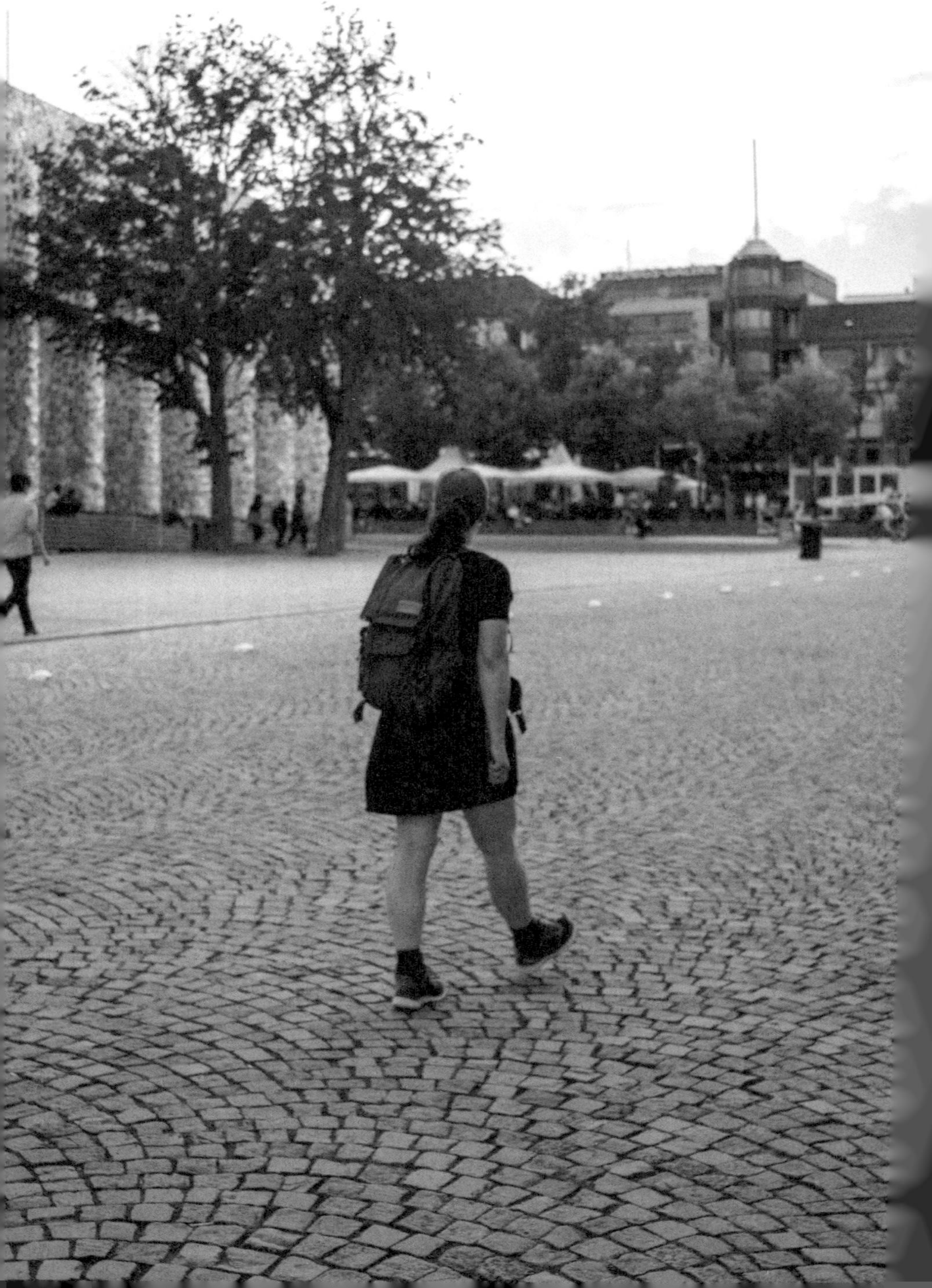

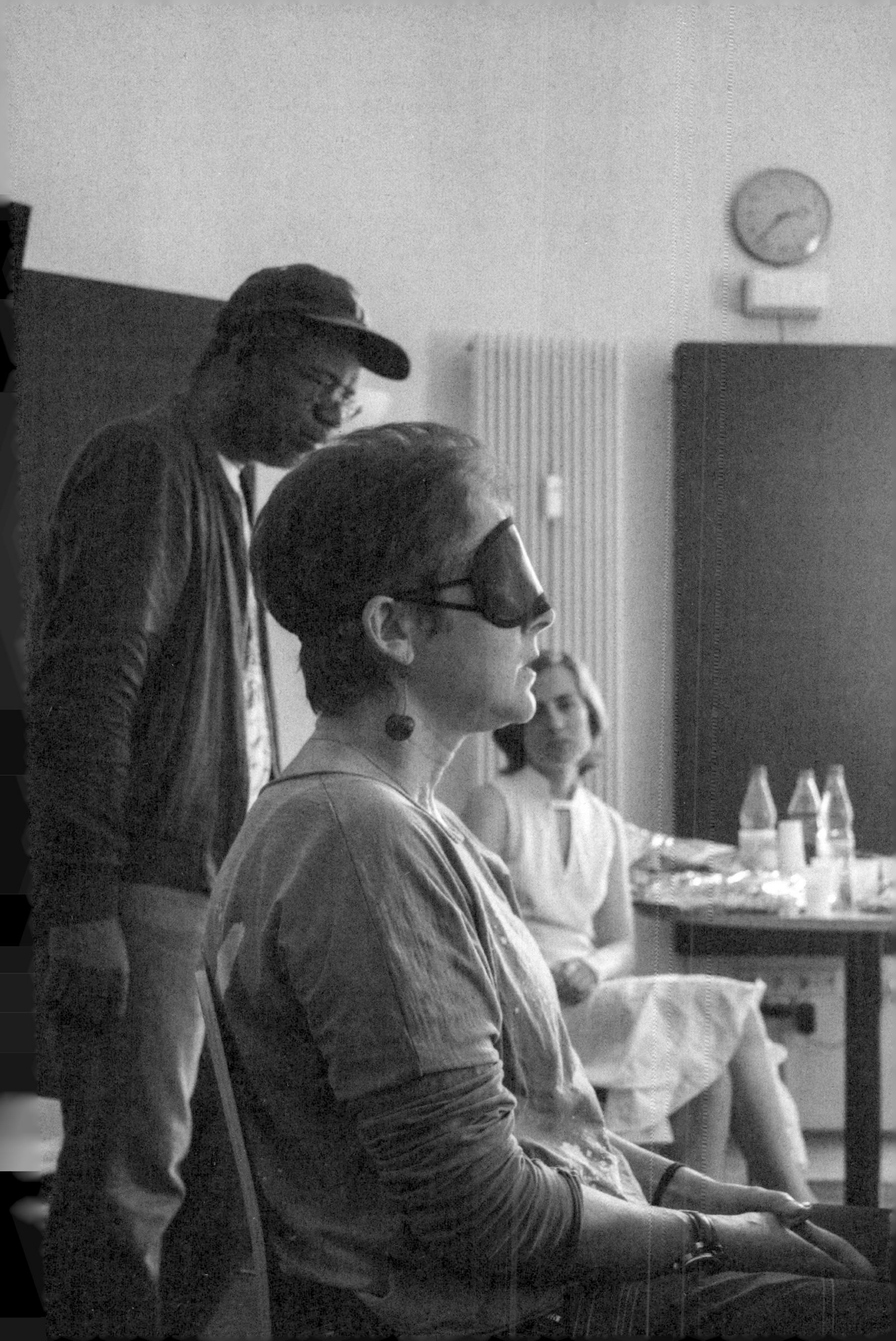

Following a Whisper
Chichan Kwong

My first encounter with *Whispering Campaign* happened at Neue Galerie in Kassel. I was strolling through a corridor; suddenly, a gentle murmur vibrated through the wood paneling. The voice had such intent that it was hard to mistake it for ambiance. “Ignorance is bliss.” I moved closer, now hearing more clearly but growing ever more frustrated with each new language that it uttered. During its pauses, people passed by quickly without noticing. Facing the wall, I appeased my limited understanding: a corridor was a pause, for galleries, for art, and perhaps for my intellect.

The second encounter: I followed a performer in downtown Kassel. She was dressed in gray, carrying a small speaker that was slung over her shoulder. It was almost impossible to make out the whisper in the lively streets: one had to get uncomfortably close to the performer. Even when the whisper interfered with pedestrians’ personal space, it never intruded or lingered long enough to call attention to itself; it dissipated quickly and prevailed like a rumor.

At the Polytechnion, in Athens, I had my third unexpected encounter. The campus felt like a natural habitat of abandonment: graffiti, wild grass, busted windows, and broken doors. In front of a rusty gate, both my friend and I heard some sound; we couldn’t say for sure whether it was a whisper or the tail end of a campus broadcast. We stood around the tree where the horn speaker was set. As we were waiting in uncertainty, a couple from Kassel came up to us. We started chatting. I told them that it was exciting to hunt for Easter eggs since the whispers were scattered throughout the city and in some cases were mobile. My anticipation and keen awareness of mundane public space were solicited by the embedded serendipity of the project. On one occasion, I heard a sound that resembled the whisper played from a moving car. Not knowing when, where, and how a whisper would happen made me want to attribute even the tiniest noise to the campaign. However, because I didn’t always understand the languages that were playing, I felt like I was missing out on the message the whisper was trying to tell me.

While we were pondering, the whisper began.

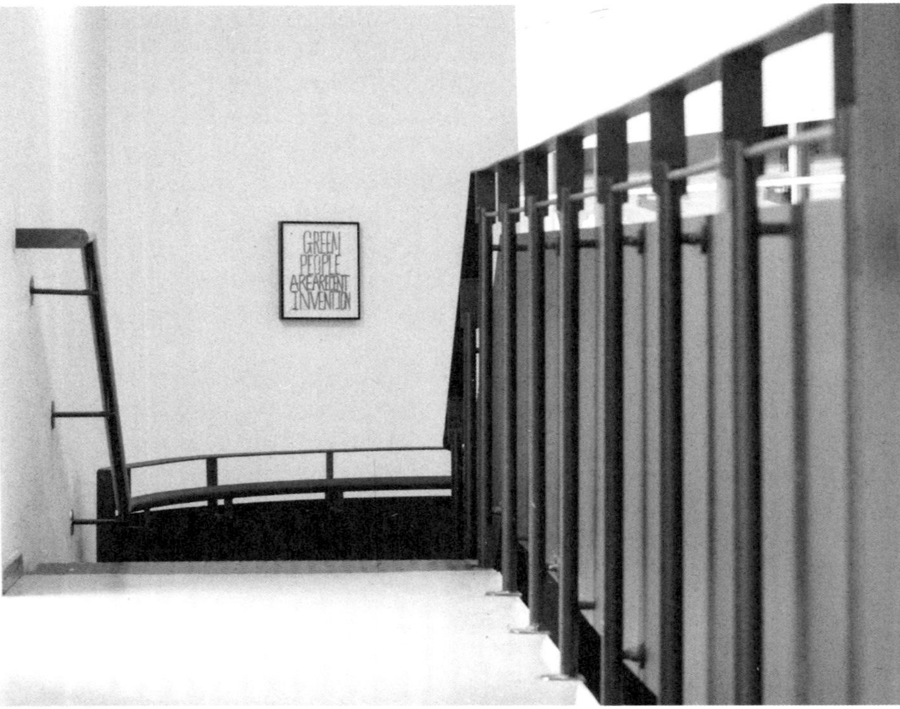
GREEN
PEOPLE
AREARECENT
INVENTION

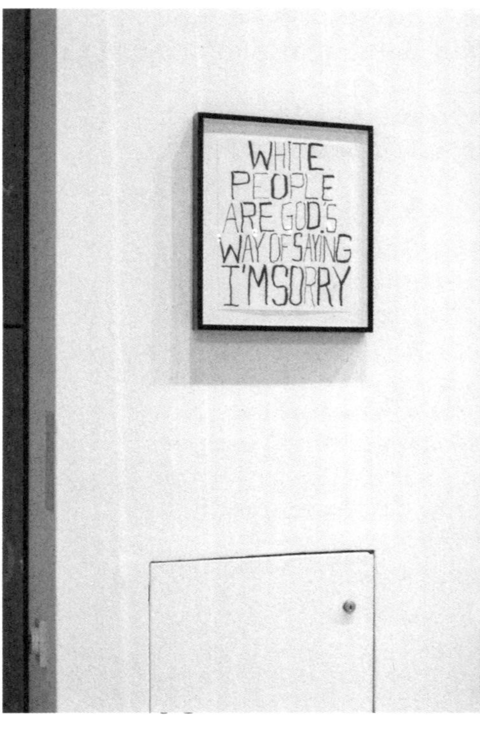
WHITE
PEOPLE
ARE GOD'S
WAY OF SAYING
I'M SORRY

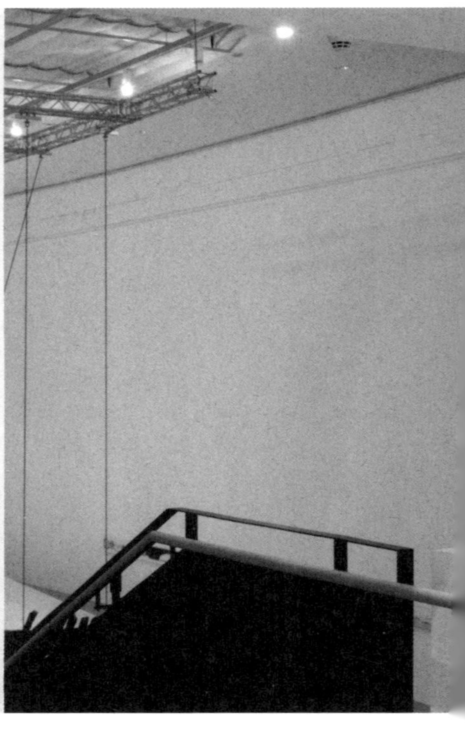

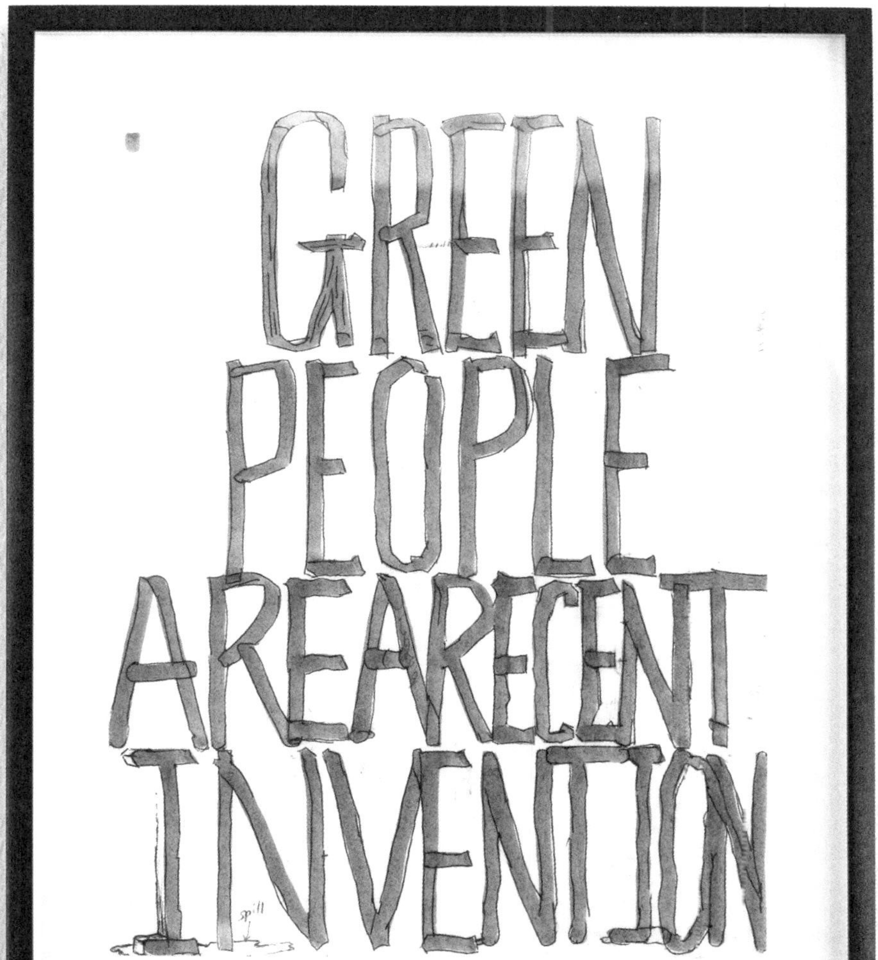
GREEN
PEOPLE
AREARECENT
INVENTION
spill

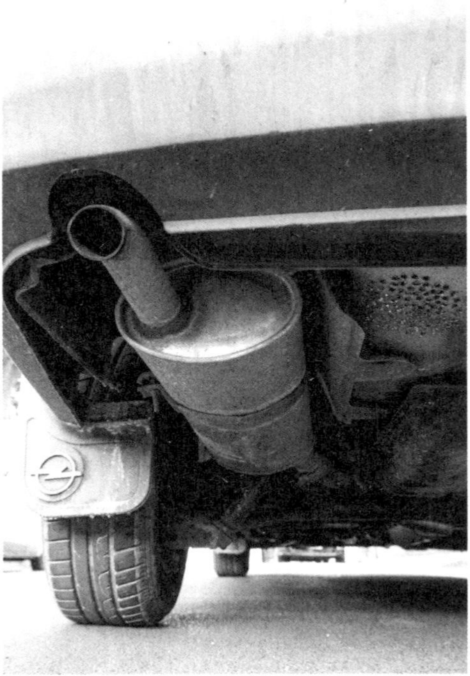

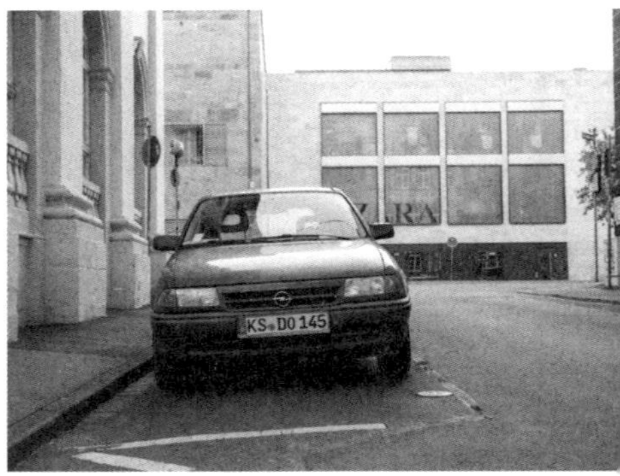
KS DO 145

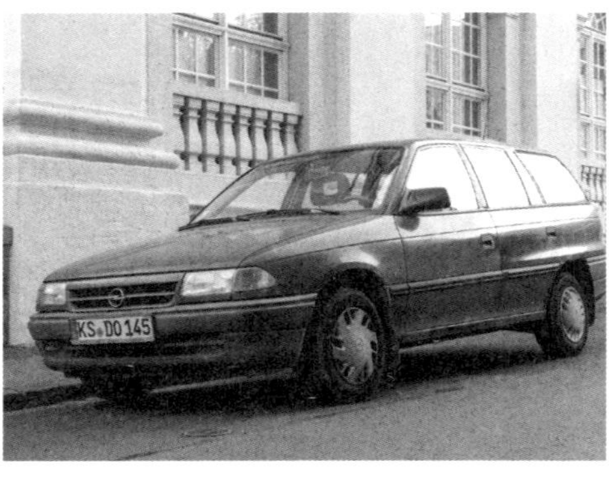
KS DO 145

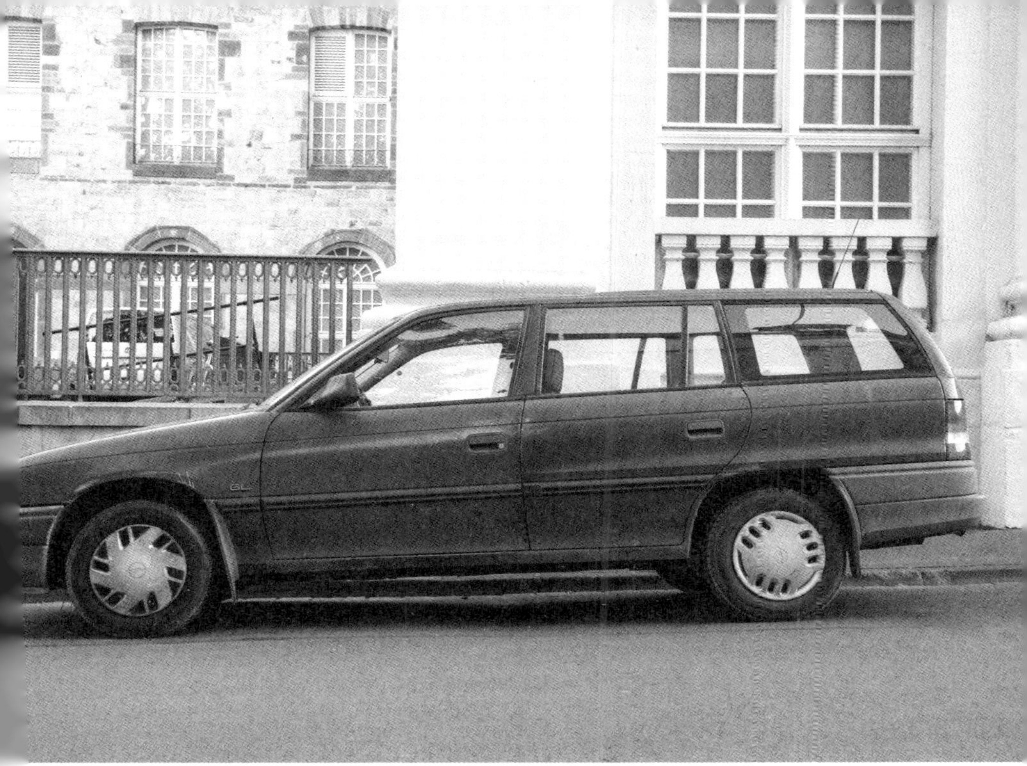

01

On *Whispering Campaign*'s Trail

Adrienne Elyse Meyers

While we were following one of the performers (or participants, or carriers of the sound), a kid on a bike stopped to ask what was going on, if it was art. I wish none of us had been around to answer that question. It was the same question that came to follow all of us through documenta in the streets and structures of Kassel and Athens. After encountering *Whispering Campaign*, the possibility of its presence seemed to be everywhere. Any little sound might be part of the project, or not. But since we're thinking about it, since it conjures the idea of the art, we greet it as something to be considered in that way. A whisper doesn't necessarily stop when the sound stops.

Brown People are the Wrens
in the Parking Lot

WHO ARE "THE BROWN PEOPLE"?

WHERE IS THE "PARKING LOT"?

WHAT DOES A "WREN" CONNOTE?

WHY WOULD SOMEONE ASK THESE QUESTIONS?

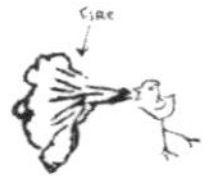

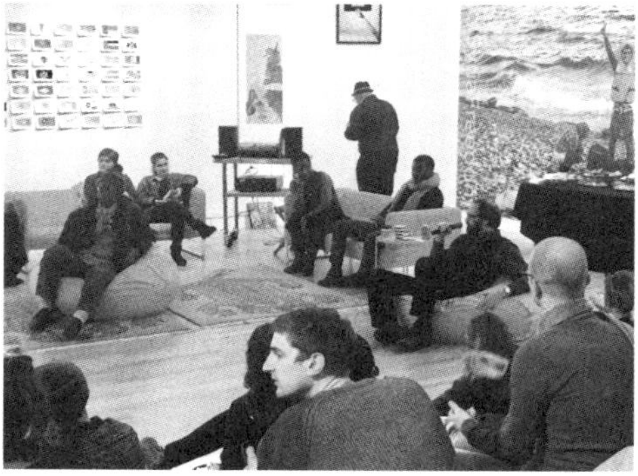

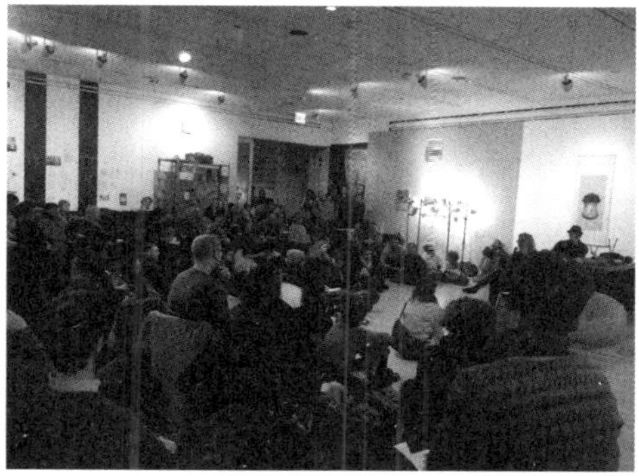

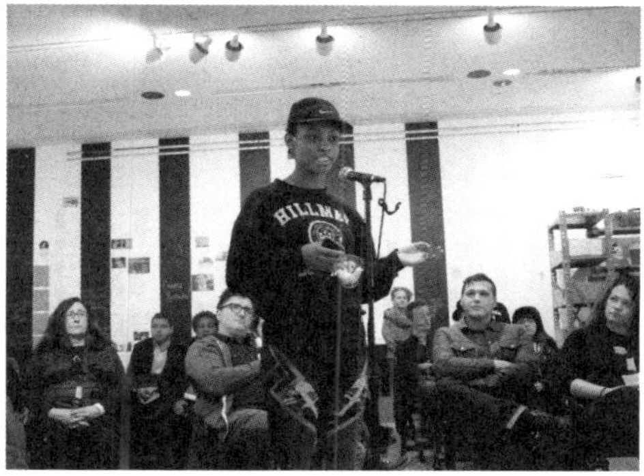

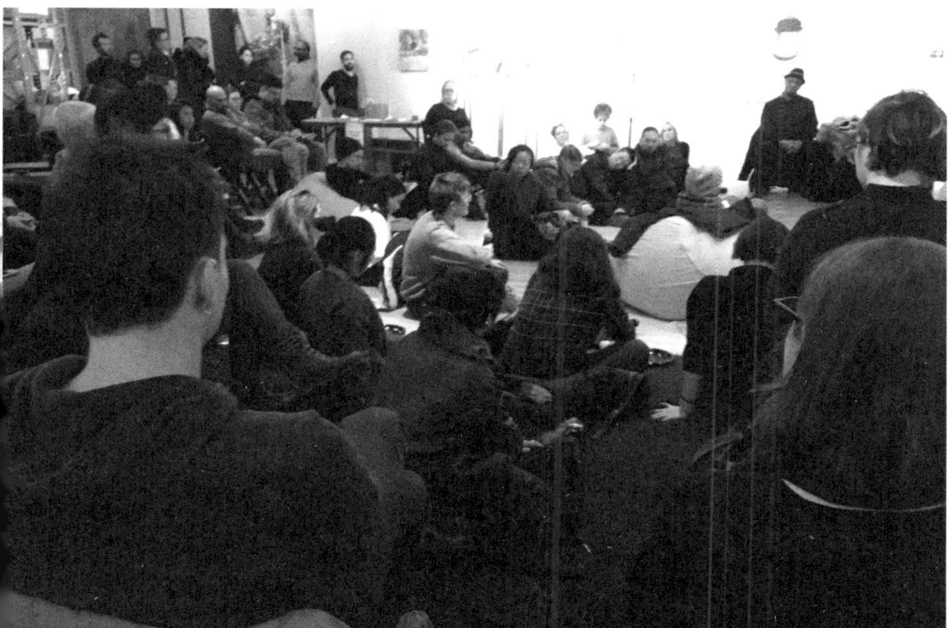

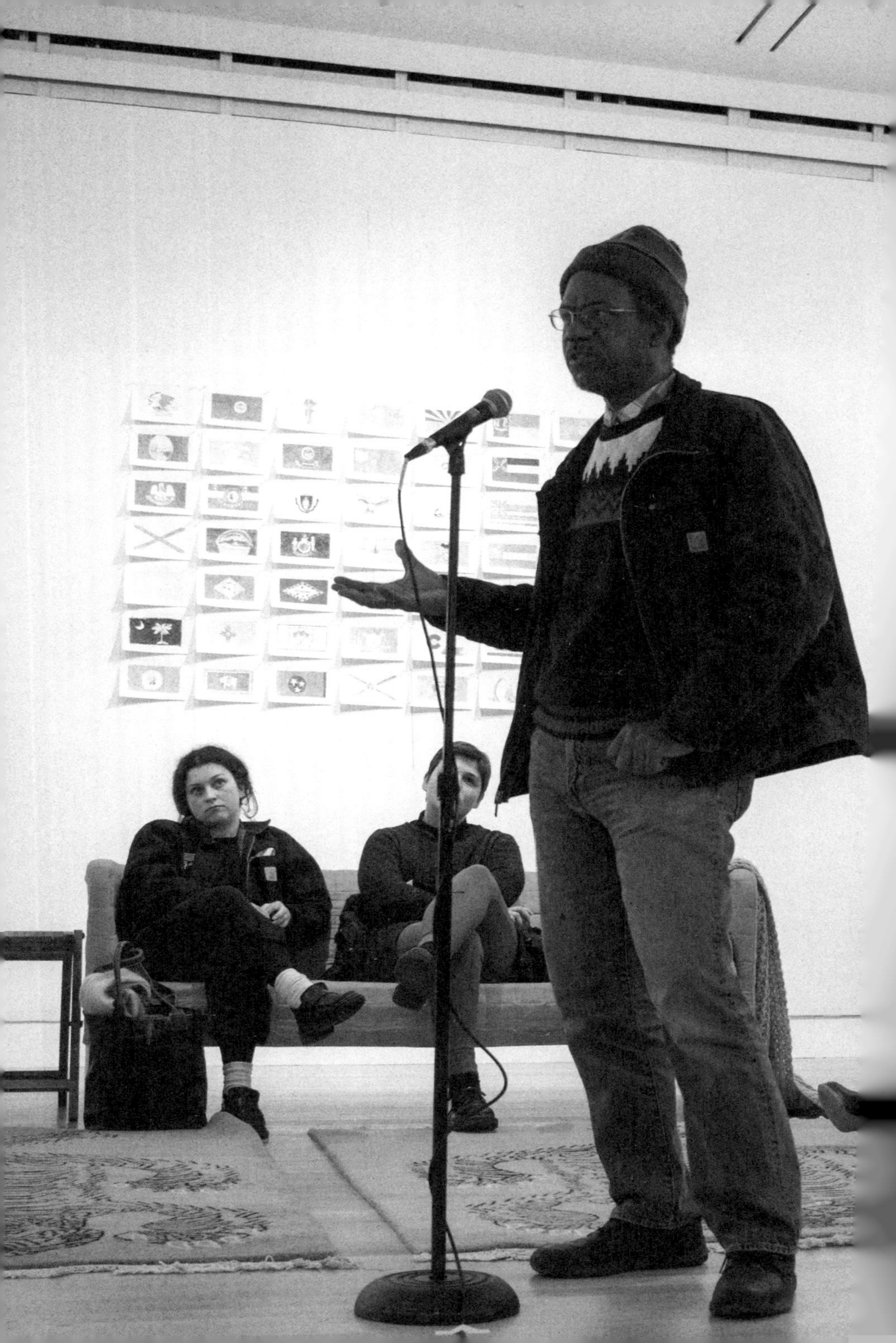

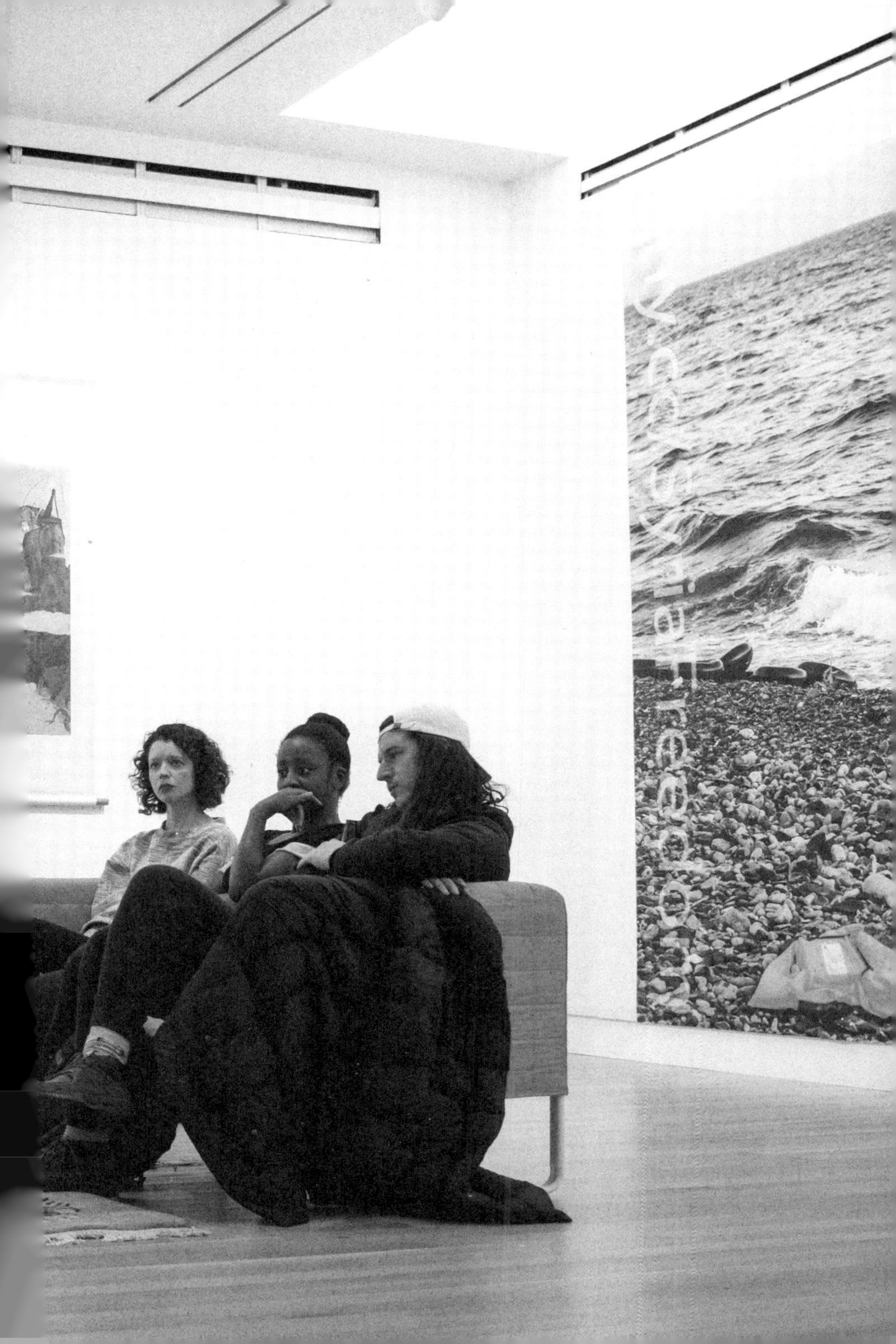

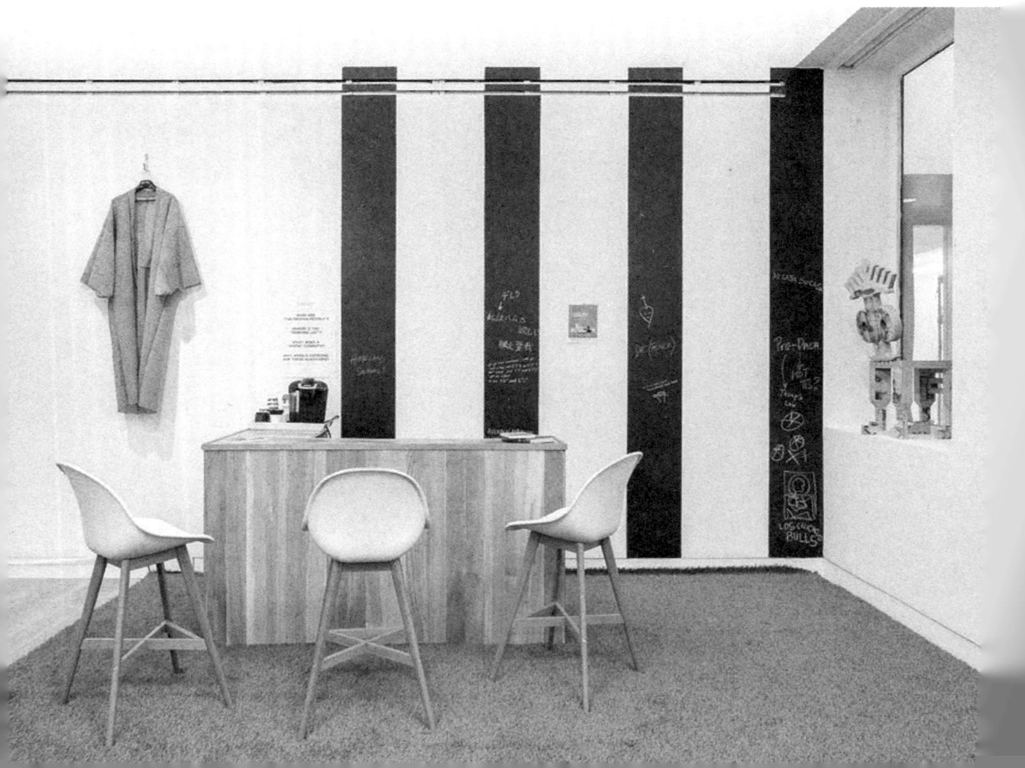

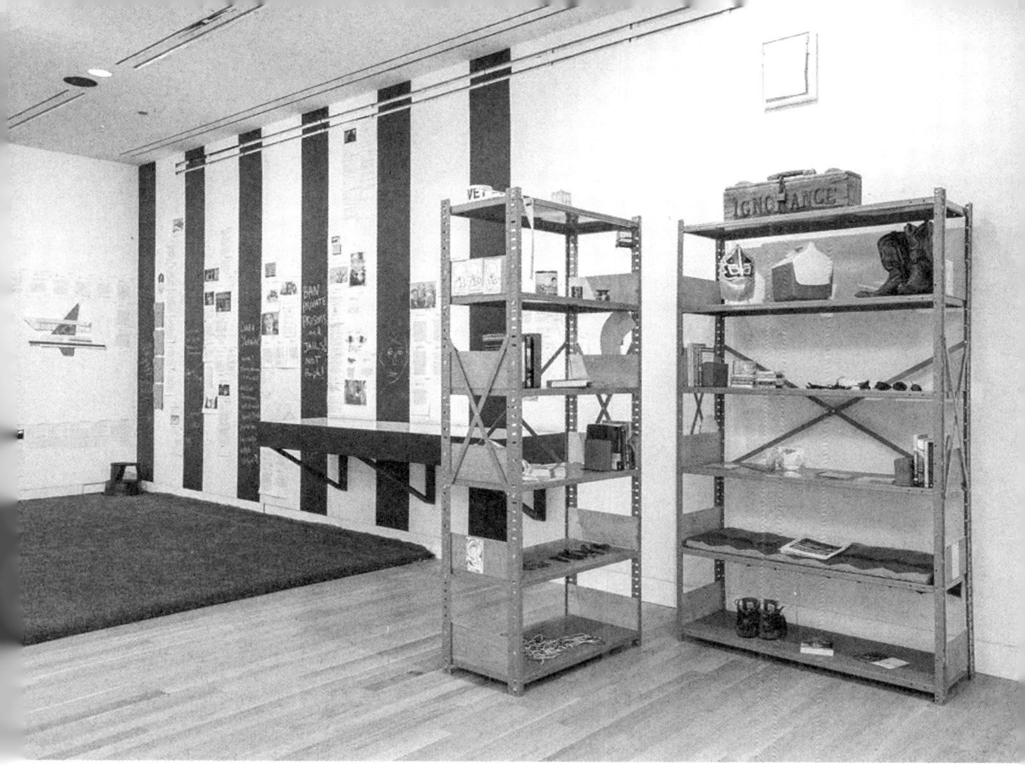

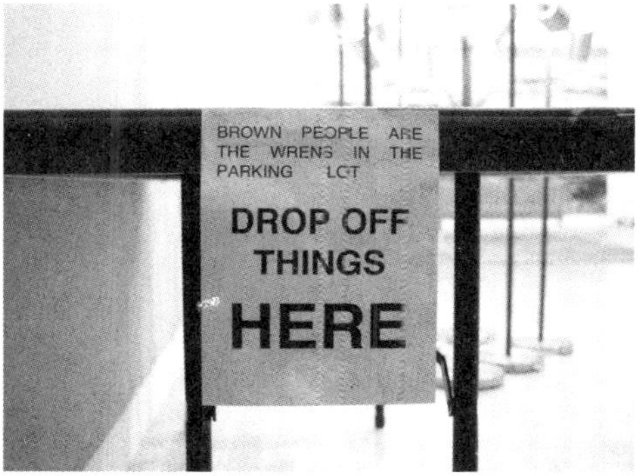
BROWN PEOPLE ARE THE WRENS IN THE PARKING LOT
DROP OFF THINGS HERE

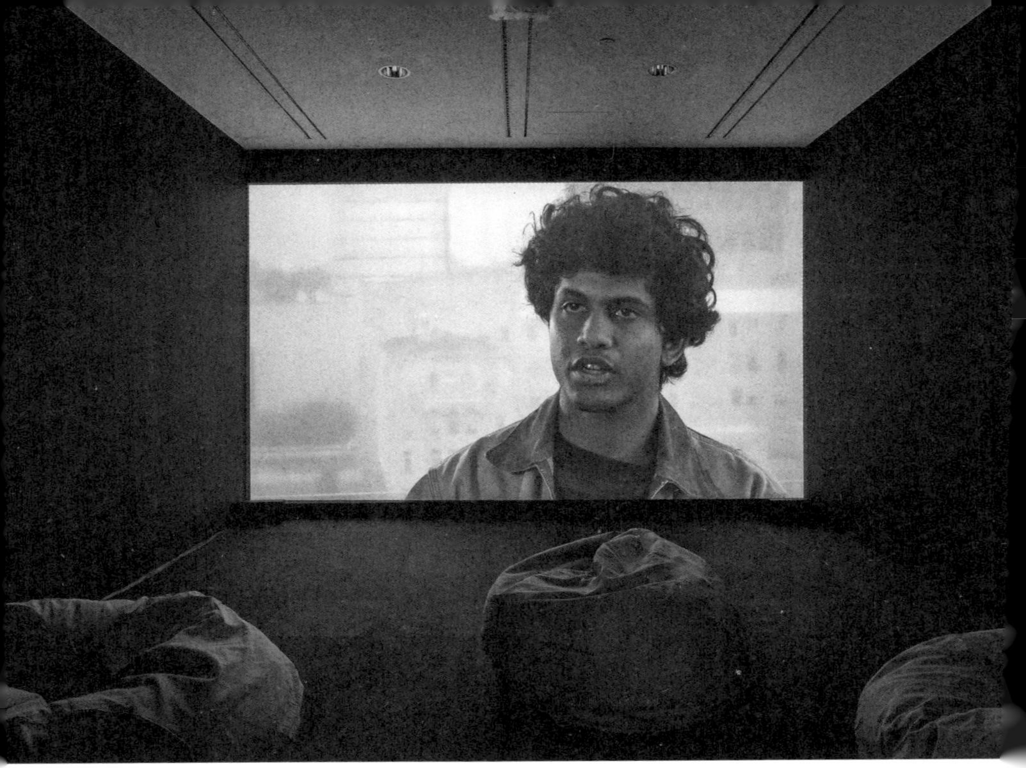

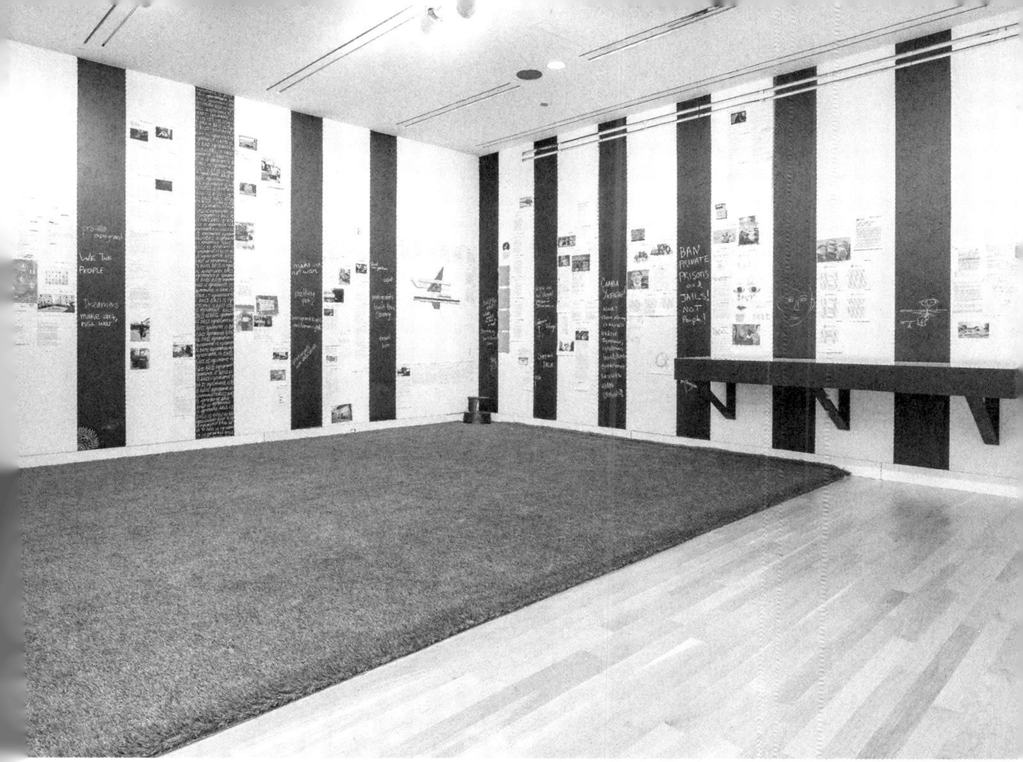
WE THE PEOPLE
BAN PRIVATE PRISONS and JAILS! NOT People!

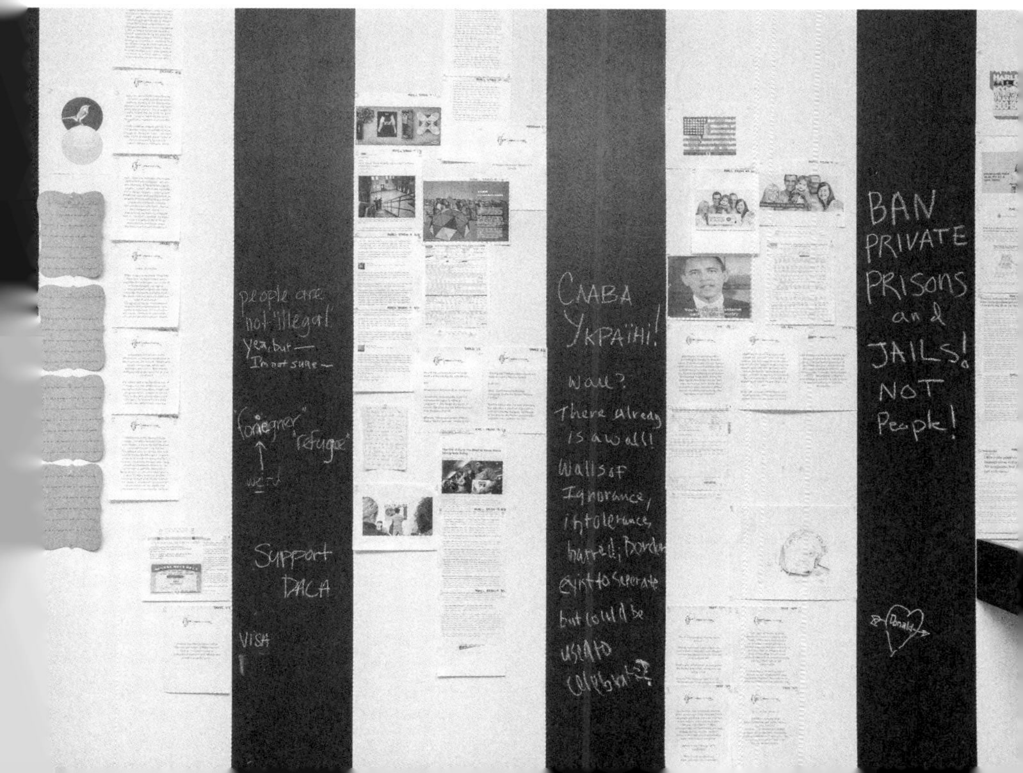
people are not 'illegal'
yea, but —
I'm not sure —
"foriegner"
"refugee"
Support DACA
VISA
СЛАВА УКРАЇНІ!
Wall? There already is a wall!
Walls of Ignorance, intolerance,
BAN PRIVATE PRISONS and JAILS! NOT People!
Donald

ARE JEW IN?
OR
ARE JEW OUT?

Come to Hillel's Hannukah Study Break!
Make cards for a retirement home, decorate cookies, & chat with new friends
Wednesday, Nov 29, 4-7 PM @ Hillel

POPE.L STUDIO 4 1/1

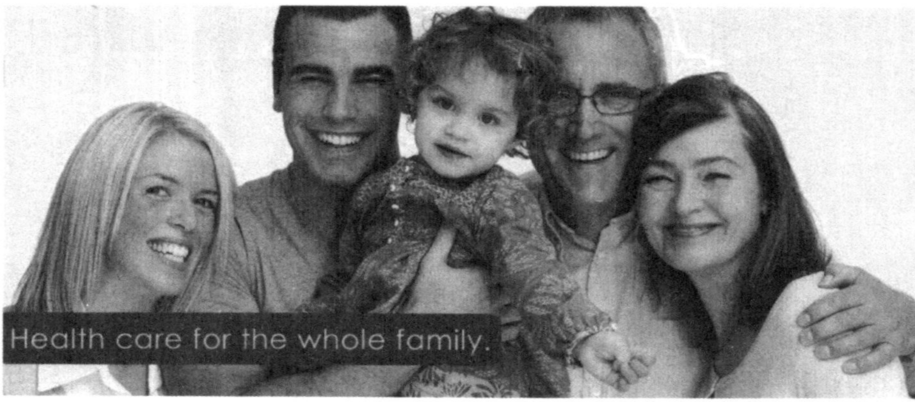

NOVEMBER 8, 2017

More than 100,000 Haitian and Central American immigrants face decision on their status in the U.S.

BY D'VERA COHN (HTTP://WWW.PEWRESEARCH.ORG/STAFF/DVERA-COHN/) AND JEFFREY S. PASSEL (HTTP://WWW.PEWRESEARCH.ORG/STAFF/JEFFREY-S-PASSEL/)

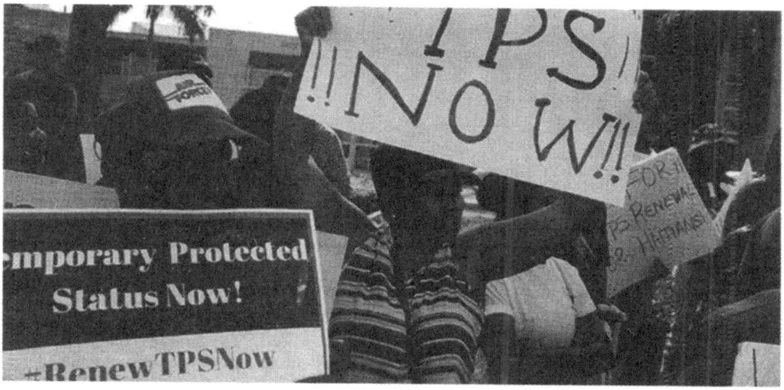

People protest the possibility that the Trump administration may overturn Temporary Protected Status for Haitians in front of the U.S. Citizenship and Immigration Services office on May 13 in Miami. (Joe Raedle/Getty Images)

More than 100,000 immigrants from Haiti and Honduras are expected to learn in the coming weeks whether they will be allowed to stay in the United States under temporary protection that was granted years ago because of natural disasters in their home countries. That protection expires next year.

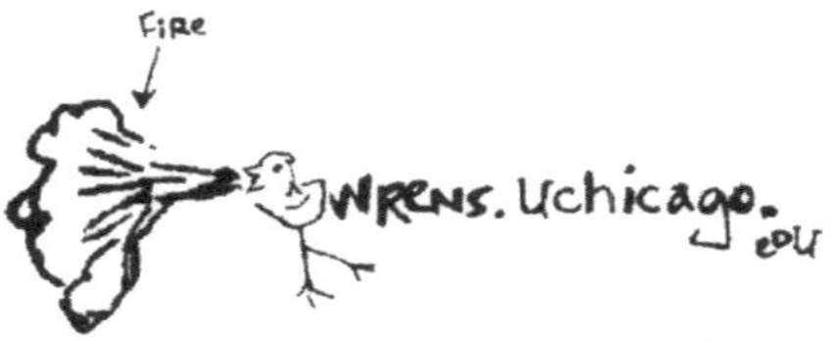

The brown people are not the white people. A wren is a survivalist. The parking lot is the United States. A provocateur asks these questions to combine poetic metaphor with a sense of irony.

DRAKE 1/1

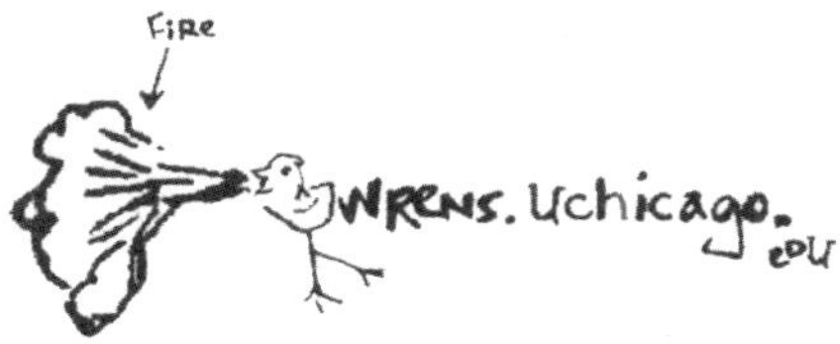

America and Mexico should merge become one nation. If Mexico would have us. This would solve all immigration problems with Mexico and create a powerful union.

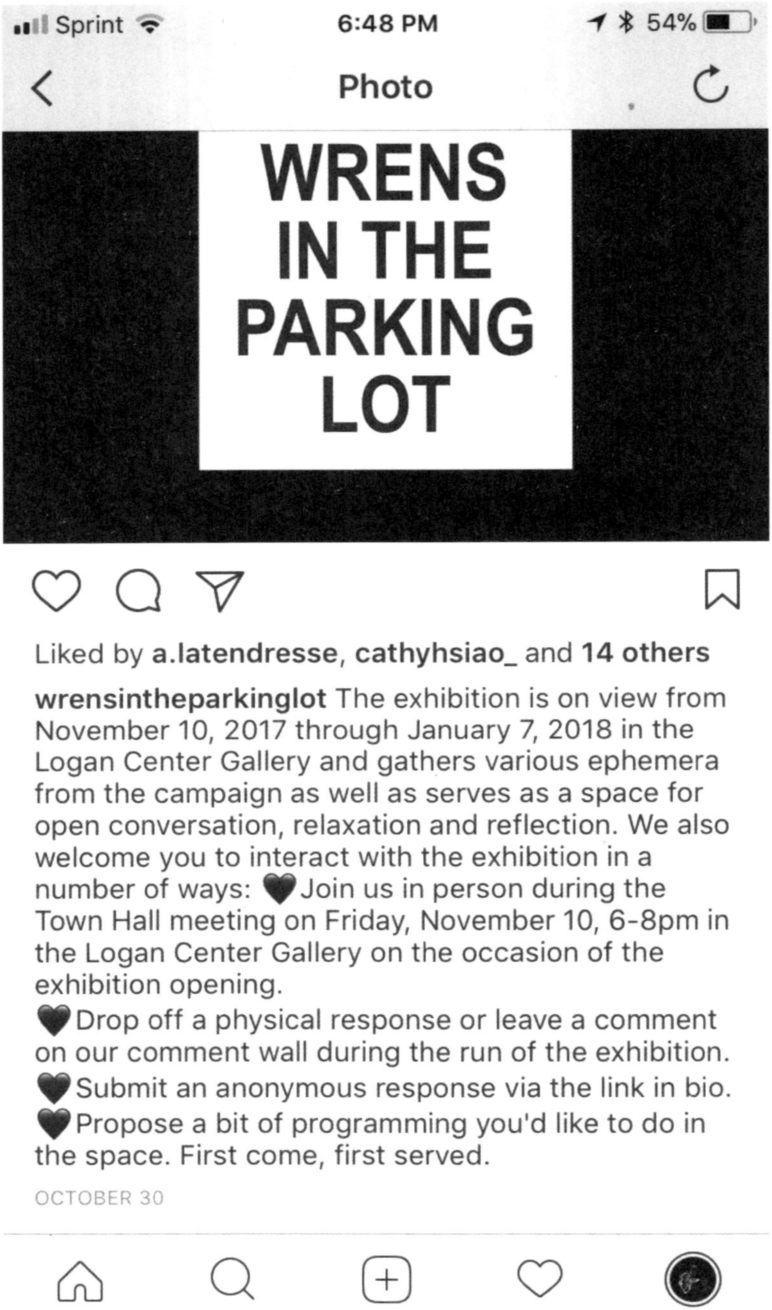
Sprint
6:48 PM
54%
Photo
WRENS IN THE PARKING LOT
Liked by a.latendresse, cathyhsiao_ and 14 others
wrensintheparkinglot The exhibition is on view from November 10, 2017 through January 7, 2018 in the Logan Center Gallery and gathers various ephemera from the campaign as well as serves as a space for open conversation, relaxation and reflection. We also welcome you to interact with the exhibition in a number of ways: 🖤Join us in person during the Town Hall meeting on Friday, November 10, 6-8pm in the Logan Center Gallery on the occasion of the exhibition opening.
🖤Drop off a physical response or leave a comment on our comment wall during the run of the exhibition.
🖤Submit an anonymous response via the link in bio.
🖤Propose a bit of programming you'd like to do in the space. First come, first served.
OCTOBER 30

Sprint 6:45 PM 55%

Photo

wrensintheparkinglot
Reva and David Logan Center for the Arts >

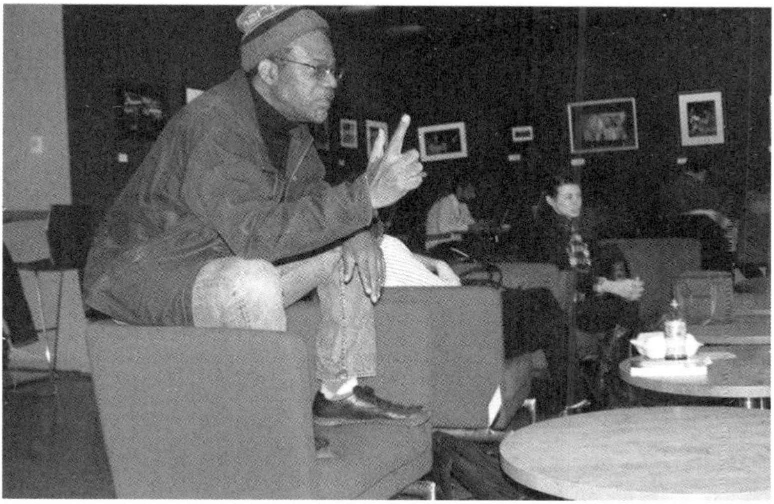

Liked by **hollyacahill**, **a.latendresse** and **26 others**

wrensintheparkinglot Here's an idea. Over 2.7 million illegal immigrants visit art museums every year. #PopeL
#williampopel
#logancenterforthearts
#uchicagoarts
#uchicago
#susannevielmetter #zachcahill
#mitchellinnesandnash #sanctuary #sanctuarycity
#daca #dreamers
#youarewelcomehere #nooneisillegal

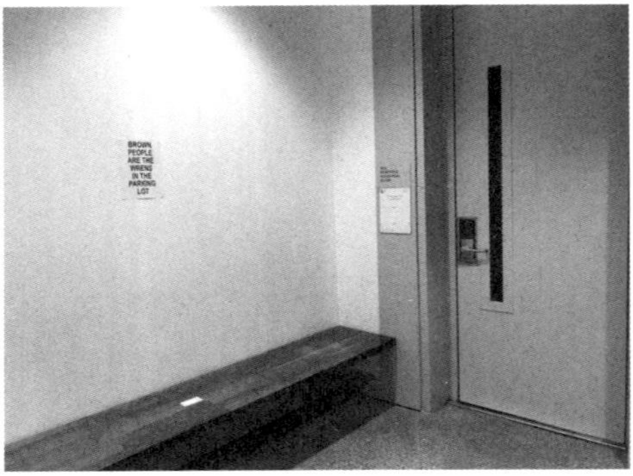
BROWN
PEOPLE
ARE THE
WRENS
IN THE
PARKING
LOT

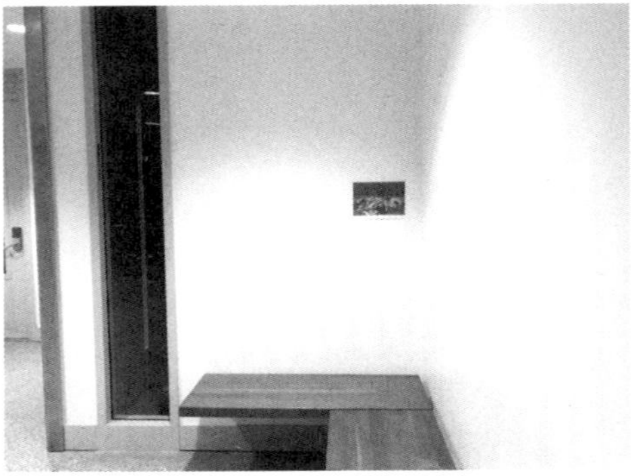

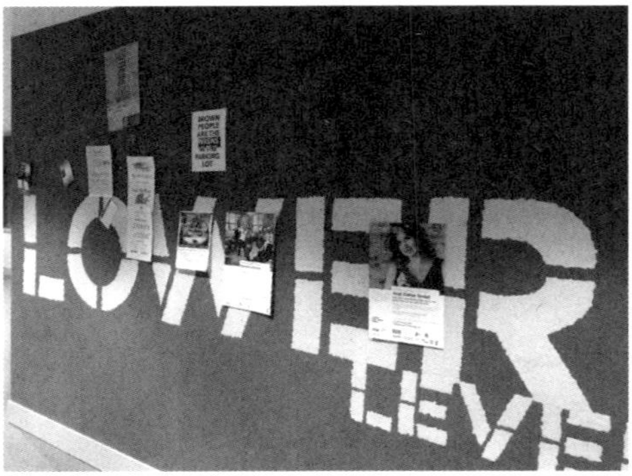
LOWER

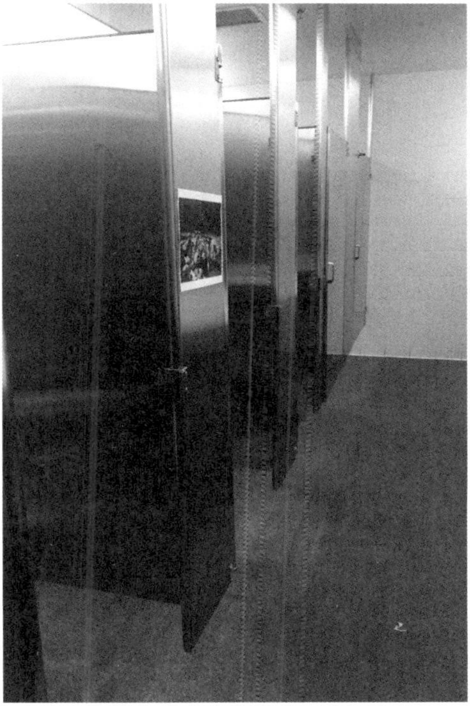

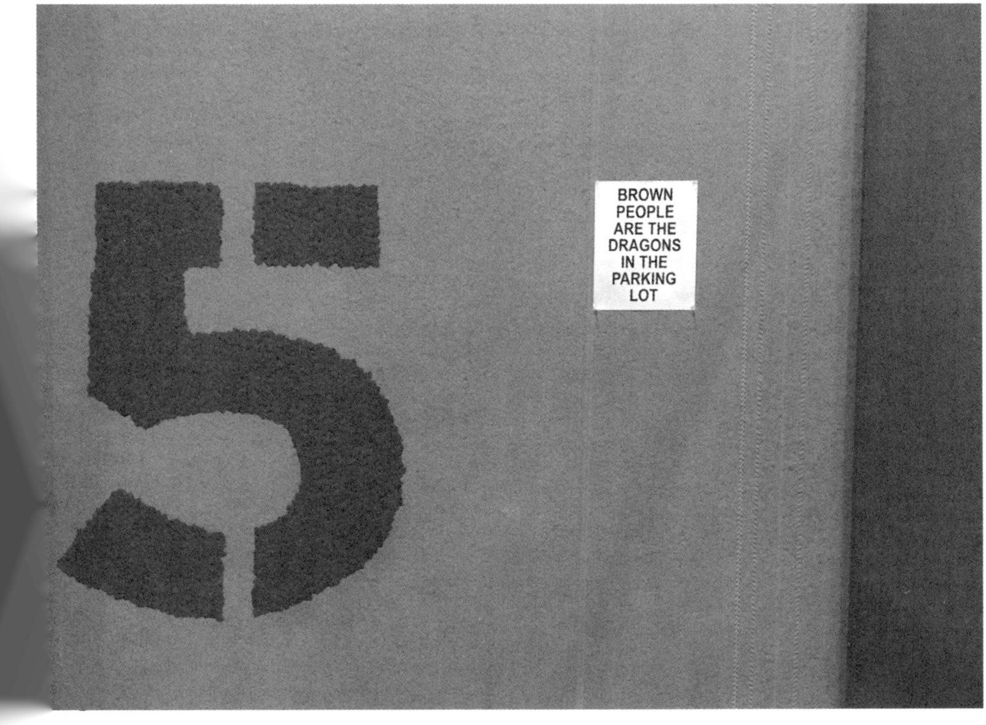
5
BROWN
PEOPLE
ARE THE
DRAGONS
IN THE
PARKING
LOT

POSTER 2

BROWN PEOPLE ARE THE WRENS IN THE PARKING LOT

POSTER 3

BROWN PEOPLE ARE THE DRAGONS IN THE PARKING LOT

THE LIBRARY IS OPEN!!!

LOGAN ROOM 039

TUESDAY OCT 24 // 2:00 - 5:00 PM
WEDNESDAY OCT 25 // 1:00 – 4:00 PM
THURSDAY OCT 26 // 9:00 AM – 12:00 PM

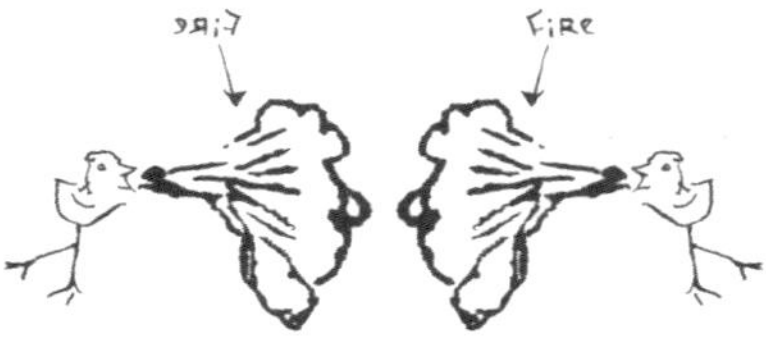

WRENS.UCHICAGO.EDU
WRENS.UCHICAGO.EDU
WRENS.UCHICAGO.EDU
WRENS.UCHICAGO.EDU
WRENS.UCHICAGO.EDU
WRENS.UCHICAGO.EDU
WRENS.UCHICAGO.EDU
WRENS.UCHICAGO.EDU
WRENS.UCHICAGO.EDU
WRENS.UCHICAGO.EDU
WRENS.UCHICAGO.EDU
WRENS.UCHICAGO.EDU
WRENS.UCHICAGO.EDU
WRENS.UCHICAGO.EDU

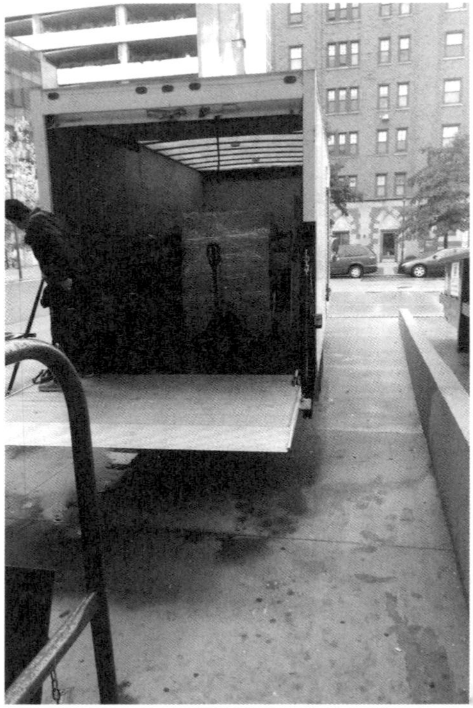

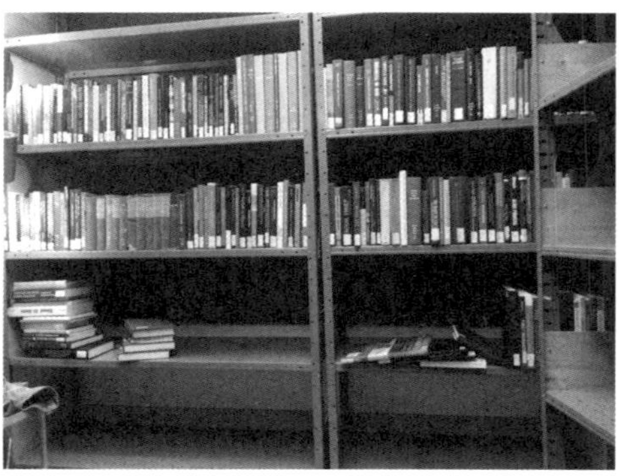

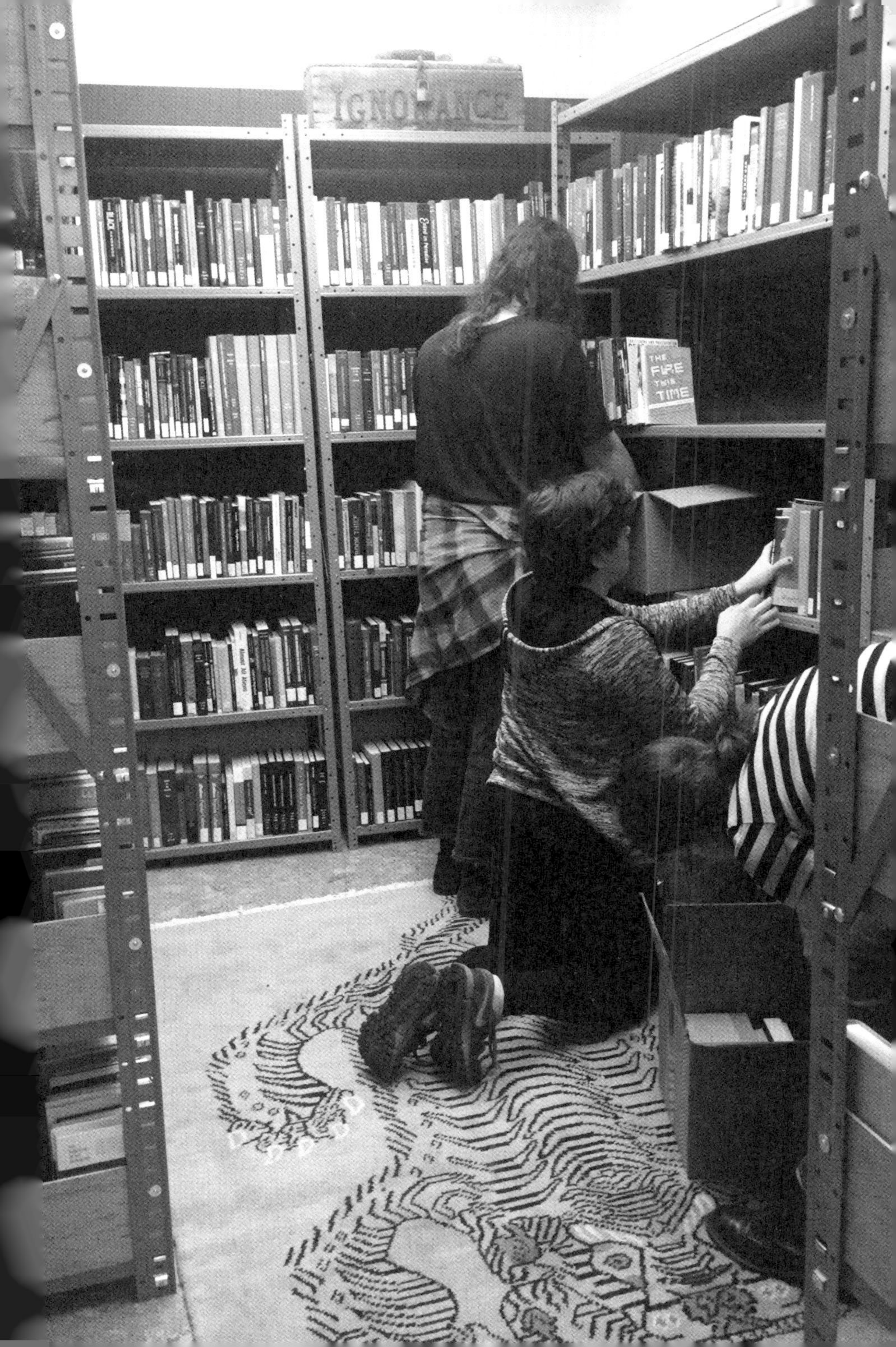
IGNORANCE
THE FIRE THIS TIME

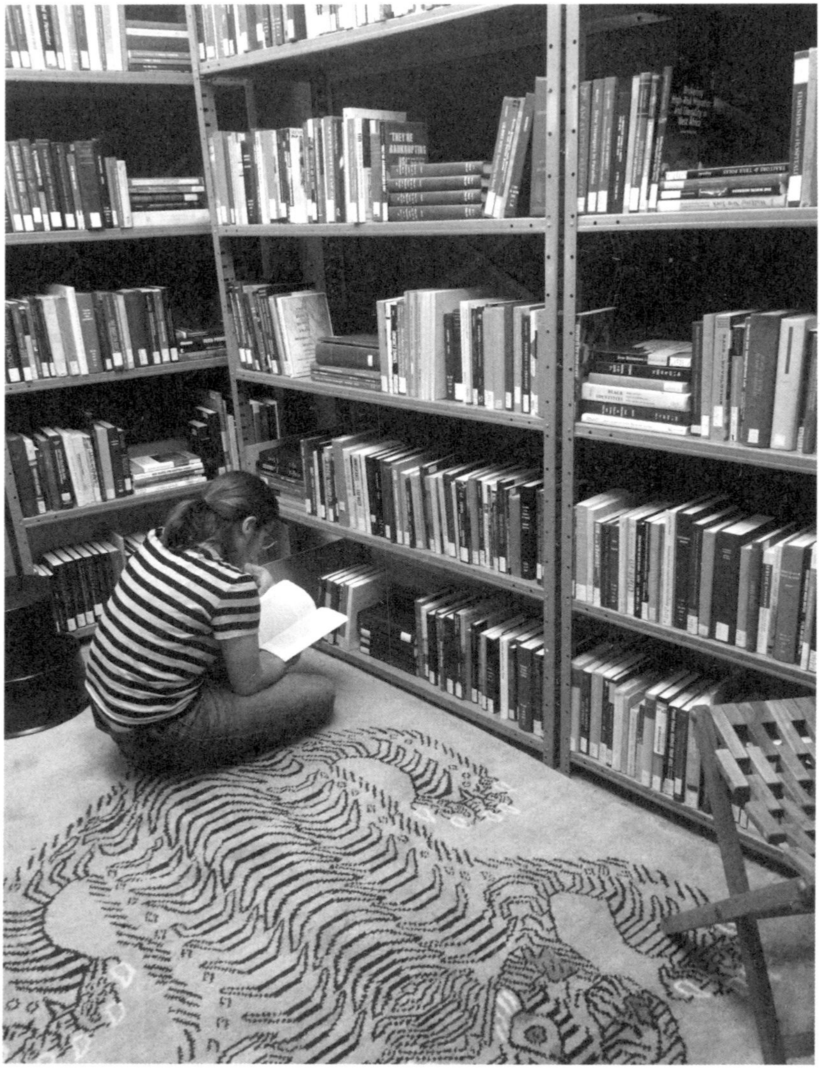

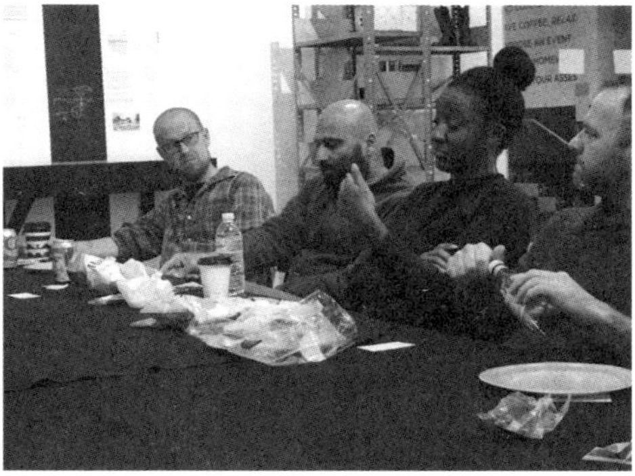

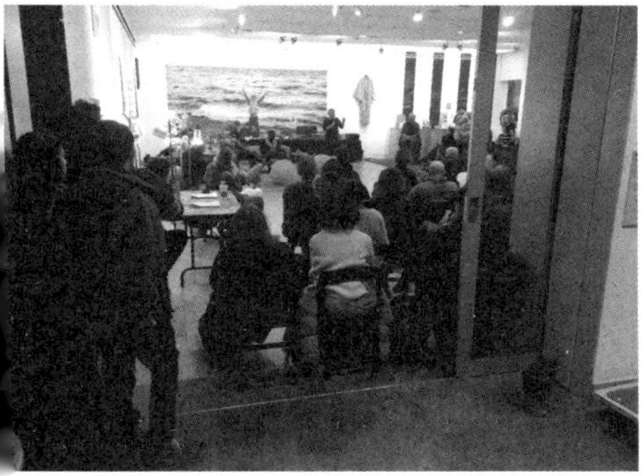

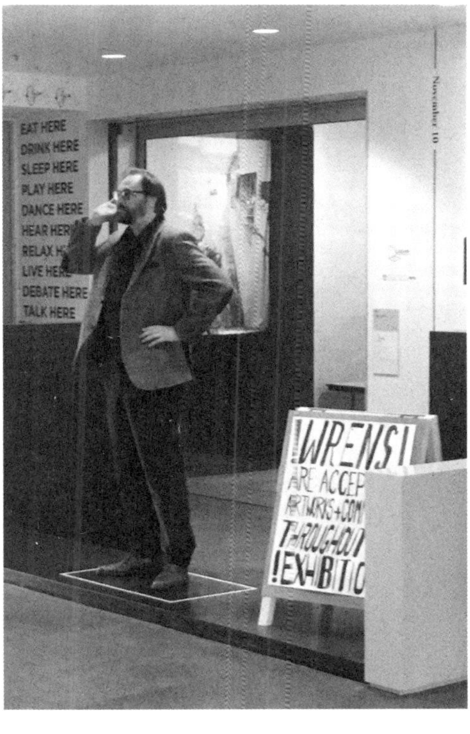
EAT HERE
DRINK HERE
SLEEP HERE
PLAY HERE
DANCE HERE
LIVE HERE
DEBATE HERE
TALK HERE
!WRENS!

November 10

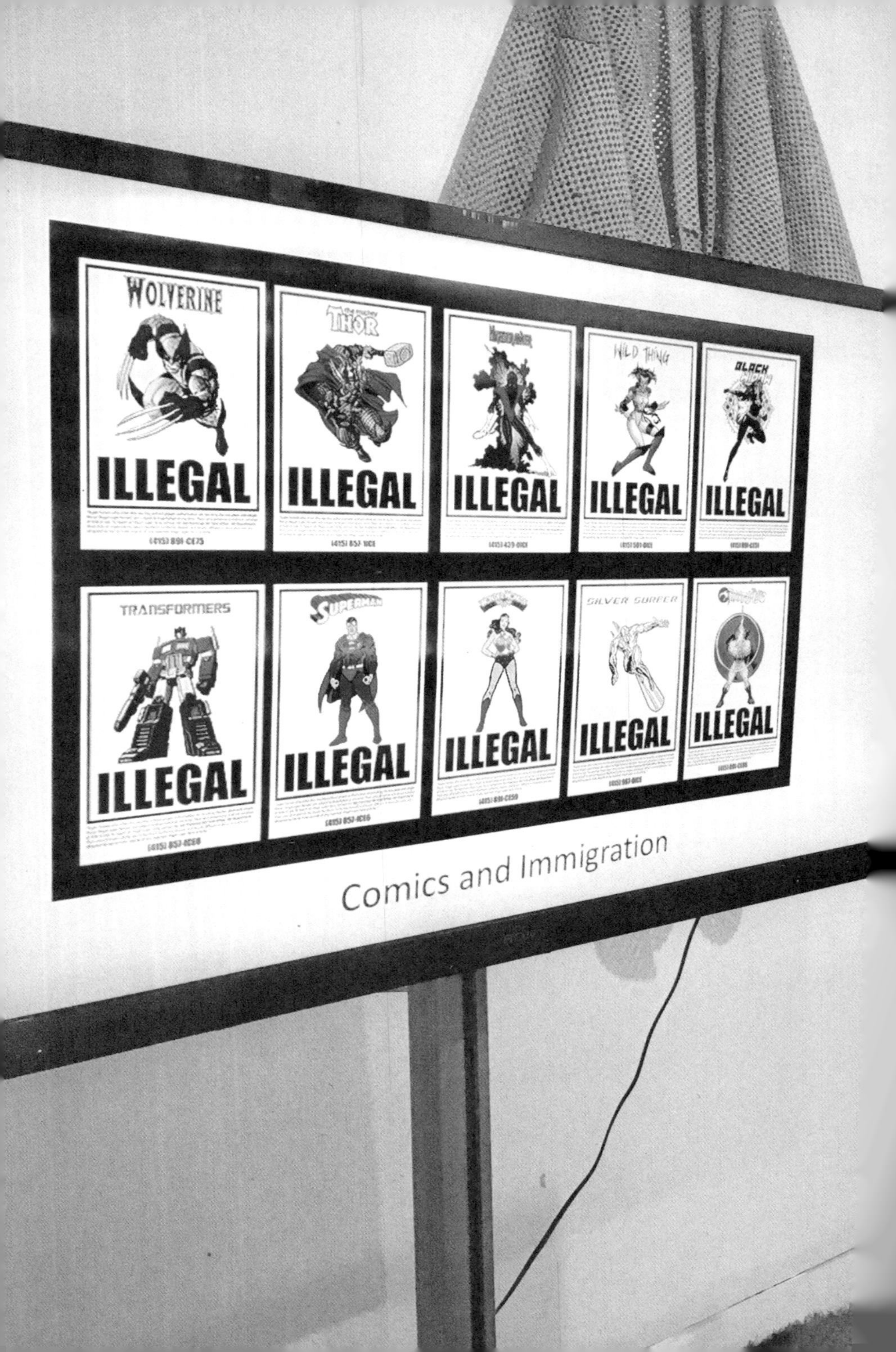
WOLVERINE
ILLEGAL
THOR
ILLEGAL
ILLEGAL
WILD THING
ILLEGAL
ILLEGAL
TRANSFORMERS
ILLEGAL
SUPERMAN
ILLEGAL
ILLEGAL
SILVER SURFER
ILLEGAL
ILLEGAL
Comics and Immigration

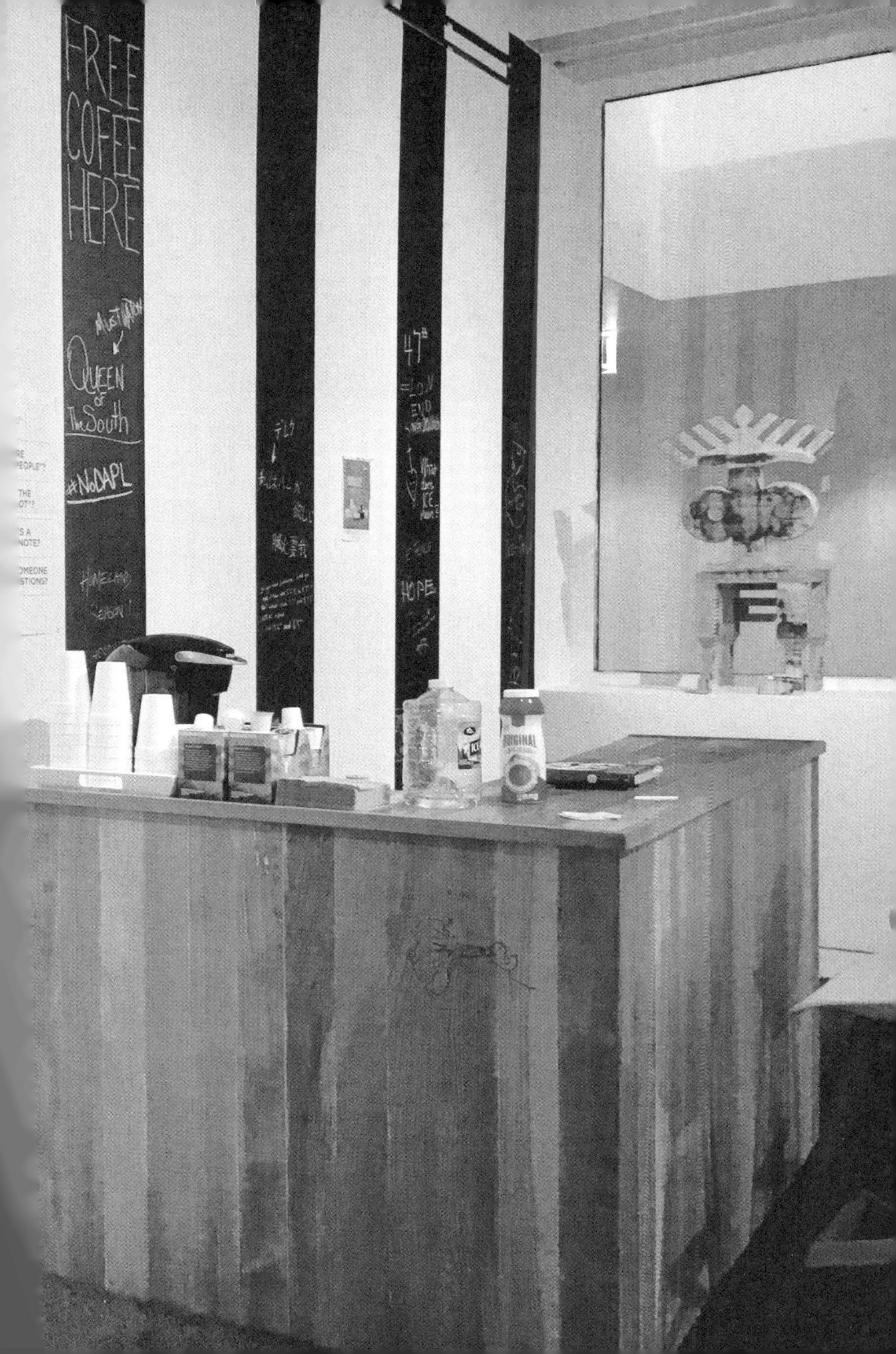
FREE
COFEE
HERE
MUST WATCH
QUEEN
of
The South
#NoDAPL
HOMELAND
SEASON 1
47th
HOPE
ORIGINAL

Immigrational Aesthetics / Pope.L and the Power of Horror

Zachary Cahill

Whoever be the individuals that compose it, however like or unlike be their mode of life, their occupations, their character, or their intelligence, the fact that they have been transformed into a group puts them into a possession of a sort of collective mind which makes them feel, think, and act in a manner quite different from that in which each individual would feel, think, and act were he in a state of isolation.[1]
Sigmund Freud

The artistic practice thus resides in the invention of relations between consciousness. Each particular artwork is a proposal to live in a shared world, and the work of every artist is a bundle of relations with the world, giving rise to other relations, and so on and so forth, ad infinitum.[2]
Nicolas Bourriaud

Human beings. What people can do in conjunction with other people is exponentially worse than what they can do alone. Society is the scariest monster.[3]
Jordan Peele

Horror begins with a whisper. A creeping sense that something is amiss. A disturbing tautness of the present hat is both unreal and indisputably palpable. A sense that he cave we are standing in is not a rock enclosure but he belly of the beast; an evil that so saturates the environment it nearly becomes invisible: it has infected vision tself. This is the stock-in-trade of the horror film genre nd the dread that so often accompanies the Freudian *Unheimlich*—the familiar turned on its head (which subsequently starts spinning and spewing bile). Horror, owever, can also begin with a shriek. A vocalized terror hat cuts the air with the maniac abandon of a brandished azor. The shriek need not necessarily be human. In fact, ne could argue that in many cases it is just the inhuman

Sigmund Freud, *Group Psychology and the Analysis of the Ego*, trans. James Strachey (New York: W. W. Norton, 1959), 7.
Nicolas Bourriaud, *Relational Aesthetics*, trans. Simon Pleasance and Fronza Woods (Paris: Les presses du réel, 2002), 22.
Jason Zinoman, "Jordan Peele on a Truly Terrifying Monster: Racism," *New York Times*, February 16, 2017, accessed January 28, 2019, https://www.nytimes.com/2017/02/16/movies/ordan-peele-interview-get-out.html.

filtered through the slimy fascia of the larynx. The shriek also resounds in the unexpected animation of a thing: the abrupt telephone ring, a creaking door, breaking glass, or a vile political pronouncement. Whispers and shrieks, the twinned specters that animate horror fantasies, are also made manifest in our day-to-day nightmarish realities.

Throughout his career, Pope.L has been labeled at times a painter, a conceptual artist, and, of course, most frequently, a performance artist. I would like to suggest here that it is perhaps time to begin to rethink his oeuvre as solidly planted in the realm of horror. The primary subject that Pope.L grapples with time and time again is the American experience and the foundational trauma produced by white supremacy and the painfully persistent legacy of slavery. For want of a better way of putting it, White guilt and Black Trauma constitute the overlapping scenes that form the difficult-to-articulate and at times barely visible tension that is the stymied encounter between the primary participants in this American horror story. Its imperceptibility is frequently willful. White Americans would rather cover it up or pretend to put the monster back in the closet, or even claim that it was just the wind knocking on the window. We can hear as much in expressions such as "Why can't we all get along," "Everyone is racist," or "I thought we were postracial now." It is a kind of "yes, but..." rhetorical alibi, by which we bracket history and the nastiness of racism in the present and move on to more pleasant things.

In his artistic practice, Pope.L seems to want us to stay with the unpleasantness for a while. Dwell on the horror and not run for the door. He invites us to have courage and to not be afraid of our monsters so that we can try to talk to them. In his effort to stay with hard truths, Pope.L is almost clinical. He labors to detect a festering sore, sticks his finger in it, and asks us, his audience: "Can you feel that? Is that where it hurts?" One of the bizarrely magical aspects of this doctor's exam is that you can feel the artist doing it to himself as well. There is a kind of acknowledgment that we are *both* sick. He feels his finger digging around in the wound too. As a patient, you derive comfort from knowing that you are not alone, that we are both struggling with the same disease.

This exploration of social horror[4] can be seen throughout Pope.L's work from his early crawling performances to more recent films such as *The Long White Cloud* (2013) and *Re-enactor* (2012/2015); his experimental theater piece at the Art Institute of Chicago, *The Escape* (2018); and his *Whispering Campaign*, featured in Athens and Kassel for documenta 14 (2017), of course. The latter had something of a double life here in Chicago—or rather, an American version of sorts, conceived as an "alternate ending" at the city's Logan Center for the Arts. If the project for documenta employed an international contemporary art venue as an opportunity to focus on the migrant crisis (let's call it what it is—a *refugee* crisis) in Europe, in Chicago, Pope.L sought to address the immigrant question on what could be described as a hyperlocal level by way of an exhibition dubbed *Brown People Are the Wrens in the Parking Lot*.

The *Wrens* project, as it became known in shorthand among participants, was difficult and experimental, even by the standards of Pope.L, who (per the *New York Times*) is known for "Answering Society's Thorniest Questions." For starters, it was to unfold anonymously: an authorless exhibition that would be preceded by a series of interventions throughout the Logan Center in the weeks before the exhibition as such opened. Again, an exhibition that was not attached to Pope.L's name but was simply (and provocatively) titled *Brown People Are the Wrens in the Parking Lot*. These interventions included an ever-growing series of flyer postings with images of refugees in various states of distress landing on the shores of Europe and/or in precarious lifeboats. These images were then captioned with the phrase *Brown People Are the Wrens in the Parking Lot*. Slowly leaking into the Logan Center's daily proliferation of flyers, their numbers began to swell so that what started out as fairly unnoticeable became unavoidable. Next, unannounced videos that discussed the subject of

4 My thanks to art historian Darby English, who, when I told him in passing that I was thinking about Pope.L's artwork in relation to horror, nodded affirmatively and with characteristic insight and precision supplied me with the appropriate term: "social horror."

immigration started showing up on the center's monitors, which were habitually used to highlight events. This was followed by a pop-up library appearing in one of the practice rooms in the basement and made up of a thousand books on the subject of immigration, which vanished after two days. Later, sidewalk chalkings appeared outside the building asking questions about immigration such as: "What is an immigrant?" "Are you pro-immigration?" "Where do you stand on immigration?" "Who are the Wrens?"

Added to these interventions was a kind of street theater occurring in the Logan Center's café, where Pope.L and I would periodically start off talking quietly about immigration; the conversation would balloon into a full-fledged shouting match in which each of us would swap sides from a pro-immigrant stance to a nativist position—after which we would let the slightly alarmed diners know that this was a staged performance that was part of the *Wrens* project, and hand them invitations to participate in an online survey about immigration. Again, most of this took place without being undersigned publicly by the artist.

These interventions constituted a monthlong windup to announce the exhibition to the users of the Logan Center. Pope.L was interested in the fact that the building had two primary sets of users: one being students and faculty, another including the café, janitorial, and security staff. That these two constituencies tended to fall along the lines of particular skin colors was not lost on the artist. Indeed, it was this very circumstance that he sought to address: Pope.L sought to make private conversations between these groups of people public, to place them in dialogue with one another by using the subject of immigration as a catalyst for conversation. All this made the university administration a bit nervous—especially given that neo-Nazis had recently been posting hate-filled and threatening flyers on campus in the wake of Donald Trump's election: grim and very real horror was stalking the South Side with banners signed Blood and Soil.

So far, one could summarize the Pope.L method as follows: Step 1, diagnose the patient (the twin users of the Logan Center). Step 2, identify a shared experience or topic of conversation (immigration). Step 3, deploy exposure therapy—a series of staged interventions and encounters.

On November 10, it was revealed that Pope.L was the artist behind the series of interventions and the exhibition. The exhibition itself looked like a quintessential relational-aesthetics event from the 1990s by artists like Rirkrit Tiravanija or Liam Gillick. In the case of the *Wrens* project, it was a place to hang out, drink free coffee at the bar, play Nerf basketball, read on one of the couches, play records, and reply on the chalkboard-painted walls to questions about immigration. To echo the typical "us-and-them" rhetoric engendered by the topic of immigration, the gallery was divided in two by artificial turf—for the grass is always greener on the other side, right? Additionally, people were invited to supply artworks and programming suggestions to the exhibition. At the opening, Logan Center exhibitions curator Yesomi Umolu and I were asked to shepherd a town hall conversation on immigration. The exchange began in fits and starts. Reluctant utterances and embarrassed commentary trailed off. It was hard. People were hesitant to open up about their views on the subject. In the spirit of "if at first you don't succeed, try, and try again," we did just that: Pope.L convened a five-hour marathon in the gallery on the exhibition's closing day in early January of 2018 with invited speakers to help move the conversation along and stimulate audience participation. This time, Pope.L himself and documenta 14 curator Dieter Roelstraete began the proceedings. Over the next five hours, people came and went, but the gallery remained full and engaged, and we learned that, even though we were inside an art exhibition, and there was a high likelihood of preaching to the choir—"of course we are all against a wall on the border with Mexico; of course we are all for the humane treatment of all people, immigrant or otherwise"—it was nevertheless the case that this choir was not necessarily in tune, or even singing the same song. The conversation was animated, lively, at times humorous, raw, often informative, and ultimately constructive.

There it sat, in the gallery: the heavy-breathing, multifaced monster that Americans are so afraid to talk about, often choosing to hide behind our own masks—*difference*. Stranger. The Other. White privilege. Racial tensions. Class tensions. Immigrants. Native speakers. Expats. It was here that Pope.L made the case for a kind of kinship with those refugees in Europe thousands of miles away, fleeing war-torn parts of the Middle East first and foremost because of America's military invasions in the region. He noted that African Americans had, in some way, also been immigrants, forced to migrate to the Americas through the transatlantic slave trade.

"Forced migration" is a term the artist posited at the marathon event. While acknowledging the important difference between the Middle Passage and the present-day refugee crisis, the artist wanted to draw a connection between the suffering of peoples forced to the Americas through the evils of the slave trade on the one hand, and those who had to flee their homes in Syria and Iraq by crossing the Mediterranean Sea because of war and deadly violence on the other hand. It is not the same thing. Equivalence wasn't the artist's goal: sympathy and common ground were. Pope.L sought to extend this common ground to everyone at the gallery who had some connection or other to migration—and because nearly everyone does have such a connection (either knowing people who had moved or been forced to move, or themselves being migrants), a dialogue became possible. Space was held, and time was given to talk beyond pleasantries.

I am not sure Pope.L ever knew exactly what would come of plastering a provocative slogan around the art center where he also teaches, or what kind of conversation might take place on the subject of immigration between people who share the same building and who exchange greetings every day, or how anyone might ever broach the horror of racism in a way that didn't only inflame old wounds and insult traumatized collective memory. In fact, I would hazard that he most surely did *not* know where his unauthored installation and clandestine performance piece would lead. And maybe that was precisely the point. But he no doubt knew where it would start: in whispers floating in the air choked with the ghosts of racism's past, present, and future. In the end, it might very well be that the "relational" art project *Brown People Are the Wrens in the Parking Lot* was a type of exorcism—which we learned needs to be practiced ad infinitum if we are ever to move our shared and migratory relations beyond the purely superficial and horrifyingly polite.

Insight
Vidura Jang Bahadur

The idea of participation is key to understanding the media campaign and exhibition initiated by William Pope.L, *Brown People Are the Wrens in the Parking Lot*. The opportunity to work on the project—in its various forms—allowed me to participate and engage in the debates surrounding questions of home, identity, and migrations and the larger concerns around the legacy of colonialism and capital flows in the global economy. A response to the recent restrictions on immigration to the United States and heightened concerns over citizenship, race relations, and the "refugee crisis" in Europe, the project resonated with me because it anchored these issues within the transnational nature of cross-border movements.

The narratives of the participants interviewed for the video projection moved me. The journeys they described, both their individual journeys and those made by their ancestors, revealed the challenges they faced and continue to face in a democratic nation at odds with its multiracial and multiethnic identity. This was reiterated in the second town hall; the performances and conversations gave a glimpse into contemporary American society and the schisms within that have festered, in my belief, because of histories that are yet to be fully addressed. The crisis of identity and the questions of belonging at the heart of this debate are not unique to the United States.

Through a discussion I led at the Logan Center under the auspices of the project, we attempted to make these connections—cultural, political, and economic—between the United States and other parts of the world more explicit. An international participant spoke about the uncertainty that comes with living under the shadow of shifting immigration laws; we discussed the colonial trade in cotton that destroyed the economy in pre-independent India, as well as its connection to cotton farming in the southern United States, slavery, and indentured labor that was shipped from India to other parts of the world in the early 1900s. The intent of the conversation was to explore the potential of transnational solidarities, acknowledging the different social and political histories of each nation, group, and community.

In an age in which we are witnessing a rise of right-wing populist leaders across the world, wherein nationhood and citizenship are being reimagined, how do we engage and participate within the social and political spheres to enable inclusive change? *Brown People Are the Wrens in the Parking Lot* attempts to raise this question and to provide a platform for debate.

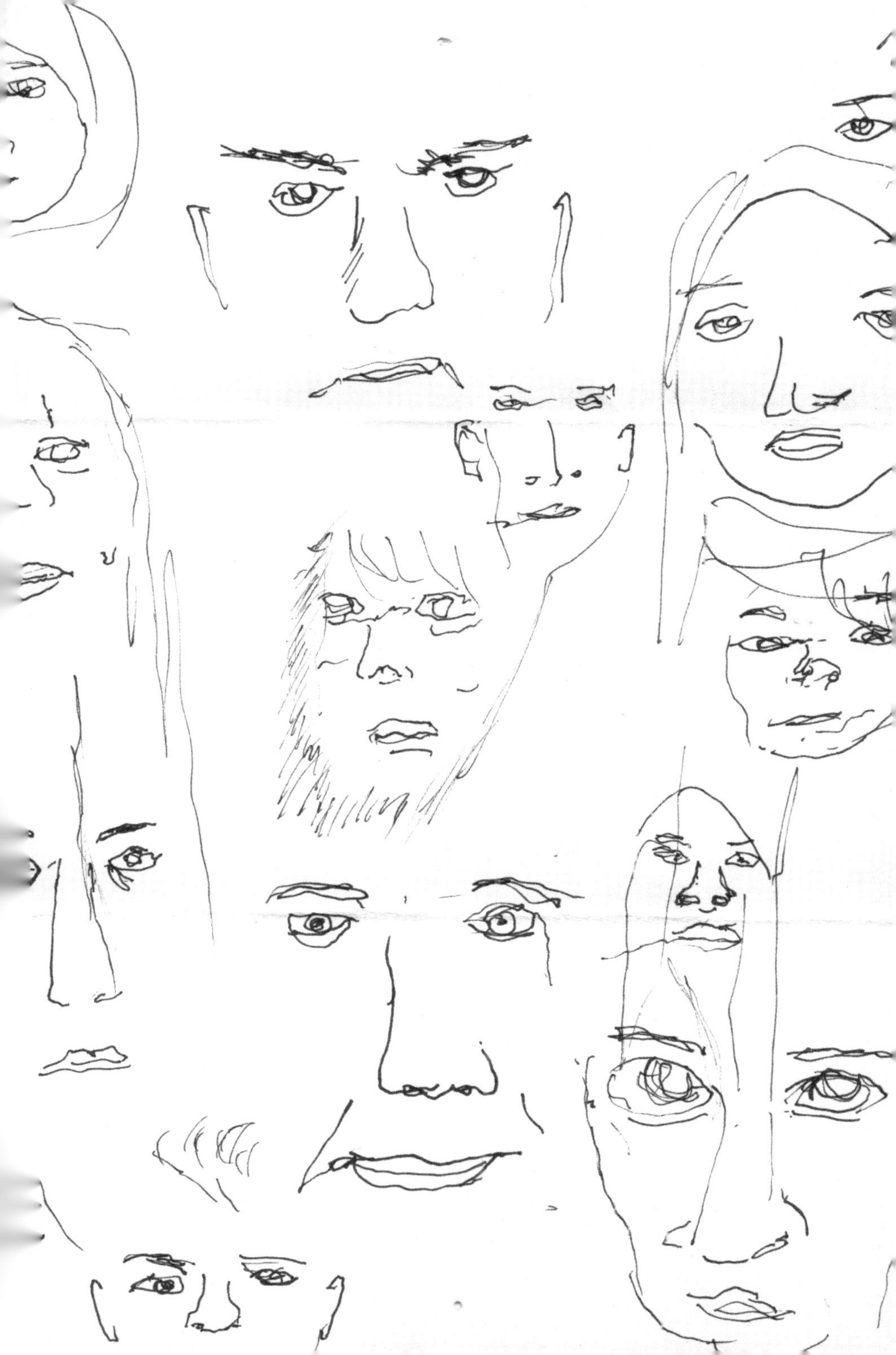

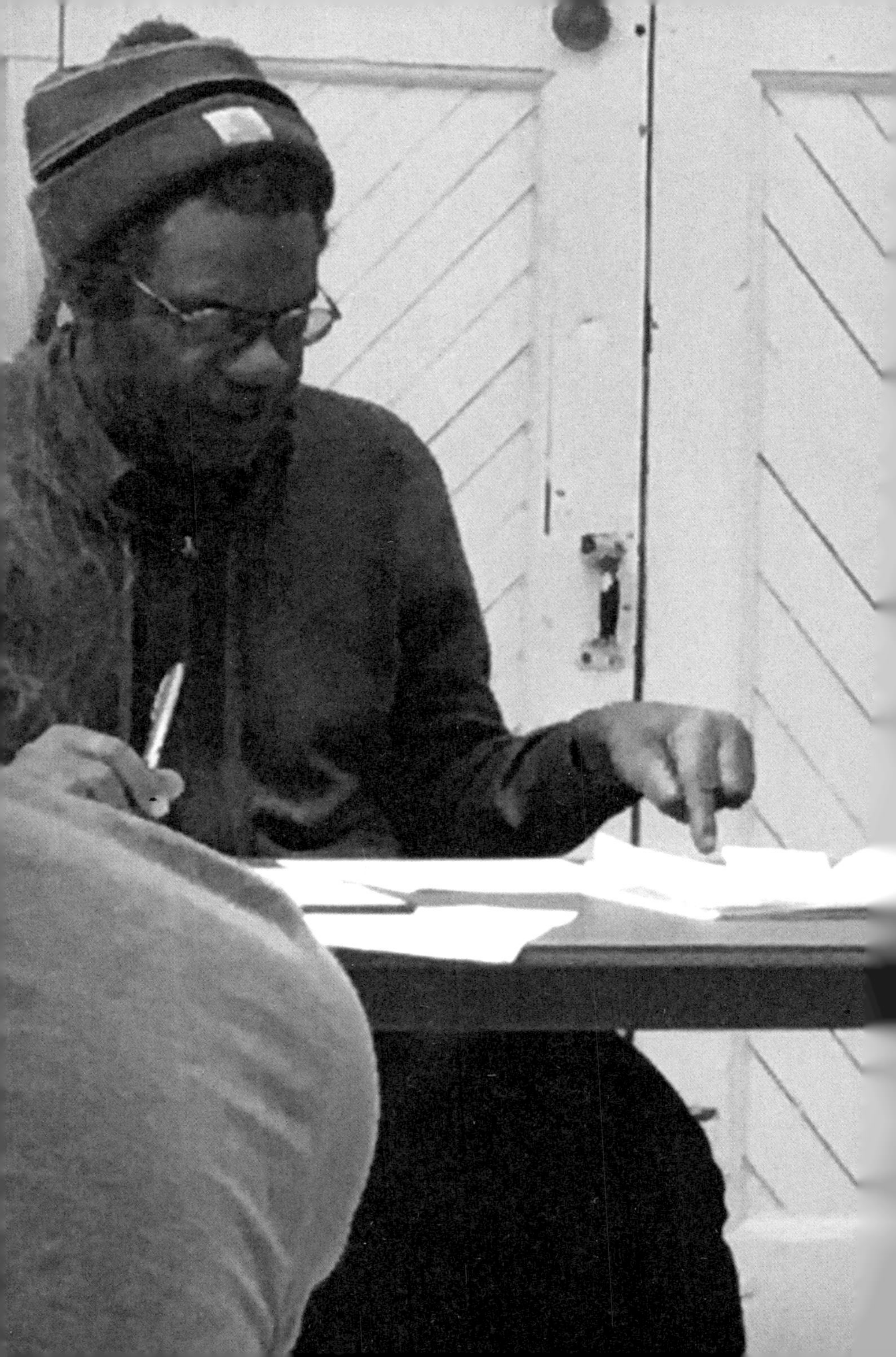

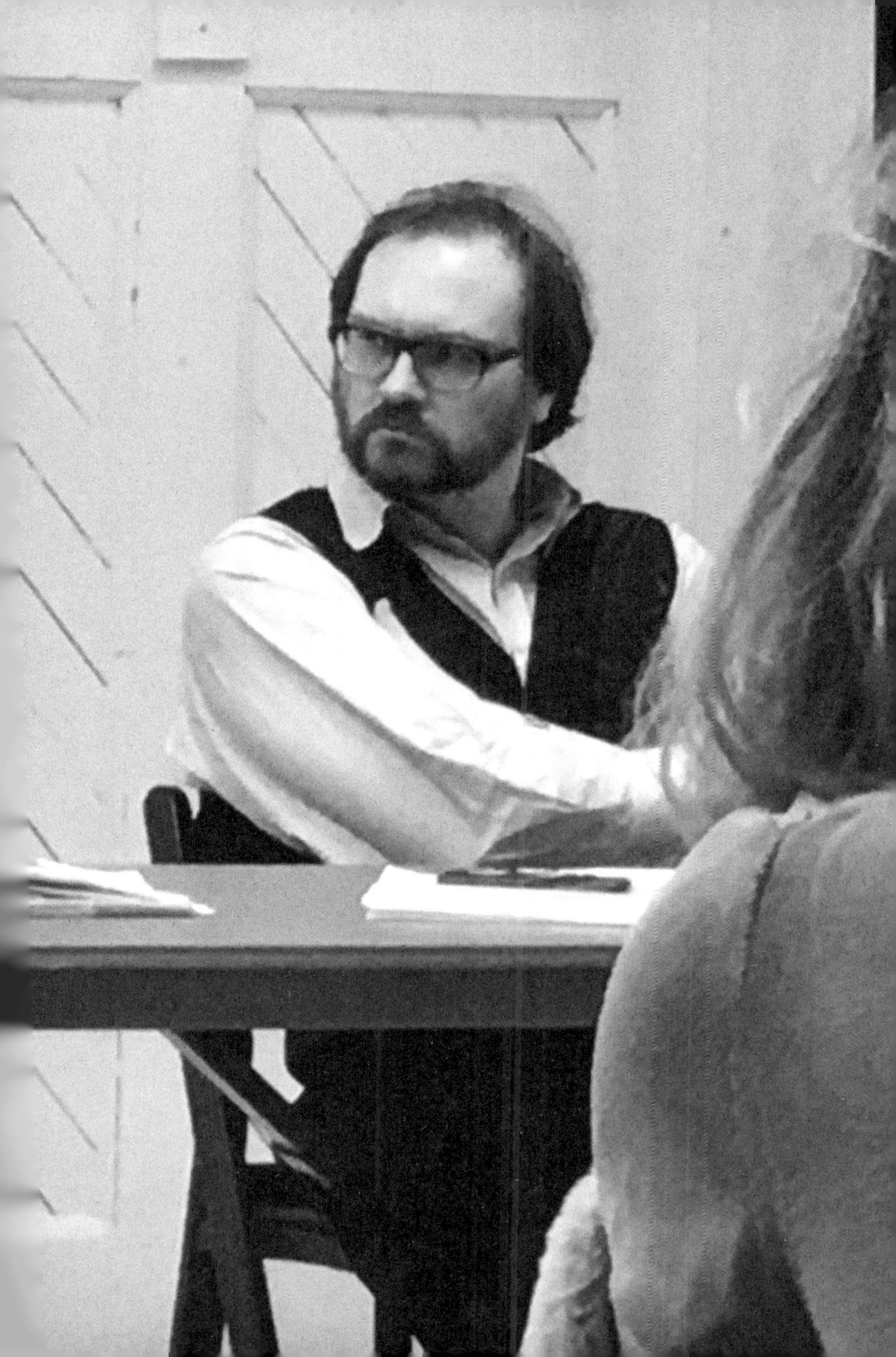

Art and Knowledge

Iris Colburn
Tianyu Guo
Jeffrey Hsu
Michal Koszycki
Jasmin Liang
Cristen Leifheit
Brock Lownes
Elizabeth McClafferty
Adrienne Elyse Meyers
Marie-Gabrielle Verbergt

Preface

In the winter of 2018, Pope.L and I taught a ten-week course at the University of Chicago's Department of Visual Arts titled "Art and Knowledge." The course was an immediate outcome of our having worked together, artist and curator, first in the context of documenta 14 and second in the framework of *Brown People Are the Wrens in the Parking Lot*. The course was conceived as an experimental, hands-on exploration of the tangle of relationships that hold art and knowledge together—and simultaneously keep them apart. One of the recurring motifs of Pope.L's *Whispering Campaign* in Kassel, the endlessly repeated slogan "ignorance is a virtue," had felt like a light-footed provocation to this listener, who has made something of an art world career as an apologist and/or theorist of the conception of art as a form of knowing ("knowledge production") or mode of research. For a couple of months, our "Art and Knowledge" course operated as a platform for articulating the various dimensions of the relationship (or lack thereof) between our respective fields' titular points of anchorage. The questions that were asked of this conjunction were, among others: does art come *before* knowledge, or *after*? Is there art *without* knowledge, or is art without knowledge? Is art *for* knowledge, or *in* knowledge? *Above* or *beyond*? Does art *equal* knowledge? Finally, and most pointedly: should "art *and* knowledge" be read as "art *or* knowledge" instead? The following selection of student submissions hints at some possible answers—in the distance.

Dieter Roelstraete

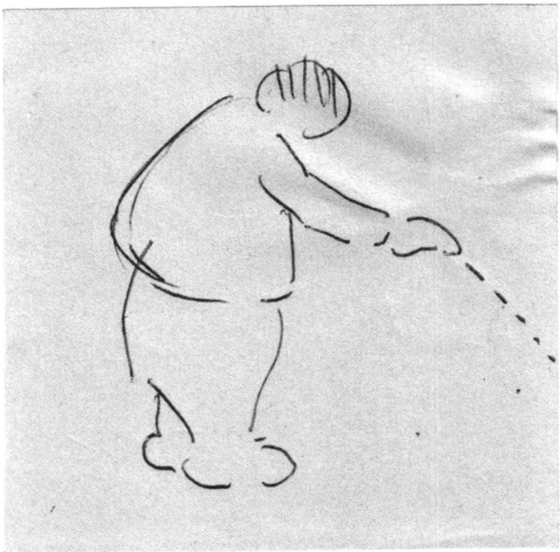

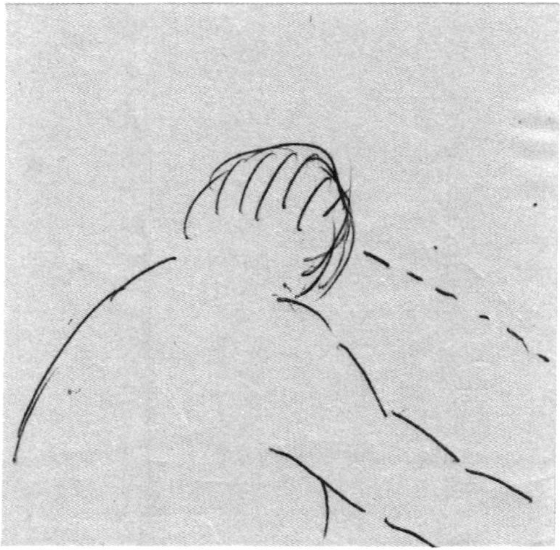

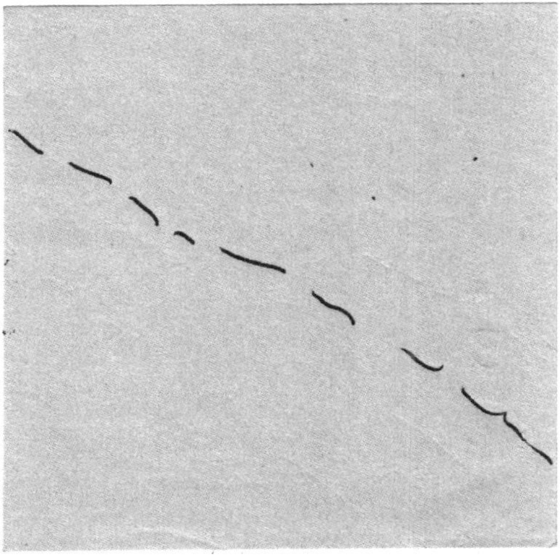

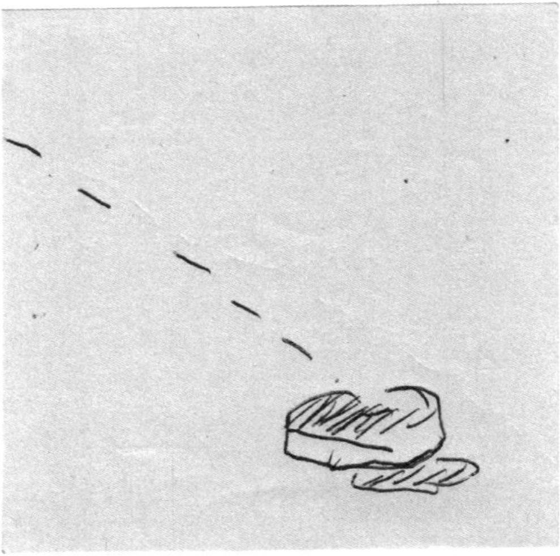

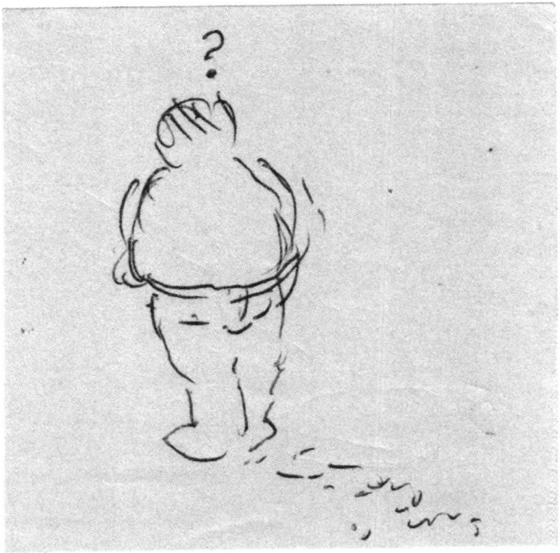

Iris Colburn

Winter Blues

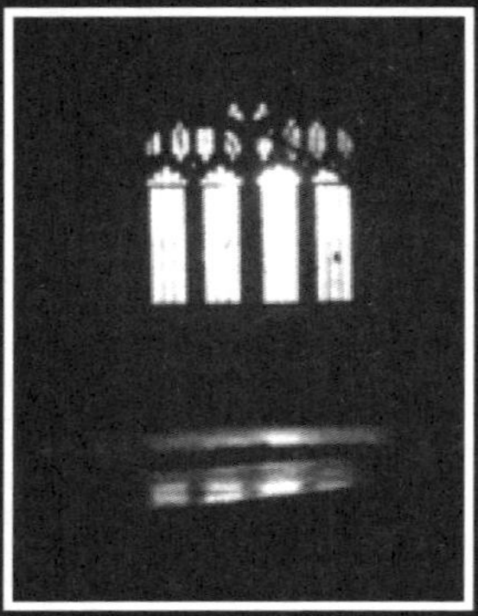

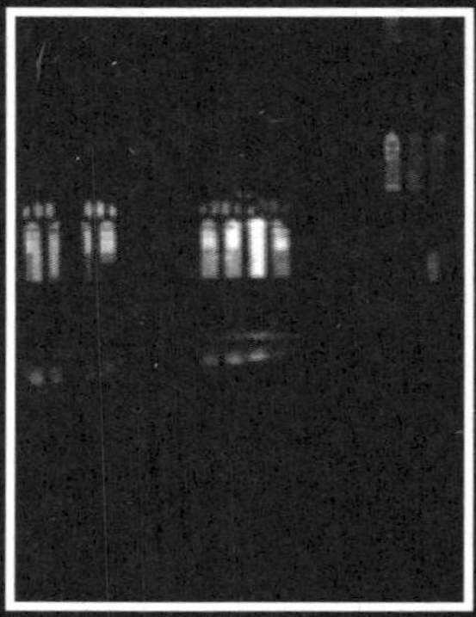

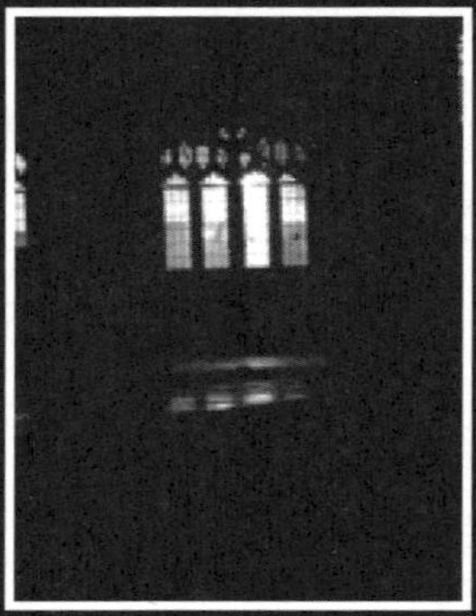

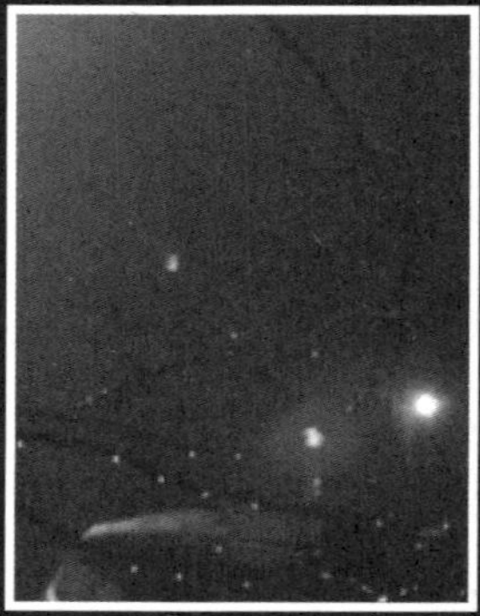

Something glowed where I did not think it belonged. The sound of a ticking fa
It could be lost forever, and I did not dare move. The glow was an even hue, not ye
lapis lazuli, and dipped once or twice into violet.

My ankles lowered, I tried not to blink. It was subtle, and I almost missed it.

It persisted. I sat up abruptly. Where did it come from? I scanned my memory-
the wall behind me and in front of the mirror was an ordinary eggshell white. I didn
understand, and I left before it could leave. I swore I would never see it again.

Over the next few weeks, I had a few encounters with blue light while walking hom
from campus. As it usually is with these kinds of things, I barely remember whe
it began.

One evening, as I stepped out of class, I caught the edge of a fluorescent scree
of radiant blue. It beamed out of the first floor of a nearby empty, dark neo-Goth
building. I detoured to see it in full. As I came upon it, something electric and war
plunged inside my body. I was struck.

I walked closer. I stopped. I stood there. I wanted to take a photo to send it to my friend. I held up my phone. I took three photos, quickly and without discrimination. Then I went home. I don't remember if I sent the photos.

A week or so later, on a walk home, I confessed my infatuation to a friend. I was vague; I didn't want to lose it to explanation. I let him do most of the talking.

We were getting close to the end of the block. I saw the blue light that defines the top of the university's emergency posts but said nothing. As we crossed the street, I saw a baby blue holding a window captive farther down the block, past the emergency post. I felt a similar piercing; it lingered and confused my step. I couldn't believe it; I was experiencing what he was struggling to understand right in front of him—"Look! There it is!" I didn't say anything else, and he kept walking.

I wondered if I should take a photo. I didn't want to lose it to the camera. This isn't something I can point to, to my friend or with the camera. But maybe a blurry photo is more telling than my words. I walked back and took one photo. I sent it to another friend. He won't stop sending me photos of objects, buildings, really anything and any blue.

Blue followed me everywhere but didn't envelop, hold, or interpellate me again. My roommate gave me an electric-blue wig. I put daffodils in front of my mirror, trying to trick the color out of it. Of course, it can still seduce me. But I've become a blue hunter, anticipating it with a squint of an eye and setting traps for our next encounter. Blue wasn't late, it just didn't care to strike back.

It came to taunt me, following me in the reflections of autonomous lights (and encircling me). I was smart enough to not give in to missing it. Missing it would be like craving the warmth of the sun in the winter.

Tianyu Guo

Tianyu Guo

Live:

"What do you want to achieve as an artist? Why art other than else?" The questions concerned with what made them chose their path of art. Based on the recurring themes, I supposed they were driven by a more personal experience: they made a decision and they were aware of it.

Derek's Recording:

"I don't necessarily think I made a decision. Well I think it's funny because I'm writing my thesis paper and thinking about this. But like... cuz it's not necessarily about making things at a certain point with 'art.' It's about existing and some kind of history or discourse: asking these sorts of questions that you ask yourself and seeing what happened. So, there are these sorts of tools for thinking and then you hope that other people can use them as tools for thinking too.

"And then you ask yourself the question of 'How did I get here?' The weird answer's sort of like, when I was a kid I could draw really well... like cartoons, like Bugs Bunny... I could just recreate in this way, and people saw that, and they were like "wow that's unusual." Or whatever it was. And then you know it just sort of like, fabric of society. It's (that) we need to put you somewhere where you make sense and then it just snowballs. And here I am I at graduate school and it's not a good answer but it's a truthful answer you know." — The environment

Recording:

I was a little disappointed at first. Without a decision made, being artist for him might be inertia blessed by environment. A prolonged childhood game that made my own "decision" seemed affected. Is there a deferred decision ahead? An exit? He is an artist only because he hasn't quit being one. If being is a continuous state of pretending, then it was the act of pushing made Sisyphus Sisyphus. Act. Doing could be the element that suffice what beyond knowledge makes art.

What is a decision anyway?

How is the natural choice compared to a "decision"

My project was presented as a performance. The performance was a conclusion of a series of interviews I conducted throughout the semester. The performance consisted of three voices: first, a monologue, performed live; second, a recorded response of an interviewee; third, a recorded monologue of my own. The first voice announced a description of the questions, along with my initiatives and strategies. After the interviewee's response, the other recorded voice was my own addressing the previous two voices with my personal experience.

One intention of the interview was to investigate a given MFA student's source for making art and their reasons for being, or choosing to be, an artist. As the project developed over time, I started to observe how more and more these conversations betrayed a projection of my own trajectory. As my interviewees dug through their own history of art making, I too opened up a pathway tracing back to my own origin story

Jeffrey Hsu

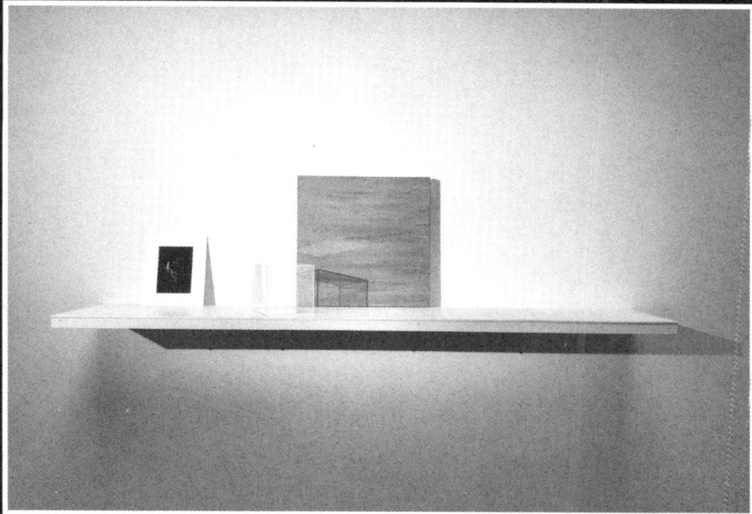

Abstraction eliminates the mundane by forcing distance between the referent and the referred. Abstraction remains empty until it acquires meaning vis-à-vis a socialized history. What results is knowledge detached from physical form: an image.

Knowledge is not an absolute reality. At the core of human understanding is a perceptual regime shaped by personal experiences and cultural schemata. Historically, we sought factual concreteness in painting—especially during the Renaissance—and then in photography in the mid-nineteenth century, only to be denied this visual stability in both mediums because they failed to form a connection between image and reality. We are left with only the image as a rupture in our understanding of what is real.

At the core of images is the play of light. The photographic instant is triggered by a chemical reaction—photons and silver form what we perceive to be an image. Paintings and sculptures require lighting to unveil their gestalt. Light is the conduit for objectivity. We see only the reflected photons. We know only because we perceive something through words, images, and thought. What we see is purely an index, a figment. Our perceptual regime remains external to what we believe is reality. Photography becomes an analogy for our understanding of the world—a method of abstraction that fails to replace object with image. The indexical becomes a symbol for the real.

Michal Koszycki

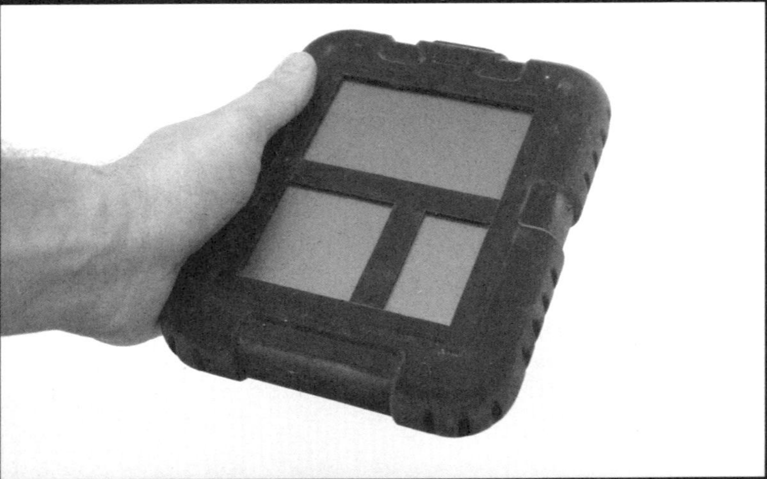

I made a phone.

Starting on March 6, 2018, it rings at random times with decreasing average frequency.

When it does not ring, a small LED in the top right corner blinks continuously.

When it does ring, it rings sixteen times, then stops, and the number of missed calls is shown.

Jasmin Liang

The Gift

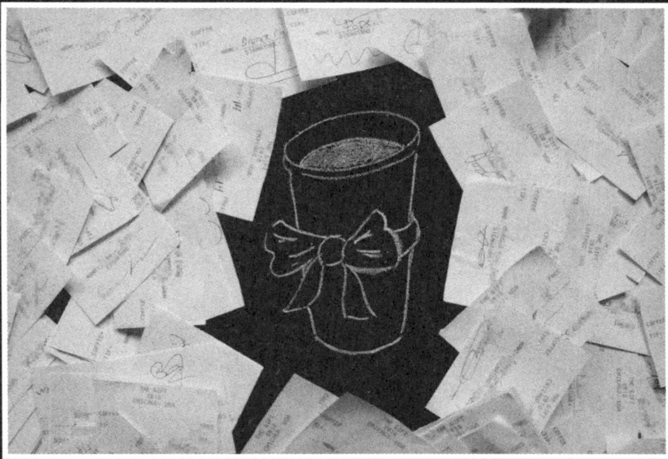

When I first conceived this piece, I was interested in using secrets as a medium and drawing out the tensions between privacy, intimacy, and human vulnerability in the age of the Internet. I wanted to set up a situation that reproduced the structure of data tracking but infused it with a kind of voyeurism.

I went around campus and gave away free coffee. In exchange for the coffee, I asked people to put down their printed name and signature on a fake receipt I made. While they were signing, I would lean over and whisper into their ear: "How old were you when you first had sex? Write down the answer at the tip section."

The reactions were varied. Some people felt embarrassed and walked away; some found it funny; some were caught off guard at first, then wrote down the answer rather indifferently. A few asked what it was for, and I would reply: "It is a project sponsored by DOVA (Department of Visual Arts)." Based on that, the participants could judge for themselves.

At the end of the day, everyone walked away with a different narrative of the experience. My understanding of the piece also changed over time, as I realized the real gift for the participants was not the coffee but their authorship vis-à-vis the performance.

Once a performance enters the public sphere, its meaning becomes predicated upon the very time and space of its enactment and upon the body of responses it elicits. Each occasion of the performance creates a new set of relationships between the performer and the viewer specific to that environment. And yet, even after it disappears from the stage, its meaning continues to mutate and multiply as each viewer's knowledge evolves over time.

Cristen Leifheit
TPS, or True Potato Seed
Single-channel video, 00:09:00 min., sound

A chorus of voices extracted from YouTube videos discuss the True Potato Seed Movement, a counternarrative to the production of potatoes in the agricultural industry. Utilizing forms of fragmentation and repetition, I reconstructed found footage from home gardeners attempting to grow potatoes from seed—a method not used by industrial farmers because of its highly unpredictable results. Visually, the video is composed of a black screen with occasional quick snippets of original footage collaged together. Unlike a platform such as YouTube, which is a massive storage device disseminating information among people and building communities over distance, *TPS* emphasizes oral culture. The predominant black screen asks the viewer to imagine that which is being described through the use of language and memory.

During "Art and Knowledge," we looked at methods of archaeology and cinema verité through artists such as Mark Dion and Laura Poitras. In *TPS*, I use similar methods to question how knowledge is evoked and shared. Does knowledge come from the tangible experiment of the potato seed, or does it come through the exchange of ideas being repeated through the online community dialogue? Does knowledge exist from the individual subjects, the collection of subjects, the reorganization of it, or not at all? How does knowledge emerge in the process of making? When we recontextualize found subjects in the world, are we creating new knowledge?

By mining footage in a platform of popular culture, this work begins to link the environment, agriculture, and media. *TPS* questions how media storage influences knowledge and information. For me, it also engages with the idea that experimentation, leisure, and failure can exist in this instance because of the safety net of the larger infrastructure of agriculture, even as the True Potato Seed Movement points to the problems of large-scale monocultures and clones.

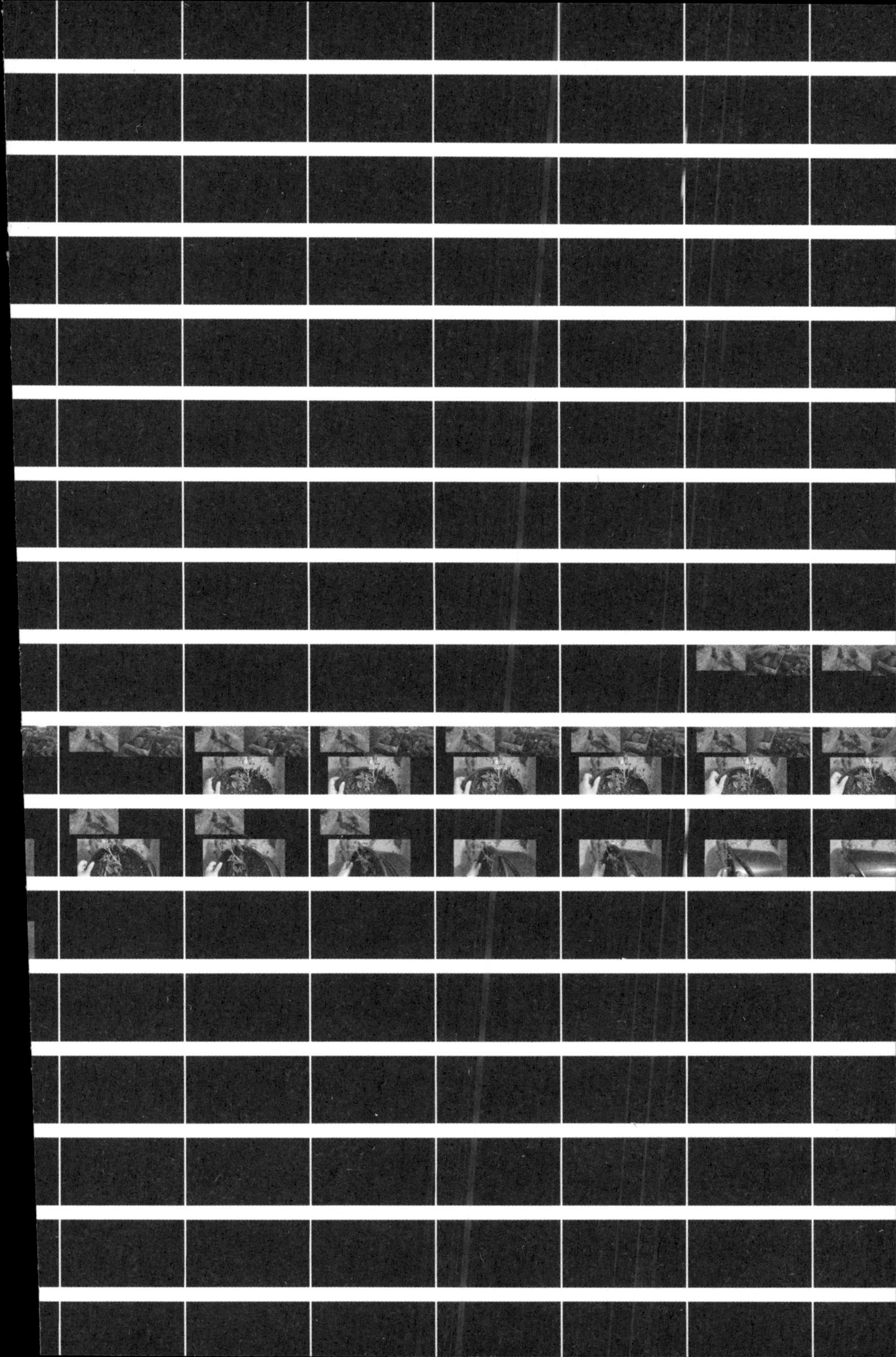

Brock Lownes
What is a Square? A Performative Lecture

CHAPTER 1: DEFINE THE SQUARE

At the most basic level, a square is a plane with four right angles and four equal sides. Squares also exist as three-dimensional forms: when six flat squares come together, a cube is formed. The cube, or square, exists as a material form in real space or as an idea in cognitive space. For example, when I say the words "green square" under the governance of collective rules prescribed by a shared visual language, everyone should have the same cognitive experience—we should imagine the form of a green square. The word "square" is perceptually self-evident, meaning our idea of the square comes from our bodily and sensorial experiences of squares in real life. To know the square, we need to have both perceived and experienced the square in real life.

CHAPTER 2: EXPERIENCE THE SQUARE

In nature there is no such thing as a square, yet the concept of a square has helped artists make the world appear natural. Artists and architects have used the square as a tool to create a system of coordinates or a grid. This grid has allowed artists to depict complex three-dimensional forms on two-dimensional surfaces, to both measure and properly depict the natural world.

Even more, depictions of nature are housed in square apparatuses called frames and on three-dimensional squares called pedestals. So, while the grid is a tool that measures pictorial space, the frame and the pedestal are tools to help define the autonomy of a picture or an object in space. What is autonomy? Autonomy is what the frame does: it defines a space, communicates the significance of the art object in contrast to the regularity of objects in the real world.

CHAPTER 3: ENTER THE SQUARE

While anybody is meant to perceive the square, only a few bodies can claim the square to be their own. The furtive craving for rationality of the square renders a strange service. Answering this call to service, the call to grasp the squareness of the square, is an almost impossible achievement. I have spent countless hours carving the foundation of my life into a square—using the square as equipment to control the nature of cognitive perception, to distill knowledge into a history of system and form Building this body of knowledge is the act of becoming an artist. I want to shape my future and dwell in the uncertainty of the square. To be an autonomous being making autonomous squares.

Elizabeth McClafferty
The Handwritten Note as Personal Archive

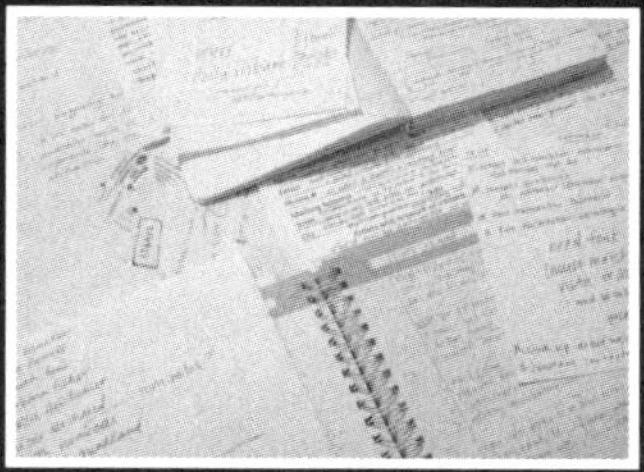

I have harbored a silent, subconscious obsession with handwriting my entire life. This became manifest, for example, in a reluctance to dispose of old school notes, grocery lists, and letters. These handwritten remnants became the trace of a developing body of knowledge, information, and experience. Moreover, embedded in anything handwritten is the physical hand of the writer. It is a fragment, or trace, of the process of thought, contemplation, comprehension, and then physical exercise. It is representative of a singular and specific human existence or being. Handwriting, like a fingerprint, is intrinsic to our person.

And so, instead of disposing of these fragments, I have collected them.

My inquiry into this process of collection sits at the intersection of three concepts: graphomania, the archive, and autobiography. Graphomania, or scribomania, is defined as a compulsive urge to write. Often used in the psychiatric context, graphomania is more specifically defined as the writing of rambling statements, which often degenerate into nonsensical successions of words.[1] My own interest in handwriting perhaps diverges from the compulsive drive to write constantly, toward an obsession with the perfection of my own writing. As a child, I would observe my mother's handwriting, or that of a friend, and mimic styles of letters that I preferred. In my fifth-grade English class I altered the way I wrote my letter *a*, and in tenth grade algebra, my letter *n*. At the core of my obsession is aesthetic value, and my handwriting, even when rushed, is as legible as the typed word. And thus, in this increasingly digital world, the information I choose to convey through handwriting gains meaning and power, importance and gravity.

This collection presents the handwritten note as personal archive. The definition of archive (noun) is "a collection of historical documents or records providing information about a place, institution, or group of people" and (verb) "to place or store (something) in an archive."[2] One synonym for archive is "record." The archive, in this sense, is ultimately a form of knowledge or information collection. The historical archive tells the story of an event—an action or existence—through the traces of that event. Mimicking that form, this personal archive contains documents that tell the story of an existence. It is indeed a collection of documents, or records, that provide information about their author—information about myself, about the people around me, my mood, the things that I have learned, eaten, produced.

And thus, this collection is effectively a form of autobiography. Because I have collected these objects, because I have chosen to present them as a record of my lived experience, as a source of knowledge production, this personal archive is autobiographic—it is a history that I constructed of myself, one I have written (quite literally) in my own hand.

1. Ossip Lourié, *La Graphomanie: Essai de psychologie morbide* (Paris: F. Alcan, 1920).
2. https://en.oxforddictionaries.com/definition/archive

Adrienne Elyse Meyers
Art and Knowledge

Looking into writings and projects from philosophers, artists, and curators, the course set out with questions about the nature of art and of knowledge, and about the places where these terms do or do not intersect. What are all the ways in which art embodies and communicates knowledge? How far can you push a definition before it falls apart? As we spent time working, talking, and writing through these questions, the categorical terms began to fade or to become less relevant. The presence of a variety of approaches and value systems dissolved the edges of art and knowledge as discrete ideas. Senses of personal interest, collective experience, and a range of fascinations were collected and presented in projects that acted out the presentation of something like knowledge and the process of something like art.

Marie-Gabrielle Verbergt

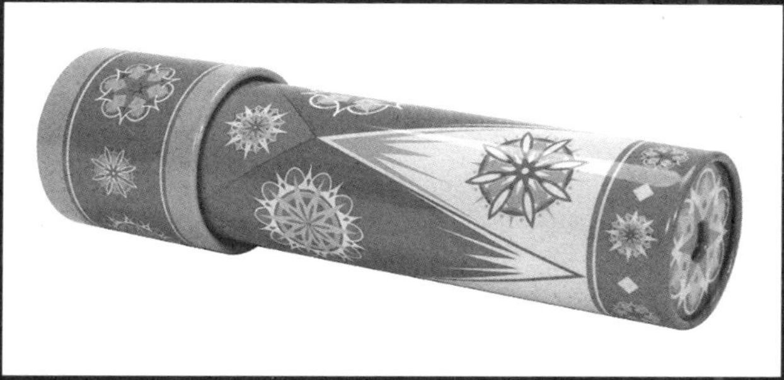

Shylling Classic Tin Kaleidoscope, $6.99 on Amazon (2018)

Q1: If Art = Kn, then what kind of Kn does Art encompass?
Q2: If Hist = Kn, then what is its relation to Art?
A: A Kal.

Art: art
Kn: knowledge
Hist: history
Kal: kaleidoscope

Through a short story about a brother and a sister, an artist and a historian, who share a love for and fascination with kaleidoscopes as their favorite toy, I developed the idea that artistic knowledge and historical knowledge are similar in structure. As contemporary art is ever more often occupied with the past, artists become our "historians of the present." Assuming, then, that historical knowledge has a structure, I explored what this shared structure could look like.

My answer became "kaleidoscopic." Inspired by the work of contemporary artists such as Mark Bradford, Jack Whitten, and Zoe Leonard, I found that art-knowledge presented itself as fractured and partial but still assumed a whole. Even behind playful lies, behind serious enigmas, there is an unironic and material world. Just as the mirrors inside a kaleidoscope break up the image of colorful beads twirling around, so do artists and historians interpret and reconstruct the real (past/present) world they draw on. The fleeting and fragile nature of historical interpretations and artistic-aesthetic fashions moreover finds a counterpart in the dynamic and circular movement of the kaleidoscope's head: with a sudden change of a hand, of a viewpoint, an entire image is gone. One artist is unlike another; no two historians read the same. Art-knowledge, just like history, is impossible to reproduce.

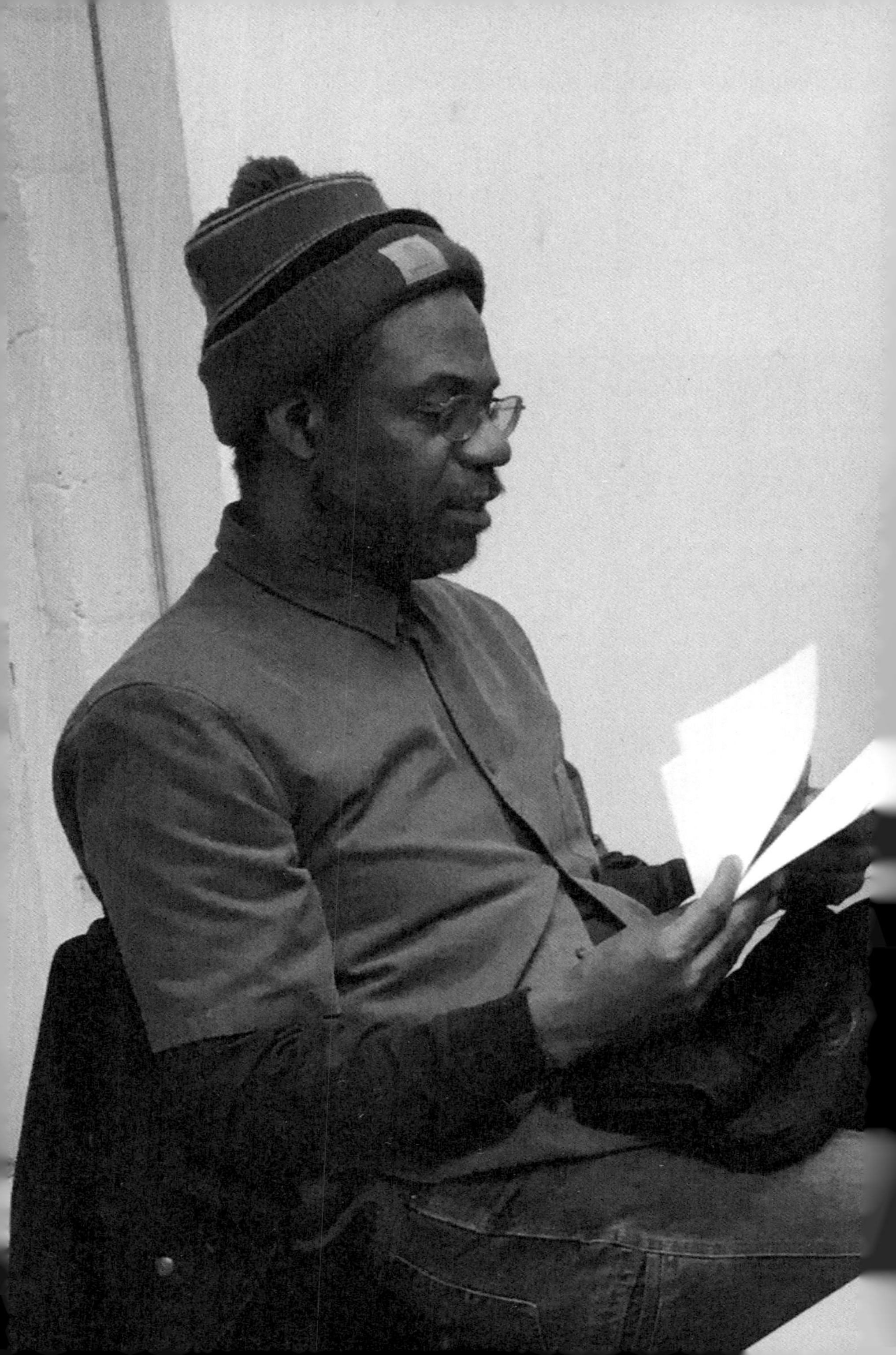

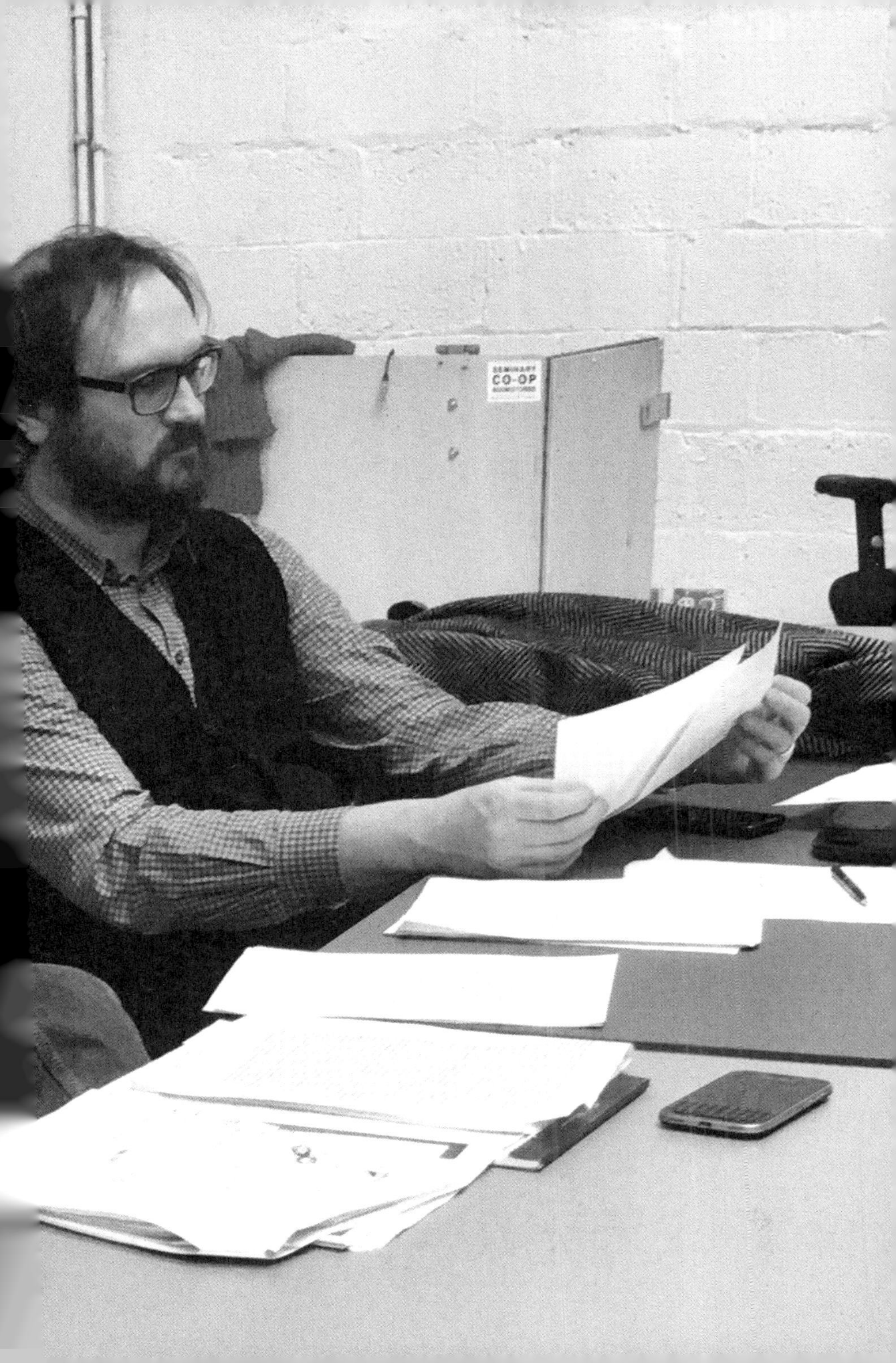
CO-OP

IMAGE INDEX AND CREDITS

Whispering Campaign
documenta 14, Athens and Kassel, spring–summer 2017

7: Pope.L, Athens, spring 2017. Photo: Freddie Faulkenberry
8–9: Pope.L and performer, Kassel, spring 2017. Photo: Mathias Völzke
22–23: Pope.L, Dieter Roelstraete, and Zachary Cahill, Chicago, spring 2019. Photo: Max Braverman
24–25: Whispering workshop, Athens, spring 2016. Photo: Freddie Faulkenberry
26–29: Speaker installation site, Athens, spring 2017. Photo: Freddie Faulkenberry
30–31: Speaker installation sites, Athens, spring 2017. Photo: Yiannis Hadjiaslanis
32–33: Speaker installation sites, Athens, spring 2017. Photo: Freddie Faulkenberry (32, top left and bottom right); Fanis Vlastaras (32, top right; 33); Mathias Völzke (32, bottom left)
45–47, 50–51: Live whisperers in the streets of Athens, spring 2017. Photo: Freddie Faulkenberry
48–49: Live whisperer in the streets of Athens, spring 2017
64: Fragment of poster designed by David Khan-Giordano
65: Radio session, Kassel, spring 2017. Photo: Leon Hösl
66–67: *Whispering Campaign* car, Kassel, spring 2017. Photo: Nils Klinger
68–69, 89, 92: Speaker installation, Kassel, spring 2017. Photo: Mathias Völzke
70–71, 88, 95: Blindfolded whispering rehearsal, Kassel, spring 2017. Photo: Mathias Völzke
72–77, 93: Live whisperers in the streets of Kassel, spring 2017. Photo: Mathias Völzke
85–87: Pope.L and Leon Hösl, Kassel, spring 2017. Photo: Mathias Völzke
90–91: *Whispering Campaign* car, Kassel, spring 2017. Photo: Mathias Völzke
98–99: *Skin Set Drawing* installation, Kassel, spring 2017. Photo: Nils Klinger (Artworks: *Green People Are a Recent Invention*, 2011, marker, ballpoint on white art paper, 30.2 × 22.9 cm © Pope.L; *White People Are God's Way of Saying I'm Sorry*, 2011, felt tip and ink on off-white art paper, 30.2 × 22.9 cm © Pope.L)
99: *Green People Are a Recent Invention*, 2011, marker, ballpoint on vellum, 30.2 × 22.9 cm © Pope.L. Photo: Fred Dott
100–01: *Whispering Campaign* car, Kassel, spring 2017. Photo: Nils Klinger

Brown People Are the Wrens in the Parking Lot
Logan Center Exhibitions, Chicago, fall–winter 2017–18

104: Social media campaign, online questionnaire
105: Event, town hall meetings I and II
106–07: Event, town hall meeting II
108: Exhibition, bar for discussion and comment wall. Photo: RCH | EKH
109: Exhibition, shelving display and comment wall; drop-off point for submissions. Photo: RCH | EKH
110: Exhibition, curated interviews on the subject of immigration
111: Exhibition, comment wall collating studio research, online responses and submissions
112: Exhibition, comment wall: submissions and studio research
113: Exhibition, comment wall: studio research
114–15: Social media campaign, responses to online questionnaire
116–17: Social media campaign, screenshots
118–19: Interventions, poster campaign. Photo: Pope.L studio
120–21: Interventions, poster campaign
122–24: Interventions, pop-up immigration library. Photo: Pope.L studio
125: Middle left: event, town hall meeting II
125: Bottom right: interventions. Photo: Zachary Cahill
126–27: Event, Zachary Cahill in conversation with Marcus Warren: on superheroes and immigration
139: Exhibition, comment wall: submission

Art and Knowledge
Richard and Mary L Gray Center for Arts and Inquiry at the University of Chicago, winter 2018

140–41: Pope.L and Dieter Roelstraete teaching, Chicago, winter 2018.
Photo: Zachary Cahill
145–49: Pope.L, *Heidegger and his Clod*, 2018. Five pieces, ink on paper, 8 × 8 cm each
© Pope.L. Courtesy of the artist, Mitchell-Innes & Nash (New York) and Susanne Vielmetter Projects (Los Angeles)
150–61: Images courtesy of the students of "Art & Knowledge"
162–63: Pope.L and Dieter Roelstraete teaching, Chicago, winter 2018.
Photo: Zachary Cahill

Vidura Jang Bahadur is an artist based in Chicago. He is currently pursuing a PhD in Rhetoric and Public Culture at Northwestern University.

Zachary Cahill is a Chicago-based interdisciplinary artist and writer. Since 2010 he has been working on the long-term project *USSA*, a series of exhibitions, performances, and publications. Cahill is director of Programs and Fellowships at the Gray Center for Arts and Inquiry at the University of Chicago and is editor-in-chief of *Portable Gray*, the Gray Center's biannual magazine.

Klea Charitou is an art historian and curator based in Athens. As part of the curatorial team of documenta 14, she was responsible for the realization of Pope.L's *Whispering Campaign* in Athens.

Leon Hösl, a Kassel-based member of the curatorial department of documenta 14, was closely involved in the realization of Pope.L's *Whispering Campaign*. He is an MA student of Art History at the University of Vienna and works as a critic and curator.

Chichan Kwong is an artist and writer based in Chicago. He is a former student of Pope.L.

Adrienne Elyse Meyers is an artist who was born in Houston and lives in Chicago. She works in publishing and is a 2019 Post-MFA Teaching Fellow at the University of Chicago in the Department of Visual Art, where she served as the teaching assistant for "Art & Knowledge."

Dieter Roelstraete was a member of the curatorial team of documenta 14. He is the curator of the Neubauer Collegium for Culture and Society at the University of Chicago, where he also teaches.

Monika Szewczyk is the director of De Appel, a contemporary art institute in Amsterdam. She previously worked with Pope.L as curator of documenta 14 in Athens and Kassel (2015–17) and visual arts program curator at the Reva and David Logan Center for the Arts at the University of Chicago (2012–14).

Editor
Dieter Roelstraete

Text Contributors
Zachary Cahill, Klea Charitou, Iris Colburn, Tianyu Guo, Jeffrey Hsu, Leon Hösl, Vidura Jang Bahadur, Michal Koszycki, Chichan Kwong, Cristen Leifheit, Jasmin Liang, Brock Lownes, Elizabeth McClafferty, Adrienne Elyse Meyers, Pope.L, Monika Szewczyk, Marie-Gabrielle Verbergt

Managing Editor
Maggie Jensen

Director of Programs and Fellowships at The Gray Center For Arts And Inquiry
Zachary Cahill

Publishing Editor
Isabella Zamboni, Mousse

Editorial Coordinator
Benedetta Pomini, Mousse

Copyediting
Erica Olsen

Graphic Design
Matteo Gualandris, Mousse

This book is supported by The Gray Center for Arts And Inquiry at the University of Chicago as part of Pope.L and Dieter Roelstraete's Mellon Collaborative Fellowship at the Gray Center.

graycenter
FOR ARTS AND INQUIRY

THE UNIVERSITY OF CHICAGO | Arts

Published and distributed by
Mousse Publishing
Contrappunto s.r.l.
Corso di Porta Romana 63
20122, Milan–Italy

Available through:

Mousse Publishing, Milan
moussepublishing.com

DAP | Distributed Art Publishers, New York
artbook.com

Vice Versa Distribution, Berlin
viceversaartbooks.com

Les presses du réel, Dijon
lespressesdureel.com

Antenne Books, London
antennebooks.com

documenta 14 map design (reprinted for this publication as an insert):
David Khan-Giordano

First edition: 2019

Printed in Italy by Tipografia Valdostana S.r.l.

ISBN 9788867493890
€ 25 / $ 30

Thanks to:

Brown People Are the Wrens in the Parking Lot

Logan Center Exhibitions, Yesomi Umolu, Alyssa Brubaker, Marcus Warren, Dieter Roelstraete, Ramyar Vala, Rambod Vala, Zespo, Frances Lee, Chichan Kuang, Takashi Shallow, Brit Barton, Aliza Hoffman, Noelle Africh, David Lloyd, Zachary Cahill, Jamila Willis, Danny Volk, Vidura Jang Bahadur, Brock Lownes, Rachel Cohen, Teju Cole, Josh Duensing, Jazmine Harris, Jessica Stockholder, DOVA, Regenstein Library, The Migration Stories Project, Hogan Movers, Earnest Dawkins, Srikanth (Chicu) Reddy, Deone Jackman, Veronica Vegna, Candida Alvarez, Marissa Chris Zain Neuman, Michael Hahn, Alexandra Small, Cecilia Resende, Max Guy, Sabina Ott, Teresa Silva, Kellie Lu, L.G., Co Sa, Laura Letinsky, Luke Clohisy, Albert Stabler, Chus Martinez, Sampada Aranke, Ben Ndugga-Kabuye, Susan Gzesh, Bettina Johnson, Kelly Kribs, Fred Schmidt-Arenales, Amber Ginsberg, Marcy Phillips, Alek Binion, Melissa Gilliam, John Harness, Silvia Gonzalez, Seth Brodsky, Jordan Carter, Marta Collazo, Melchior Dikkers, Ruth Erickson, Hannah Feldman, Hendrik Folkerts, Leslie Guy, Kelly Jones,

Ayan Kassim, Michal Koszycki, Mark Linn, Courtney Mackedanz, Gabriel Moreno, Solveig Nelson, Tricia Van Eck, Kristen Vosberg, Lukey Walden, Amy Babinec, Ionit Behar, Staci Boris, Lynne Brown, Ivan Bujan, Suzette Bross Bulley, Joan Cairney, Mirga Chowdhary, Tessa Clark, Katya da Silva, J Lepez Espinoza, Margarita Flores, Marcia Epstein Fraerman, Ashley Gillanders, Karen Greenwalt, Anneasha Hogan, Josefine Kocian, Kristin Korolowicz, Anna Chiaretta, Jin Lee, Jaewook Lee, Jasmin Liang, Mev Luna, Karsten Lund, Nicky M. Lutsky, Isabelle Frances McGuire, Monique Meloche, Chloe O'Neill, Suzie Oppenheimer, Roni Packer, Jameson Paige, Joshua Plekkenpol, Jeff Prokash, Joseph Rabensdorf, Kathleen Rapp, Michelle Lynn Rinard, Adam Schachner, Daniel Schulman, Malte Stiehl, Brandon Sward, Suzy Vogenthaler, Zhucen Wei, Anne Yoder, Abbas, Naomi Beckwith, David Bottorff, Jeremiah Hulsebos-Spofford, Dev, Assaf Evron, Jersey Fonseca, Gael, Deana Haggag, Tim Hargrove, LaShonda Kirk, Kent Lambert, Gautama Mehta, Bill Michel, Dan Peterman, Greg Redenius, Abraham Ritchie, Mike Schuh, David Schutter, Aram Han Sifuentes, Jacqueline Stewart, Sheridan Tucker, David Wolf, Ben Chandler, Andrew Yale, Studio Chew, RCH | EKH, DoVA MFA's 2017 & 2018, Richard and Mary L. Gray Center for Arts and Inquiry, Pope.L Studio, Mitchell-Innes & Nash, Susanne Vielmetter, Artforum, Arts in Creative Writing at the University of Chicago Center for the Study of Race, Politics, and Culture, Logan Center Exhibitions, Logan Media Center, Logan Center Security, Open Practice Committee (OPC)

Whispering Campaign

ATHENS, GREECE
Dieter Roelstraete, Monika Szewczyk, Hendrik Folkerts, Klea Charitou, Leon Hösl, Andrea Linnenkohl, Eleanna Papathanasiadis, Benjamin Kiel, Christina Assimakopoulou, Antigone Tsagkaropoulou, Bianca Maria Fasiolo, Angeliki-Hatzi, Iraklis Kopitas, George Moraitis, Aikaterini Kotsou, David Zarbock, Emma Ladji, Jyreika Guest, Brendan Cushing, Fanis Vlastaras, Freddie Faukenberry, Mathias Völzke, Yiannis Hadjiaslanis, Stathis Mamalakis, Areos Park, Athens Concert Hall, Athens Conservatory, Athens Metro, Athens School of Fine Art, Cantina Social, Cine Paris, City of Athens, Delta Pi Productions, Department of Visual Arts (University of Chicago), Documenta, Ebony L. Haynes, First Cemetery of Athens, Galaxy Bar, Richard and Mary L. Gray Center for Arts and Inquiry, The Hellenic Olympic Committee, Kiosk at Praksitelous 1 Street, National Museum of Contemporary Art Athens, National Technical University of Athens, The University of Chicago, Aliza Hoffman, Anja Lindner Anouar, Ariel Pittman, Ben Brix, Christian Bulwien, Christoph Steinau, Courtney Willis Blair, Dan Norman, Danny Volk, David Khan-Giordano, David Lloyd, Dimitris Politakis, Eva Kotanidi, Jacqueline Stewart, Josh Duensing, Katerina Kafentzi, Konstantinos Tzoumas, Lorenzo Conte, Lucy Mitchell-Innes, Manolis Economou, Melina Spathari, Mickey Craft, Natascha Werner, Natassa Sideri, Nikolas Konstantinou, Odysseas Megalooikonomou , Polytechnic Workshoppers, Quinn Latimer, Saskia Trebing, Susanne Vielmetter, Thalia Karamolegou, Wanderers, Zachary Cahill

KASSEL, GERMANY
Dieter Roelstraete, Monika Szewczyk, Hendrik Folkerts, Klea Charitou, Leon Hösl, Christoph Steinau, Christian Bulwien, Natascha Werner, Martin Dege, Lou Hardt, Andara Shastika, Allison Peacock, Andra Schumann, Nella-Larissa Walsch, Tanja Böhme, Daniel Kauffeld, Felix Werthschulte, Erol Ögel, Felizitas Fritz, Natalia Escuerdo, Frank Weißenborn, Susanne Holbein, Lisbeth Nelleßen, Alina Moller, Andrea Holler, Jutta Millich, Jonas Buerleh, Martina Thoneick, Heidrun Siegesmund, Talat Kaya, Ulla Lux, Dieter Kindl, Nils Klinger, Mathias Völzke, Fred Dott, Alta Grafica, Citizens of Kassel, City of Kassel, Department of Visual Arts (University of Chicago), documenta, documenta Halle, Freies Radio Kassel, Fridericianum, Friedrichsplatz Tiefgarage, Gottschalkhalle, Hauptbahnhof, Richard and Mary L. Gray Center for Arts and Inquiry, Il Convento, Karlsaue Park, Kassel School of Art and Design, Kassel University, Königs-Galerie, Königsstraße, KulturBahnhof, L'Osteria, Neue Galerie, Neue Neue Galerie, Palais Bellevue, Parkplatz Universität Holländischer Platz, The University of Chicago, Aliza Hoffman, Anja Lindner, Anouar, Ariel Pittman, Ben Brix, Christian Bulwien, Christoph Steinau, Clara Brandt, Courtney Willis Blair, Dan Norman, Danny Volk, David Giordano, David Lloyd, Dimitris Politakis, Eva Kotanidi, Jacqueline Stewart, Jochen Laube, Josh Duensing, Kafka, Konstantinou, Lorenzo Conte, Lucy Mitchell-Innes, Manolis Economou, Melina Spathari, Mickey Craft, Miro Schawalder, Nikolas Konstantinou, Odysseas, Megalooikonomou, Polytechnic Workshoppers, Quinn Latimer, Saskia Trebing, Susanne Vielmetter, Thalia Karamolegou, Wanderers, Zachary Cahill